WALDO FRANK

WALDO FRANK

WALDO FRANK

Prophet of Hispanic Regeneration

Michael A. Ogorzaly

Lewisburg
Bucknell University Press
London and Toronto: Associated University Presses

Associated University Presses
440 Forsgate Drive
Cranbury, NJ 08512

Associated University Presses
25 Sicilian Avenue
London WC1A 2QH, England

Associated University Presses
P.O. Box 338, Port Credit
Mississauga, Ontario
Canada L5G 4L8

The paper used in this publication meets the requirements
of the American National Standard for Permanence of Paper
for Printed Library Materials Z39.48-1984.

Library of Congress Cataloging-in-Publication Data
Ogorzaly, Michael A.
    Waldo Frank, prophet of Hispanic regeneration / Michael A.
Ogorzaly.
        p.   cm.
    Includes bibliographical references and index.
    ISBN 0-8387-5233-0 (alk. paper)
    1. Frank, Waldo David, 1889–1967—Knowledge—Latin America.
2. Frank, Waldo David, 1889–1967—Knowledge—Spain.   3. American
literature—Latin American influences.   4. Authors, American—20th
century—Biography.   5. American literature—Spanish influences.
6. Latin America—Historiography.   7. Latin America in literature.
8. Spain—Historiography.   9. Spain in literature.   I. Title.
PS3511.R258Z77   1994
813'.52—dc20   92-55007
                                                                          CIP

PRINTED IN THE UNITED STATES OF AMERICA

To Fredrick B. Pike

CONTENTS

PREFACE

This work is a revision of my Ph.D. dissertation, a study that originated with a suggestion from my adviser at the University of Notre Dame, Fredrick B. Pike, that I might find a possible topic by exploring the curious relationship between Waldo Frank and the Hispanic world. Largely forgotten in his native land, Frank is still respected in some quarters in Spain and Latin America.

Upon examining the scant biographical material available, I found that Frank's "Hispanic adventure" received only summary treatment in the United States. Nevertheless, among those professing to be knowledgeable on the matter, he came to enjoy the reputation of a keen interpreter of Hispanic culture. My own research would soon lead to the conclusion that Frank's writing on Hispanic themes rested on superficial study and observation. All too often, moreover, study and observation were employed only to bolster Frank's preconceived conclusions. Significantly, these conclusions often coincided with Latin American self-evaluations formulated during the generations and resting on the conviction that spirituality was more highly prized in the lands to the south of the Rio Grande while North Americans, in their excessive materialism, tended to ignore higher values. Essentially, Frank told Latin American cultural elites what they wanted to hear, and thus assured himself a high standing among them.

The purpose of this book is to establish the true nature of Frank's relationship with Spain and Latin America. This objective has been approached through a careful evaluation of the facts that surround this aspect of his life and an analysis, hopefully more probing than that contained in previous studies, of the five books that culminate each critical phase in his lifelong role as "prophet of Hispanic regeneration."

The text is divided into five chapters. Chapter 1 examines the various influences that combined to help form Frank's prophetic sensibility; chapter 2 deals with Frank's relationship with Spain; chapters 3 through 5 cover Frank's relationship with Latin America (chapter 3: 1919–31; chapter 4: 1932–43; chapter 5: 1943–67).

Several people contributed to the successful completion of this work. At the dissertation stage, my brother Dave and his wife Donna, with the help of the Schaumburg Township Public Library, assisted me in obtaining copies of numerous articles by and about Frank. Domenico Bommarito and Terry McGovern used their access to the libraries of Northwestern University and Loyola University of Chicago on my behalf. My friends John Nerone, Owen Lippert, Jeff Burns, John Stamatakos, and Rajani Alexander helped me in countless ways. Catherine Box faithfully typed the manuscript. I thank them all.

Upon reading my dissertation, Gary Hamburg generously offered me a number of cogent suggestions should I ever decide to revise for publication. Then John Ryan got me a computer and taught me how to use it. Without them, this book might never have been attempted.

As always, my sister Karen, her husband Tom, and my mother were there throughout the entire process, doing those things that I couldn't do for myself. I am blessed to have them.

Finally, I am most grateful to my dear friend, Fred Pike. From start to finish, his guidance and support were crucial to the consummation of this study. I am forever in his debt.

1
THE MAKING OF A PROPHET
An Introduction

On a June day in 1929, a crowd of two to three hundred intellectuals filled the rows of heavy mahogany high-backed chairs in the *Gran Salon de Actos* of the University of Mexico. Outside in the yard, an overflow crowd of more than a thousand students stood before a loudspeaker.[1] They had all gathered to hear the U.S. writer and thinker Waldo Frank, the author of *Virgin Spain* (1926). This book presented Spain as a land that had forged a spiritual synthesis of its warring religions, a land whose people had achieved a kind of wholeness that would serve as an example for the disparate cultures of North and South America in their striving for organic fusion.

Frank had received from the university an invitation (hand-delivered in New York by Mexico's assistant minister of education, Moises Sáenz). The university had offered to compensate Frank generously for a series of six lectures. Now, as he stood on the mahogany dais under a gilded candelabra, the small, compact man with the black hair and mustache was excited, for he had been welcomed by his hosts not as an academician but as a celebrity. Speaking in Spanish, he began with the statement: "I have come to Mexico to learn." Then he proceeded to deliver his lecture. His thesis was that the New World did not exist; it had yet to be created. He said that America was Europe's burial ground, i.e., the repository of European culture, and that it was her destiny, responsibility, and spiritual mission to create the new culture, the true New World, that must appear. He challenged Mexico to work with him to achieve this vision.[2]

Frank's message struck a responsive chord with his listeners. And why not? He spoke to them as brothers, as equals, treating them with respect. Moreover, he assigned them the importance that they had longed to have recognized by a *Yanqui*. But while the leading morning paper, in its lead editorial, enthusiastically accepted his challenge, no less a person than Moises Sáenz would tell him: "Frank . . . you are a fraud, a cheat, a second-rater. Your visit will accomplish nothing and will bring nothing about." Frank was stung by the attack, but he understood it as aimed more at the United States than at him personally. Besides, he himself did not expect any immediate results. For he had not come to Mexico as a diplomat trying to put some new policy into effect, nor as a businessman trying to make a deal, nor as a political activist or social reformer trying to effect change. As he records in his *Memoirs*: "In Mexico, I had been a prophet. . . ."[3]

Such a characterization was not mere posturing on the part of an aged man. Without a doubt, on that first visit to Mexico he saw himself as a prophet. It was a role he relished. Furthermore, it was a role for which he had prepared himself from early on.

The Waldean

Born in Long Branch, New Jersey, on 25 August 1889, Waldo Frank grew up in his father's four-story brownstone on the Upper West Side in Manhattan.[4] The youngest of four children, Frank started life with many advantages. Besides being something of a wunderkind, he enjoyed all the benefits of upper-middle-class life: books, music, trips to Europe, and no money worries.[5]

His father, Julius J. Frank, was a successful lawyer. He was an attorney for the Hamburg-Amerika Line and often took the family with him on his European travels.[6] Furthermore, he had an office on Wall Street. The elder Frank was no conservative, however. Progressive and liberal in his politics, he was a reform Democrat opposed to Tammany Hall.[7] He was not so progressive when it came to his family. Waldo characterizes his father as "imperious" and a "tyrant in matters of deportment."[8] And yet, while Julius Frank reigned supreme in his household,[9] he had what his son calls "a respect for the personality of others,"[10] a quality that undoubtedly gave young Waldo some breathing room during his formative years.

His mother, Helene Rosenberg Frank, was a Southerner whose father had been a blockade runner during the Civil War. According to William Bittner, she was "more pretentious, more cultivated, and less idealistic" than her husband. Music was the common thread that held the Rosenbergs together.[11] Mrs. Frank's brother Herman played second violin in a string quartet; a cousin,

Alexander Bloch, played the viola. She herself was an accomplished singer who had studied under Leopold Damrosch.[12]

Julius Frank shared this love of music. Indeed, he made music a family affair. Each week the Franks assembled for play, with the father at the organ (or piano), one sister on the piano, and the other sister on the violin. When Waldo was old enough, he was assigned the cello. Apparently he learned to play well, for while at Yale he earned himself a seat in the university orchestra.[13]

This inbred musicality perhaps naturally attracted Waldo to the aesthetic movement that joined music and literature,[14] but the question remains of where he got his spiritual sensibility. His father, the son of a German Jewish immigrant, had forsaken the ceremonies of Judaism, though he remained true to the ideals of that religion through membership in the Society for Ethical Culture. His mother was of Jewish descent, but she and her family also seem to have abandoned the customs of that faith.[15] Recalling the Friday night family gatherings at his father's house, Frank asserts that no sign that any of his relatives were Jewish ever surfaced in their conversations. Not that they were ashamed of their heritage. In fact, they took pride in it. And yet, none of them ever went to a temple or synagogue. They were, perhaps, too sophisticated for that.[16]

Thus, the Franks might be characterized as cultural Jews. To be sure, no deliberate instruction in Judaism or participation in its customs existed within the family. While Julius Frank might gather the family members in his library every evening to read from the Bible, Shakespeare, or other standard European and American authors, that was the extent of the spiritual direction he gave them.[17]

Jerome Kloucek does say that Mrs. Frank had a "religious nature," which was perhaps the strongest connection she had with the youngest of her four children.[18] Does that mean that she was a major influence on his spirituality? In none of his writings does Frank credit her as such. He only refers to his mother as a "generous, intuitive, imaginative artist."[19] But since, to Frank, the artist works to realize God, an artistic nature and a religious nature are synonymous.

The evidence suggests that Waldo Frank was born with a predisposition toward spirituality that was made manifest as early as the age of seven. In his *Memoirs* he recalls the moment: it was a Friday night and he was in the tub. As he lay on his back the only part of his body above the water was his erect penis, "the island apex of a continent. . . . This is the Waldean continent, with the male organ as its center. . . ." This place he called "Waldea" was no mere geographical or political entity, however; Frank was not content with being just an emperor. He made himself a "high priest—and the body—of a religion." Though there were no teachings or ceremonies to this religion,[20] it is significant that its god, also Frank, was, therefore, immanent. Thus, not only does this incident disclose a "heady illusion of potency and omnipotence,"[21] but it also points to the organicism that would later capture his allegiance.

Thereafter other episodes that further expose his spiritual nature occurred regularly. Around the age of ten, as he walked home one snowy afternoon, upon reaching the lamppost in front of his house, he

> saw on the first step of the stoop a small black cat with a white patch on his face. He stopped to look at it, while the snow, muffling the white street, welded together the houses, patched with lights, his body and the little beast. His mind framed a question: *What would it be to be this kitten?* And an immediate answer overwhelmed him: *Nothing would be changed.* With the instantaneousness of touch, he knew this. The kitten peering at him, he looking down at the kitten within the silent moving street, would be as they were![22]

This "experience of relation" would be repeated when in the woods he sensed the trees "as erectile arms of earth that reached for him and absorbed him" while he needed "to embrace them as the child embraces its embracing mother," or when on a summer night he "felt his identity with what the stars were made of." Frank admits that it took another ten years or so before he realized these incidents were "a share of the central experience of prophets and poets."[23] But well before that, around the age of twelve (ca. 1901), he announced to his older brother that he had founded a new "Waldensian" religion and that he, Waldo, would be its prophet. As Joseph Frank told William Bittner: "He nearly drove me wild with his nonsense on a European trip we took together." Another couple of years later, after young Waldo decided to be a writer, he wrote in his notebook that his every book would be a "proof of God."[24] These adolescent notions reveal a spiritual sensibility that combined with his mature intellect and his other plentiful gifts to make him feel that he possessed "magical powers" with which he might change the world. He felt that this was something he had in common "with a long succession of religious prophets, major and minor."[25] It is to that early intellectual maturity that we must now turn.

To be sure, Waldo Frank was precocious, as exhibited by his

academic career, which was one of impressive achievement. Early on, however, his personality seems to have prevailed over his intellect. As he himself admits, he was a bad little boy[26] who became arrogant and opinionated as he grew older, and throughout his youth he maintained a constant state of rebellion against his strict father.[27]

Some of this rebellion seems to have been misdirected toward his siblings. While his feelings toward his older brother (almost seven years his senior) were a mixture of adoration, envy, and hate, for his sisters he had only envy and resentment because they looked up to Joseph and down on him, the baby of the family. From his point of view, the situation was akin to a state of war, and Frank offers several examples as testimony to his belligerence. For instance, on one occasion, he broke his sisters' dolls. On another, he threw a brush at his brother, which struck him on the cheek.[28]

Adults, however, were always his main target. At age six (ca. 1896), for example, Waldo heard the table talk about the "monster" William Jennings Bryan who, if elected, would "ruin the country." Yet, upon seeing a big man with a kind face wearing a Bryan button, he couldn't understand and carried his trouble home. Two years later, in the midst of the Spanish-American War, he made heroes of the U.S. military men who were helping the starving Cuban children; he had seen their pictures in newspapers and he also wanted to help them. He disapproved of his father, who opposed the war.[29]

The rebellion eventually carried beyond the walls of his home. He was expelled from Horace Mann School before reaching the sixth grade when, after engaging the class bully in a fight, he refused to apologize to his teacher for her plaster statue of Jupiter that was broken during the scuffle. He finished his primary education in one of New York City's public grammar schools, which had to accept him.[30] Perhaps as a result of his emotional immaturity, Frank was double-promoted only once. Kloucek surmises that because Frank was short and slight, that one year's difference between him and his older classmates might have isolated him from them and exacerbated his feeling that he was not appreciated by his family.[31]

It was at DeWitt Clinton High School, just north of Hell's Kitchen, that Frank's intellect finally predominated. In 1905, he not only won the gold medal in the annual oration contest for his "passionate partisanship" of Walt Whitman, but he even had a novel, "Builders in Sand," accepted for publication by Putnam's, only to have his father withdraw it.[32] Furthermore, during his

senior year, he was an associate editor for both the yearbook and
the literary magazine as well as the captain of the debating team.[33]

By Frank's own admission, he loved his time at Clinton. And
yet, he was not allowed to graduate from there. He had refused to
take a required course in Shakespeare during his final semester because he felt he knew the subject better than the teacher. Was this
the old rebellion surfacing again? Frank recalls that he was motivated by his love for the head of the English department, and that
the only way he could make love to her was by defying her.
Perhaps there was more to it than that. A year earlier, when the
woman with whom his father was having an affair tried to seduce
him, Waldo ran away from home, only to be persuaded by an old
"pervert" to return for his mother's sake. Besides flight, his only
other response to his father's indiscretion at the time was illness,
for which he was shipped to Maine to pass the summer with a couple of friends.[34] It seems likely that Frank's refusal to take the
Shakespeare course was a kind of revenge, a belated resumption of
his revolt against his father.[35]

While Julius Frank couldn't have been more accommodating in
his acceptance of his son's brashness, perhaps because Waldo had
already passed the entrance exams for Harvard, he nonetheless
decided to place his seventeen-year-old son in Les Chaumettes
Pensionnat, a private prep school in Lausanne, Switzerland, for
the 1906–7 academic year. There Waldo learned French and began
his extensive reading of French literature.[36]

As his time in Switzerland neared its end, Frank chose to stay in
Europe to study at Heidelberg University. Upon hearing this news,
Joseph Frank become convinced that his brother was becoming too
much of a European. On his summer vacation from Cornell (where
he was a chemistry instructor), he went to Paris to meet his younger brother and convince him to return to America and Yale, a
college that would make an American out of him. Waldo ac-
quiesced, and as he recalls, it was on the train to New Haven in
September of 1907 that he resolved: ". . . what *I* became was
going to be America! The infantile god of Waldea was still
living."[37]

The accomplishments continued at Yale. A "superior but not
startling scholar,"[38] Frank won two literary awards for essays that
had earlier in his university career been turned down by the college
publications, probably to keep the upstart underclassman in his
place.[39] He got his B.A. in three years but stayed on for an M.A.
so that he could graduate with his class. That last year at Yale was
perhaps his happiest. Having found the curriculum a bore, as he

did most of his teachers, he found refuge in the library, reading a book a day. At the same time he worked as drama critic for the New Haven *Courier Journal*. Also, amidst all the extracurricular activities, which included beer, sports, and, of course, sex, he found time to begin work on another manuscript, "On the Spirit of Modern French Letters."[40] When he graduated in 1911, his two degrees were conferred together, and he was made an honorary fellow of the university and awarded a Phi Beta Kappa key.[41]

After Yale came the years of "finding himself." Following graduation, he traveled to Wyoming to spend the summer on a classmate's ranch. On the way there, he stopped in Chicago and visited the notorious Everleigh Club, supposedly the most "luxurious" bordello in the country. Then in the fall he took a job as a reporter with the New York *Post*. "Eased out" of the position in January of 1912, he joined the staff of the *New York Times*, only to lose the job in mid-January of the following year owing to his "naïveté."[42]

Perhaps journalism was not enough to fulfill his ambition to be a writer. In any case, he journeyed to Paris and lived among other artists from February till September. Though he wrote mostly for the stage,[43] his only success during this stay in Europe appears to have been the completion of his book on French letters, which was accepted by the head of Yale University Press. But Frank's thinking was in such a state of flux that he never finished the required revision and it was never published.[44] The Paris "exile" was important, though, for it was during that period that he began his study of Bradley, Freud, Nietzsche, and, most importantly, Spinoza.[45]

Back home in America in the fall of 1913, Frank lived in Greenwich Village and other addresses in and around New York City. Writing popular fiction and drama throughout 1914, he met with no success in getting anything published. He did, however, meet his future wife that year. Margaret Naumburg introduced him to psychoanalytical techniques. These, coupled with his own background in Viennese psychology, came to influence his writing, and publication soon followed.[46]

But 1914 is most important as the year that witnessed his conversion to Spinozism, a conversion that marked the beginning of his mystic awakening.[47] The career of the writer was joined by the vocation as a seer. A prophet was born and began to grope toward a vision that, in one of its many manifestations, would be articulated in the speech given in Mexico City in 1929.

Frank, of course, was more than simply a creation of his own impulses and abilities. He was also a child of the times. His crusade for a new world was simply an upsurge of the belief that the world faced an imminent transition period after which a stage nearer perfection would be achieved.[48] This belief began in the second decade of the twentieth century and lasted throughout the 1920s and even the 1930s. It was the product of the convergence of every kind of influence—every contemporary blueprint that promised to create a new culture: e.g., Marxism, Freudianism, and Theosophy, to name but a few. Frank was often critical of these plans for growth. He claimed them fraudulent because they were incomplete; they were not "mature enough" to fathom "the cosmos within the American self."[49] Frank's criticism, however, was from the perspective of one who had had firsthand experience with them all. Indeed, these influences that pointed to an apocalypse of sorts converged in the person of Waldo Frank, as the following pages will make clear.

The Cultural Revolutionary

In *The End of American Innocence*, Henry F. May has shown that the cultural revolution that "everybody knows" America underwent at some point in the twentieth century had its beginnings in the years 1912–17. By cultural revolution, May meant that "the sense of what life means" began to change during those years.[50] This revolution coincided with an upsurge in the "utopian longing." Indeed, within the North American context, they might be construed as the same thing.

An important element in both events was a wave of ideas that

> consisted of a special kind of mysticism, a rejection of both utilitarian progress and aesthetic despair in favor of a rather vague, cheerful, wide-open universe, a doctrine of flux and chaos, a suggestion that since nothing was certain, everything was possible.[51]

Henri Bergson was not only the most important authority for this kind of belief, but also "for a brief spell the most influential thinker in the world as well as the rage in intellectual America." One basic concern of his philosophy was evolution ("Evolution . . . to Bergson was both creative and unpredictable. The organism itself played a major role"). The other was thought ("In order to look at any phenomenon, the mind had to stop the flow of time; like the camera, it had to break actual duration into separate instants").[52]

Not surprisingly, the photographer Alfred Stieglitz was attracted to Bergson's philosophy, and the magazines he edited or sponsored contained contributions that illustrated Bergson's influence. In 1917, Waldo Frank became associated with the Stieglitz group, among whom "Bergson was very much in the air." By that time, Frank was probably already familiar with Bergson's works. His reading list for the years 1908–19 contains Bergson's *L'evolution créatrice* and *Essaie sur les donnees immédiates de la conscience.* Furthermore, his former English professor at Yale, William E. Hocking, had recommended Bergson to Frank, emphasizing Bergson's thinking on the powers of intuition. Whatever the direct influence might have been, the major similarities between Bergson's thought and Frank's are their conceptions of intuition and their interest in the mystic experience. Also, Bergson's concept of *élan vital* resembles Frank's concept of desire or will.[53]

Another important element common to the cultural revolution of 1912–17 and the "utopian longing" was the thought of Friedrich Nietzsche. According to May, "Of all the Europeans who repudiated the nineteenth-century world of scientific progress and moral advance, Nietzsche enjoyed the greatest popularity in prewar America." To the young people of this generation, Nietzsche offered liberation and confidence. His doctrines expressed the necessity of moral revolution. To him, modern civilization, with its concepts of progress, utility, reason, and democracy, was sick unto death; "joy and health lay only in the self-fulfilling and self-transcending individual" who would bring about the reversal of Christian values.[54]

Nietzsche's thought received various interpretations by American thinkers. Most commonly he was seen as an aesthete whose enemy was modern culture. American aesthetes made him into "an apostle of art and joy" and an "anti-Puritan" who could only be appreciated by those "who really understood Europe."[55]

Waldo Frank, however, found deeper meaning in Nietzsche, to whose works he was first exposed in 1902–7 while attending the private preparatory school in Lausanne, Switzerland.[56] He began serious study of Nietzsche in 1913 while living in Paris.[57] By his own admission, Frank read probably all of Nietzsche. In the German, he discovered ideas that he could take seriously. In fact, he so absorbed some of Nietzsche's insights concerning psychology, aesthetics, creativity, suffering and pain, culture, and history into his own writings that Nietzsche can be deemed "a major influence in Frank's intellectual growth."[58]

The extent of Nietzsche's influence on Waldo Frank can best be measured by reading Frank's *Our America* (1919), a book that criticizes mainstream American culture while praising what he calls its "creative minority." It is the book that represents the "credo of Frank's career." Significantly, the book concludes with a sentence that epitomizes the Nietzschean turn of mind:[59] "And in a dying world, creation is revolution."[60]

Like philosophy, literature contributed to the cultural revolution in the United States and the renewed faith in the imminent achievement of perfection. The Russian Revolution of 1905 captured the imagination of many Americans, who saw the Russian peasant as the embodiment of the social ideal. This attitude contributed to the admiration of all things Russian. Indeed, as May points out, "Wherever one looked in these years Slavic genius seemed to be flowering. Some of it new, some of it newly popular." Tolstoy was admired as "sage and saint;" then, around 1912, Dostoevsky, with his "mystery and profound emotion," came into vogue.[61]

Waldo Frank first came to Russian literature while in high school. "Beginning with the chance borrowing of *Resurrection*, he read all the Tolstoy he could find."[62] This early absorption of Tolstoy did much to influence the adolescent Frank's ideas on socialism and reform. Frank, of course, was to go beyond the Russian's thinking on these matters, but Kloucek is certain that because of the influence of the Russian novelists on the writers who followed, Tolstoy was sure "to impress Frank even indirectly, the most notable example in Frank's apprenticeship being Romain Rolland, whose debt to Tolstoi was heavy." As for Dostoevsky, Frank told Kloucek that the Russian was "the greatest of all novelists." To Frank, Dostoevsky was a prophet "capable of nourishing the future," like Nietzsche and Whitman.[63]

The contribution of French literature to the worldwide belief in the coming of "Utopia" provides additional proof that the American cultural revolution was part and parcel of an even broader movement. Before the First World War, May writes, "aside from the small groups of critics who read French fluently, Americans were denied access to the major sources of neo-romanticism." However, one of these critics, James Huneker, not only read the neoromantics, but, "ahead of critical fashion," praised them. Significantly, his praise tended to focus on Stendhal.[64] Waldo Frank read Huneker on Stendhal; and, between 1908 and 1912, Frank, who also read French fluently, came to regard Stendhal's *Le rouge et le noire* as "the most powerful novel between *Don Quixote* and *Anna Karennina* [sic]." According to Kloucek, Stendhal portrays the new individual whose will to power generates a chaos that results in his death and that of his world. From this prophetic vision, Frank gained "a vital insight into the chaos of the modern world."[65]

Like Stendhal, the French Symbolists, whose significance to the subsequent aesthetic movements in France through the first half of this century cannot be underestimated,[66] were only known in America to "a very few students of poetry."[67] Frank, who admitted that France had contributed more to his intellectual formation than the United States, was familiar with their work, which he quickly digested. From the Symbolists, Frank derived the basis for his own method of writing. The Symbolists "overthrew conventional syntax, altering the normal word sequence, avoiding rhetorical development, seeking always to find the rhythm naturally inherent in the thought"—a revolutionary technique, indeed.[68]

French literature also influenced Frank through Romain Rolland, whose multivolume *Jean-Christophe* appeared in American translation between 1910 and 1913. Many Americans responded to *Jean-Christophe* with the hope that the new type of realism embodied in the massive novel would take root and flourish in their national literature.[69] In 1913, Waldo Frank read *Jean-Christophe* in its entirety. He identified with the main character, who fought "to achieve recognition in a hostile world," and he poured out his soul to Rolland in a long letter. The letter began a relationship that lasted until Rolland's death thirty years later. It was a relationship that by Frank's own admission exerted a great influence on his personal life and career. As an example of this influence, the following is significant. In 1916, Rolland wrote Frank, expressing his ideas on revolution, the creative life, and his dream of a new world. Rolland saw America's destiny as that of saving and rebuilding civilization. Through self-expression in the arts and by creating "a nation that integrates, not suppresses, the unconscious yearnings" of its diverse population, America could lead the world toward his ideal of an "international culture." Such a revolution would mean a "rebirth of mankind." In essence, Frank made these aspects of Rolland's thought his own.[70]

The one American writer who contributed significantly both to the cultural revolution and to rekindling utopian longing was Walt Whitman. Frank discovered Whitman while in high school, where in 1905 he won a literary contest with "an exciting and almost spell-binding speech" on Whitman.[71] But Frank "found more corroboration for his boyhood enthusiasm for Whitman in France than in America." In fact, the cult of Whitman flourished in France after 1900, a development that also intrigued Frank's associates on the magazine *Seven Arts* (1916–17),[72] Van Wyck Brooks and Randolph Bourne.[73] The interest of Frank, Brooks, and Bourne in Whitman is significant; together with James Oppenheim, "it was these writers who, more than any others in the period, revived the spirit of Whitman as a regenerating force in American thought."[74] Whitman's appeal to American writers lay in his idealism, his use of the language, and his "contagious democratic gospel." For these reasons, Daniel Aaron concludes, "of all their literary forebears, Whitman alone spoke most directly to them."[75] Frank believed Whitman had seen the "apocalyptic vision," a vision that Frank shared.[76] Kloucek draws this parallel between the two: "Both seek the new world, which shall be created by man, through man, and from within man."[77] Finally, John R. Willingham places Frank squarely in the Whitman tradition:

> His theory of art is one with his political and social viewpoints, and all are blended with a rare mystic zeal to make the earthly state of America a fitting symbol of and preparation for the cosmic unity which man perceives slowly but which the artist following Walt Whitman knows intimately in flashing insights. The revelation of such insights in organic forms is thus the highest social good the artist can perform in America; this is the fundamental position of the theories of both Whitman and Frank.[78]

Along with the departed Whitman, the living voice of D. H. Lawrence contributed to the utopian longing and cast a spell on Waldo Frank. Around 1912, Lawrence had begun "to interest the extreme avant-garde" in the United States,[79] and, as Alfred Kazin notes, Lawrence's *Sons and Lovers* (1913) was part of a European current that seemed to point the way toward the new culture for which America hungered.[80] His work represented the revolt against social regimentation. Americans applauded him for his censure of society's decadence, for his championing the freedom of the spirit, and for emphasizing the unconscious.

> Life for Lawrence was a series of emotional tensions. Emotional crises whip the blood into strenuous activity. Intellection, associated with any natural act, deprives it of its vitality. Thus his attack upon modern morality, modern science, modern squeamishness of all sorts.[81]

Kloucek credits Lawrence's work merely as serving to inspire Frank's "poetic style" as well as the way he described feelings and emotions.[82] But to Paul Rosenfeld, Frank's colleague on the *Seven Arts*, Lawrence was Frank's "master." Rosenfeld notes Lawrence's stress on the "projections of the subconscious mind" and "the voices of the earth behind the intellect." Following this lead, Frank "focussed his attention more directly . . . upon the hidden ground of the psyche."[83] Lawrence's stories were welcomed at the *Seven Arts*, for Frank believed Lawrence's work could "give to the nation's outlook a vision which would honor the complete man rather than the person whose single obsession was property and its value."[84] In recalling his days in Greenwich Village (ca. 1914), Frank admits that everyone read D. H. Lawrence, and refers to the Englishman as "the prophet angered because he had no church."[85] What Christopher Lasch has written of the influence of Lawrence on American intellectuals in general seems particularly applicable to Frank: "It was as a prophet armed with a new religion that he caught their imagination and as a prophet that they accepted or rejected him."[86]

The Freudian

Of all the influences that contributed to the utopian expectation, that of the psychology of Sigmund Freud is the most curious. And Frank's assimilation of this influence is peculiarly American. A. A. Brill, an American doctor who had studied Freudian clinical psychology at Carl Jung's Clinic of Psychology in Zurich, in 1908 arranged with Freud to translate the latter's principal works into English. Brill published his translation of the third edition of Freud's *The Interpretation of Dreams* in 1913, and followed that with his translation of *Three Contributions to a Theory of Sex* in 1918. These works "contained most of what was to be tagged 'Freudianism' by the layman."[87]

Brill's translations were widely reviewed and the outlines of Freudianism came in for considerable discussion by the popular press.[88] In 1916 Freud "was in the air,"[89] with his theories impressing one American enthusiast as "the most fantastic cult of the coming decade."[90] Greenwich Village and the circle of Mabel Dodge (who "all but established the pattern of the 'free-lance intellectual' of the twentieth century") were where one went to learn about the "new psychology," which rivaled the war in Europe as a topic of discussion.[91] May explains the "sudden rush of interest . . . partly by the chaotic state of American psychological theory at the time, partly by the deep splits and strains beginning to be apparent in American thought as a whole."[92]

But of what interest was Freudian psychology to those who

dreamed of Arcadia? Much of the enthusiastic welcome that Freud's works received "was due to his being catalogued as an irrationalist." Freud's works were perceived as a major threat to the "accepted rationalist approaches to knowledge." This perception sprang from the interpretation some gave to certain Freudian terms. First, there was Freud's concept of the *unconscious*. For Freud, the unconscious was a reservoir of what we are not conscious of. And the unconscious was of two kinds—"the simple, latent mental states, which are easily accessible, and the states which appear, through some obstruction or other, to be permanently hindered from being conscious." Coming at a time when orthodox psychology was limited to the conscious, the concept of the unconscious was thought by some to be "a sharp attack upon rationalism," and a final disposal of "the hampering limits imposed upon thinking by the too rigid syntactic systems."[93]

Secondly, the term *repression* was given an American twist. For Freud, repression was "a question of psychic energies purely; and a 'cure' which makes the repressed material conscious to the patient does not allow him free use of it; it merely points him a way of dealing with it intelligently within the world in which he has to live." But for those Americans who resented the Puritanical morality of the country, *repression* became a term of "disapproval," and to recall the repressed suggested "relaxed disciplines and smoothed the way to seduction."[94]

Finally, Freud's concept of the *libido* became "confused with the *unconscious*, as though the terms were interchangeable," even though to use libido in reference to instinctive life is almost pointless. But as Hoffman makes clear, most of those who read Freud did not study him carefully and mistook him for "an advocate of free love who argued that sexual freedom was the only pathway to happiness."[95]

Thus, armed with clues to the knowledge of the unconscious and a rationale for revolution against accepted standards of behavior, radicals and dreamers alike adopted Freud as one of their own, "a patron of a new cult of happiness." This perception of Freud as a "liberator of the soul, or at least the creative psyche" was ironic, for Freud "hated false optimism and above all mysticism."[96] Despite efforts of those like Walter Lippman, who in 1915 invited Dr. Brill to speak at Mabel Dodge's salon "in order that Freud might be better understood and not distorted,"[97] by the 1920s Freudianism was even being linked to Marxism "in the fight against bourgeois economic and social convention."[98]

Waldo Frank was introduced to the writings of Freud by his future wife Margaret Naumburg (they were married on 20 December 1916). She had studied with Montessori in 1913 and founded the Children's School (later named the Walden School) in 1917.[99] Waldo Frank read all of Freud's published works, and found that the writings "amazingly corresponded with much of the intuitive thinking . . . on human motivation" he himself had carried out.[100] Yet Frank freely acknowledged his debt to Freud.[101] For example, recalling his days in the Village (before World War I), Frank writes, "Freud . . . was a guide to our immaturities and the balm to our guilt of having abandoned the house of our fathers." Moreover, Frank credits Freud with revealing to the prewar generation their desire to be released from the outmoded middle-class morality of their elders. Significantly, Frank recalls that the "world of Freudian wish" was a "fantasma befitting the disintegrating world of Western Culture."[102] Earlier Frank had written that Freud systematized "the lines of continuity between the person and the objective world."[103] This was the cue that Frank took from Freud as he strove to sketch "the lineaments of a new culture."[104]

Waldo Frank also found in Freud support for his belief in human perfectability. Frank took Freud's ego-ideal, to which Freud assigned the role of realizing man's "higher nature," and harmonized it with his faith in Spinoza's system "for consciously guiding and controlling the passions."[105]

Frank's differences with Freud, however, are just as important in revealing the extent of Frank's commitment to his faith in the future. Frank was critical of Freud for being overly insistent on the rational, and for not allowing for "the mystical vision in the unconscious."[106] He maintained that the ego possessed an aspect that Freud disregarded, "the direct conduit to Cosmos." Rather than reject Freud for such discrepancies with his own thought, however, Frank reinterpreted him even more than most American contemporaries would have dared. He contended that Freud was wrong in defining himself as antireligious, for his concept was correct. "For him the human world, even unto the will to die, was a structured organism suffused with an energy" as vital as Hegel's "Absolute" or Spinoza's "Substance." Thus, Frank believed Freud's goal was the same as that of real religion. To Frank, Freud's confidence in the power of the ego to transform the id and "make man whole" was, indeed, religious.[107]

In characteristic fashion, Frank then credits Freud as an influence on the apocalyptic vision. He insists that with the appearance of the new religion, the one that will change the ego so that man can relate to the cosmos within himself, "Freud's part in it—a method for revealing and classifying the dynamic elements of the individual—will then be seen as central."[108]

The religious sense of Waldo Frank, his belief in a means of victory over death—what he called "the mystic x" that Freud hesitated to allow[109]—contributed greatly to his apocalyptic vision. Indeed, religion influenced the utopian longing; this subject will be dealt with next.

The Spiritualist

E. L. Doctorow, in his 1975 best-selling novel *Ragtime* (a historical novel of the pre-World War I era, set in New York City), describes at one point how J. P. Morgan gave Henry Ford the exclusive privilege of viewing his most prized possessions—ancient artifacts, "souvenirs," that proved the existence of the "secret wisdom" of the ages. Morgan then suggested that Ford was but an instrument of trends that affirmed the ancient wisdom, and tried to persuade Ford to join him on an expedition to Egypt in search of truth. Ford replied that a book entitled *An Eastern Fakir's Eternal Wisdom* only cost him a quarter, yet told him everything he needed to know to put his mind at rest.[110]

That Doctorow included such an episode in a book on the Ragtime Era is no aberration. There was during the late Victorian period a revival of occultism that lasted well into the twentieth century. The occultists operated outside established religion; they concerned themselves with the esoteric knowledge, a continuous body of wisdom dating from ancient times "which had remained rejected from the mainstream of European culture because of historical accident."[111]

The ancient wisdom embraced a wide variety of ideas, all of which were unquestioningly assumed to be absolutely true by the believers.[112] Some of these ideas deserve mention, as they contribute to the faith in the imminent perfection of the world. The oldest Western source was the mysterious Pythagoras (ca. 580–500 B.C.), who, as legend has it, viewed the universe as an orderly, harmonious cosmos composed of numbers that reflected its divine arrangement. Pythagoreans regarded "the understanding of the cosmos and its forces as paths leading to ultimate salvation in an afterlife."[113] To Pythagoras's "mystical mathematics" was added the literature attributed to Hermes Trismegistus—ancient Egyptian wisdom that included alchemy, the "symbolic rendering of the quest for self-transformation."[114] Pythagoreanism and Hermeticism converged in Gnosticism, the name given to a number of systems that "embody the doctrine of divine ensnarement in matter."[115] Put another way, man could only find salvation through *gnosis* (knowledge) deriving from a godlike vision; after death he would ascend to God.[116] Gnosticism was thus a source of the ancient wisdom, as was Neoplatonism (also sprung from Hermeticism). Founded by Plotinus (A.D. 205–270), it "taught an emanationism: that the cosmos is made from emanations from the One and that man can return to the One by mystical experience." Rooted in Neoplatonism is the Cabala, a speculative Jewish mysticism that also contributed to the ancient wisdom.[117] The Cabalists attempted to gain a vision of the throne of God that is described in the first chapter of Ezekiel.[118] Like all associated with a gnostic tradition, they believed ultimately in the immanence rather than the transcendence of God.

These early sources of the ancient wisdom were reflected in movements such as Rosicrucianism, in which a group of seventeenth-century Lutherans attempted "to present an apocalyptic message of universal reform." Such occult traditions, combined with mesmerism, Swedenborgianism, American transcendentalism and revivalism, formed the basis of Spiritualism. Beyond its belief in life beyond death and the ability of spirits to communicate with the living, this variety of religious liberalism believed in the notion of human perfectionism. The revival of Spiritualism in America in the 1870s, combined with a new knowledge of Asian religions, gave birth to the Theosophical Society.[119]

The term *theosophy* means "divine wisdom" and it was used to refer to the combination of the aforementioned systems of occult, mystical speculation. The force behind the Theosophical movement was Mme. H. P. Blavatsky. Basically, her writings presented the "ancient wisdom-religion" as "the answer to the religious strife of the modern age"; for Theosophy "calls the individual to a life of sacrifice, both for the sake of others and also as a means to his own salvation," thus harmonizing religious life with life in the world— the answer to a perennial problem in religion.[120]

In 1907, a year when Theosophical activity was peaking in Russia, P. D. Ouspensky discovered the movement and its literature. Already influenced by Nietzsche (who "had become inextricably entangled with the occult and Symbolist literature"), Ouspensky, as James Webb describes it, "sucked out the yolk from his Theosophical reading." He followed this with an intensive reading in occult and mystical literature, and in 1911, with a thorough knowledge of Theosophy, he began to write the book that made his name—*Tertium Organum*. The book expounded the idea that man must try to expand his consciousness to the world beyond appearances. Differing from Theosophical literature that generally saw "the evolution of humanity toward higher consciousness as a process occupying millenia," Ouspensky thought Utopia was close at hand. In Nietzschean terms, he wrote, "The future belongs not to man, but to *superman*, who is already born and lives among us. A higher race is rapidly emerging among humanity, and it is emerging by reason of its quite remarkable understanding of the world and of life."[121]

In 1915 Ouspensky met the mysterious Georgei Gurdjieff, "a seeker for esoteric knowledge, a student of the unconscious mind, a 'physician-hypnotist', a professional occultist," who had developed a "Method that can only be described as having as its aim to show the best way for men to attain whatever aims they may have." There now began a relationship with Gurdjieff as the teacher, Ouspensky as the pupil. Though the two eventually broke over philosophical differences, their names remained associated— an association fostered in his native England as well as America by A. R. Orage, who taught Gurdjieff's ideas after the 1920 United States publication of *Tertium Organum* was enthusiastically welcomed in that country's occult circles. Orage presents quite a story in himself. In the late twenties he had "an extraordinary underground influence." As Webb explains, "Although psychoanalysis was a more enduring movement, in Orage's New York heyday the revelations of Professor Freud were no match for his captivating charm."[122]

How does the influence of occultism and mysticism in shaping the apocalyptic vision apply to Waldo Frank? Bittner shows that at Yale "the reading of Strindberg seems to have inspired Frank to investigate mystical philosophy and to have led him eventually to the Orientals."[123] Kloucek adds that the renewal of interest in the philosophies and religions of the East, which began in the nineteenth century, was initiated by the idealists, whose philosophies, in turn, stimulated a revived interest in mysticism; therefore, "it is not surprising to find Waldo Frank reading in Hindu, Brahman, and Vedantic literature" while he was in college.[124]

Whatever the sources of his original interest, Frank, upon graduating from Yale in 1911, began studying Oriental religions; his reading included the Rig-Veda, the Upanishads, the writings of Lao-tzu, and Buddhist works.[125]

While still at Yale, however, Frank also studied the organicist philosophy of F. H. Bradley. Since organicists agree that their position derives from Hegel (although Hegel would not have classified himself as an "organicist"), only a few of the general postulates of organicism significant in Bradley's work need be mentioned. First, organicists see the universe as a "creative process which integrates into an organic whole." The final integration is "the Absolute, . . . Whole, . . . God." Every part of the Whole plays a role "in the creative process but assumes its form and its aim through its relations with all other parts and with the Whole." As for man, his goal is to achieve the heights of "self-consciousness, wherein his knowledge, willing, feeling integrate into an awareness of a self which knows no limits, but rather expands into a vision of a total self, which is the universe as a whole, or the Absolute."[126]

It was probably Frank's professor, William E. Hocking, who introduced him to Bradley's work; in his book *The Meaning of God in Human Experience*, Hocking calls Bradley the "elder metaphysician to our time." Frank credited Bradley with influencing his intellectual development. Kloucek, however, concludes that Bradley's greatest influence upon Frank was that he prepared the way for Frank's conversion to "Spinozism," a conversion in which Nietzsche also was "most influential."[127]

Indeed, Baruch Spinoza was "the only person to whom Waldo Frank avow[ed] discipleship." This is not surprising in light of the fact that "every organicist philosopher from Schelling to Bradley to Whitehead has been in some measure indebted to Spinoza," whose "system is organic."[128]

Frank was indebted to Spinoza for his "idea of God," his "theory of knowledge," his "naturalistic view of man as part of nature," and his belief in a "conduct of life that leads to the intellectual love of God."[129] Frank summarizes Spinoza's vision thus:

> Spinoza is the prophet who has completed the purifying of the knowledge of God into the God of inwardness, of substance and action. . . . It is he who has best established the organic belief of God *in* matter and in human thought; who has made rational the ancient mystic intuition that the cosmic dwells within the man in so far as the man grows self-conscious.[130]

According to Kloucek, all of Frank's work was an effort to carry out that vision.[131] William Bittner, however, interprets Spinoza's influence on Frank somewhat differently. He writes: "It is not that he took his ideas from Spinoza, but he took Spinoza as a model in centering his knowledge of society, modern psychology, and phenomena of the material universe on the unity he felt to exist."[132]

Frank sees Spinoza's ethic as "revolutionary," due to the impossibility of its fulfillment within a world constrained by the prevailing tenets of modern rationalism, positivism, and empiricism. He writes, "If a man knows the presence of the Creator within him, how can he hate, how can he lust, how can he fear—even death?" Moreover, Frank accepts the basic insights of Spinoza's assumption "that man by intellectual effort can free himself from the bondage of his affections and passions, attaining reason whose grasp of reality is authentic and autonomous." After all, Spinoza had written, "By reality and perfection, I mean the same thing."[133]

It is worth mentioning that Frank also studied Christianity. Having been "fully acquainted with the Catholic resurgence in France around 1900 with its strong revival of medievalism and mysticism," Frank was attracted to Catholicism, which he came to see through his reading of the church fathers, Aquinas, Dante, and other writers as "a structure founded on the intuitive knowledge of man's brotherhood in God and so ordered as to give a specific and organic place for every one of the parts of the whole man." In addition, he read the Bible, Talmud, and the medieval Jewish mystics and Cabalists down to Spinoza. By 1920 "Judaism in a modified form won his allegiance."[134] But more importantly, between 1914 and 1919, probably beginning with his conversion to Spinozism, Frank experienced what has been called "the gradual awakening of a mystic illumination." It culminated in a number of mystical experiences in 1920.[135] As Bittner explains:

> First comes the awareness of personal inadequacy . . . ; and finally an illumination that cuts through the complications of the mystic's problems with an experience leaving him full of a sense of the unity of all things. The mystic feels personally involved, with unity expressing itself through him.[136]

Even before his mystical experiences of 1920, Frank had written in *Our America* (1919): "Ours is the first generation of Americans consciously engaged in spiritual pioneering. . . . We go forth to seek America. And in the seeking we create her." Then, as Webb notes, following his illuminations, "Frank read *Tertium Organum*, and lost no time passing on his enthusiasm to his friends." The book "seemed to provide the basis for the leap into that American superconsciousness which Frank so hopefully expected."[137]

Kloucek argues that *Tertium Organum* could hardly "stimulate anyone as well grounded as Waldo Frank in metaphysics and Eastern mysticism."[138] The evidence suggests otherwise. In 1923, when Frank was a "literary lion" influencing a circle of writers including Hart Crane, Gorham Munson, and Jean Toomer, this group became so fascinated by Gurdjieff that they secured a hearing for Gurdjieff's ideas in America. Furthermore, by 1924, with Orage beginning his career as an independent teacher of Gurdjieff's ideas, Waldo Frank numbered himself among a group of Orage's devotees who met weekly for study of the Gurdjieff system. He attended one of the groups for three years, and defended Orage "against critics who despised the worldly brilliance of his following."[139]

In 1927 Frank went to France to see Gurdjieff at his Institute, apparently believing that "the Master would welcome him as a fellow sage." Instead, the visit saw Frank humbled and embarrassed by Gurdjieff—to such an extent that Frank left in a rage, discarding his "investigation of the possibilities of becoming a more perfect individual" and reverting to the "possibilities of the nation as the more perfect communion of the individual with his kind"—an idea suggested in *Our America*. Frank's *Re-discovery of America* (1929) contained his new vision in its more developed form. Showing the influence of his wide mystical reading, he poses the idea of "the symphonic nation in whom all selves adumbrate to wholeness [*sic*]."[140]

The Social Revolutionary

The ideal of social revolution as the means of fulfilling the apocalyptic vision is something of a constant in utopian thought. Consider the following observation by Melvin Lasky:

> The utopian dream of the future . . . implies the nightmare of the present. . . . There has always been a new world to win; and, as a consequence, the perennial question—phrased in identical words from More to Burke to Owen to Lenin—"What is to be done?" . . . It would appear throughout all of history man has tried to fulfill some of his highest moral and political aspirations through some form of revolutionary act.[141]

In America, the ideal of social revolution was much in evidence, and Frank was quite naturally exposed to it.

At the end of the nineteenth century the anarchist ideal gained new adherents in Western Europe and the United States. "A label of fascination and even pride to some intellectuals," anarchism was "most effectively popularized" by Mikhail Bakunin, Peter Kropotkin, and Leo Tolstoy. In fact, Tolstoy with his nonviolent religiosity was "anarchist counselor to the world until his death in 1910."[142]

Anarchism fragmented prior to World War I, and "worked more as a catalyst within other revolutionary movements than as a unitary force." But more importantly, the anarchist ideal "kept alive a quasi-religious, totalistic belief in revolution during an era of positivism, skepticism, and evolutionary progressivism." The major proponent of this faith was Emma Goldman, who combined "Russian revolutionary hopes along with the Judaic idea of the promised land."[143]

Closely linked to anarchism was the American version of revolutionary syndicalism, embodied in the Industrial Workers of the World (IWW), founded in 1905. Its leader, William D. ("Big Bill") Haywood, advocated the general strike as the vehicle that would produce the revolution to bring about worker control. At its peak in 1912, the IWW claimed 100,000 members.[144]

Goldman and Haywood were heroes to the young artist-rebels of prewar Greenwich Village. This should come as no surprise, for as Oppenheim recalls of the Village, "Everyone was cooking up some kind of revolution."[145] But this radicalism was not confined to the Village. One contributor to this atmosphere was the wealthy avant-gardist Mabel Dodge, whose "evenings" at her Fifth Avenue house were famous.[146] Of her salon, Kazin writes, "It was the entrance to Bohemia and a preparation for it."[147] And Aaron tells us that "here young men and women of the middle class could consort with notorious radicals who were happily subverting the social order by word and deed."[148]

Despite the war and the ensuing "Red Scare" of 1919–20, the "revolution" continued to arouse new hopes. The rhetoric of revolution, as Lasky observes,

> moved from a traditionally vague utopia of scientific socialism, with its imprecise and uneasy mélange of technological and humanist aspirations, toward the urgent seizure of state power by the true party of the proletariat in the name of all the masses.[149]

But even if the 1920s and 1930s saw Marxism "discovered" and Leninism "embraced, . . . the sentiment was often Bohemian."[150]

And why not? Gorham Munson writes, in recalling the years 1916–24, "bohemianism was characteristic of my generation."[151]

What influence did revolutionary activity and ideology have on Waldo Frank? Frank's childhood probably predisposed him favorably toward revolutionary concepts. Lewis Mumford observes that Frank, having started in life with all the advantages of the upper-middle class, was uncomfortable with such "economic favoritism," and fantasized that he was on "the side of the deprived and the subordinate."[152] Furthermore, his reading of Robert Hunter's *Poverty* in 1906 and similar works on social injustice aroused not only his curiosity but probably his indignation; and "he took walks through other parts of the city, getting to know the slums and to observe their inhabitants."[153] These experiences combined with his boyhood idolization of Tolstoy to inspire him toward anarchism—at least he admits to having "anarchist leanings" as late as 1924. Upon his arrival in Greenwich Village in 1913, Frank recalls that he was "a revolutionary like all the starters of my generation."[154] Kloucek, though, contends that as of 1917 Frank, even after having read Marx, "was no more than a 'philosophical radical' . . . who could accompany John Reed to an anarchist meeting where Emma Goldman spoke, but could not be impressed by either personage." Nevertheless, Frank registered for the draft in June of that year as a conscientious objector on the political grounds of his repudiation of "imperialism."[155] (Or was it really cowardice? Frank was in such anguish over his real motives that by September he was ill.[156] An incorrect diagnosis of appendicitis was followed by an unnecessary operation that almost killed him, and as a result he was despondent throughout the winter of 1917–18.[157]) Whatever his motivation, his action aligned him with the radicals of his day, the anarchists and the socialists. Thus, if Frank's revolutionary tendencies were not born of his sojourn in Greenwich Village among the radical intelligentsia, they were undoubtedly nurtured and strengthened by it.

The next fifteen years saw Frank act on his revolutionary proclivities in a political way. In November of 1919, he went to Kansas, where he helped organize the Non-Partisan League, "a socialist-front attempt to revive the old Populist vote." At the same time he wrote propagandistic editorials for the *Ellsworth County Leader*. But disillusionment set in a month later when he witnessed the sellout of the membership by the League's representatives at the national convention in St. Paul.[158]

His experience probably caused him to confine his political work

to writing. In November of 1925, he became a contributing editor
to *The New Republic*, a post he maintained until his resignation on
5 June 1940. Then, in May 1926 he was named contributing editor
for the *New Masses*, beginning with its inaugural issue, and was
carried until February 1930.[159]

It was not until 1931 that Frank, following a trip to the Soviet
Union, was swayed by the romance of communism[160] and finally
convinced that the Communist party was the only organization that
had the means to change society from capitalism to socialism. He
decided, however, not to join the Party but to accept its basic goal,
"the creating of free persons; even if its doctrines . . . and its practice, barred free persons and suppressed them."[161] In November
he spoke of his Russian sojourn to a meeting of the Friends of
the Soviet Union. He also joined a committee that protested the
persecution of Chinese writers by their government.[162]

The following year, the fellow traveler was named chairman of
the Independent Miners' Relief Committee, which aided strikers in
Kentucky and Tennessee. In an attempt to get food to the striking
miners, he and other members were arrested outside of Pineville,
Kentucky. Though the charges of disorderly conduct were dis-
missed, the committee was urged to leave the county. Before they
could, however, he and his companions were rounded up from
their hotel rooms by vigilantes, and taken out by cars to the out-
skirts of town, where they were assaulted. Frank was struck from
behind by some metal object; the blow resulted in a slight
concussion.[163] Two days later, on 12 February, he testified before a
U.S. Senate committee that investigated the brutalities surrounding the famous Harlan County miners' strike.[164]

In August he and his onetime close friend Sherwood Anderson
headed a writers' delegation of the National Committee for the
Defense of Political Prisoners. The group meant to protest the
treatment of the Bonus Army in Washington, D.C., but his group
was snubbed by President Hoover.[165]

In 1935, the cracks in his loyalty to the Party begin to show. He
joined the International Committee for Political Prisoners and
penned a lone minority statement that disapproved of Stalin's mass
executions. Yet he did not break with the Communists, and in the
fall of the following year he did political work for the Committee
of Professional Groups for Browder and Ford. This activity got
him arrested on 30 September along with Earl Browder's party in
Terre Haute, Indiana. Five days later, the indomitable Frank was
the main speaker at a rally for Browder at New York's Town
Hall.[166]

By 1937, however, his defense of Leon Trotsky and his call for an international Trotsky trial got him denounced by Browder, and this ended Frank's relations with the Communists.[167]

Frank's path had followed two detours from Marxism as he pursued realization of his apocalyptic vision. These detours were determined by the nature of his utopian-revolutionary thinking. Specifically, it was Frank's thought regarding his chosen profession that set him upon his first detour from Marxism. He had joined the literary revolt against the "genteel tradition" in American letters; he hoped to regenerate America through his art.

The Literary Revolutionary

According to Daniel Aaron, literary revolts "seem to have occurred periodically from the early nineteenth century to the present." There is a preparatory stage, "usually marked by the pursuit and discovery of a philosophical system . . . to sanction the movement." Marx, Nietzsche, Tolstoy, Freud—these "are only a few of the European prophets who have been domesticated and sometimes vulgarized to serve American intellectual purposes."[168] Then,

> In sermons, essays, poems, and plays, in fully realized works of art and in thinly concealed tracts, the artist conveys his vision of society. Sometimes he remains a party of one; sometimes he is associated with other literary or quasi-literary alliances.[169]

The first literary revolt of the twentieth century began, according to Aaron, between 1910–12 and ended in 1919. What did these writers-in-revolt believe in? "'Released personality', 'expression of self', 'emotion', 'intuition', 'liberation', 'experiment', 'freedom', 'rebellion'—these phrases and words connote[d] the prevailing spirit."[170] As early as 1913 George Santayana rendered a contemporary diagnosis of the period. In his judgment,

> the age . . . was one of transition. Traditional Christian civilization was dying, and the nineteenth-century forces of atheism, democracy, and progress still gaining. . . . Instead of defending reason and tradition, the current age was reacting to the materialist and progressive threat with various kinds of irrationalism. Everywhere in art, literature, religion, and philosophy, anarchy had broken out. This upsurge of instinct, barbarism, anarchism, and sheer whim was not altogether to be despised; it was what made the age interesting. But it could not make it great.[171]

Ironically, Santayana became perceived by some as a partisan herald of this transition period. After all, in his 1911 essay "The Genteel Tradition in American Philosophy," an analysis of "the malady of American intellectual life," he had depicted "gentility as the prime enemy of a vigorous and imaginative cultural life." As Douglas Wilson points out, "Santayana's strictures were welcomed by the younger, resurgent generation, once they became known, not only because they expressed something important and useful, but because they put the 'custodians of culture' on the defensive."[172]

Thoroughly familiar with Santayana's writing on American life was one of his former pupils, Van Wyck Brooks. Clearly, Brooks profited from Santayana's ideas, and Santayana's influence shows in the characterization of America's intellectual tradition that Brooks offers in "America's Coming-of-Age" (1915).[173] In this essay, as well as in his writings for the *Seven Arts*,

> Brooks diagnosed the central disease of American civilization as an insane individualism. This historic obsession with self-reliance and personal achievement not only distorted economic practice but made it impossible for the nation to develop the spiritual and emotional resources necessary for a truly healthy society.[174]

To cure these ills, Brooks urged the "formation of a genuinely organic social and cultural experience" that in turn "depended on the substitution of self-fulfillment for self-assertion."[175]

Brooks's faith was that of his literary forebears, Melville and Whitman, of whom he writes:

> . . . their ideas were not of their own time but had a long future before them, and a long past behind. . . . They spoke for a democratic socialized world with a humanist philosophy based on the positive elements of all religions; and this was the world I too hoped to see.[176]

Brooks was the "intrepid pioneer," but one who dug deeper than Brooks in the very veins prospected and marked out for mining by him was Waldo Frank.[177] Indeed, Frank was a leader in the revolt against the Genteel Tradition. Of that tradition, he writes in his *Memoirs*, ". . . let the violence speak, let the 'Genteel Tradition' be blown up, with Melville and Walt Whitman to conduct the explosive obsequies."[178]

Frank's outlet, of course, was the *Seven Arts*. Along with Oppenheim and Brooks, Frank led "a group that saw in the late teens an awakening of national self-consciousness, a restless yearning for a finer vision of destiny than the land had previously known."[179] His passion was "to let a word be collectively created,"[180] and he had this in mind when he laid down in his first issue a manifesto as to what the magazine was to be: "an expression of artists for the community."[181] Against the "cold madness" of the world at war, Frank believed a new world had to be made. To his delight, numerous stories were submitted that proclaimed "the world's dawning sense of death and transfiguration."[182]

But the life of the *Seven Arts* was short—only twelve issues from 1916 to 1917. According to Frank, the magazine folded "because its leaders could not counter-balance their egoisms with the stronger social and cosmic elements of their selves."[183] Another reason, no doubt, was that the *Seven Arts* took an editorial position opposing America's participation in the war, and the magazine's sponsor, Mrs. A. K. Rankine, withdrew her subsidy. "Thus the magazine died with its task barely begun."[184]

The death of the *Seven Arts* released Frank to write books. Now his main concern became "the deprivations of American culture, the barriers thrown up by Puritanism, by mean-spirited reflexes of the pioneer experience, by technological willfulness, to the achievement of personal integration."[185] The result was *Our America* in 1919, in preparation for which he toured the country, mainly the Midwest and Far West, the year before.

Paul Rosenfeld points out that "many of the apocalyptic plunges of *Our America*" followed the lead that Brooks set in "America's Coming-of-Age."[186] Indeed, Frank had read the essay and declared it "clear and luminous as flame."[187] But *Our America* was more a "vision of an America to be" than an "analysis of contemporary society and its background."[188]

Brooks probably also had a more subtle influence on Frank—an influence that would send Frank traveling the country in search of America after the literary revolt waned in 1917: Brooks helped initiate Frank in the new cult of "primitivism." It is not surprising that Frank would take to this cult, for primitivism was yet another manifestation of the upsurge in utopian longing.

The Primitive

Van Wyck Brooks recalls that as the 1920s dawned "there were those who were drawn to the primitive."[189] At first glance, primitivism and utopianism seem diametrically opposed. As Henri

Baudet explains, ". . . primitivism mourned the past, utopianism looked toward the future;" and "despite their deep interaction, . . . the two categories are still essentially different."[190] But it is precisely the interaction that made utopians become primitives, for utopianism and primitivism "are at opposite sides of the same coin of human aspiration for a way of life dramatically opposite in complexity and organization from the present." While utopianism looks at the future, "primitivism dreams of a paradise on earth that does or did prove an alternative to the present age could exist." More explicitly,

> primitivism postulated people dwelling in nature according to nature, existing free of history's burdens and the social complexity felt by Europeans in the modern period and offering hope to mankind at the same time that they constituted a powerful counter-example to existing European civilizations.[191]

Primitivism, like utopianism, was a recurrent phenomenon. In the seventeenth and eighteenth centuries, primitives had served as models "of all that was admirable and uncorrupted in human nature."[192] Then, during the 1920s and 1930s, a similar view emerged. A small number of intellectuals and reformers had, by the 1920s,

> repudiated the stress upon racism and Anglo-Saxon institutions in favor of cultural pluralism. Rather than wanting to stamp out minority groups, . . . these thinkers and social reformers favored instead their preservation as a vital part of a better American life for all. In immigrants, Blacks, and Indians, these intellectuals found the virtues and a humanity they thought lost in the White, Anglo-Saxon, Protestant world.[193]

In explaining the change in attitudes, Fredrick Pike has offered a valuable insight as to why primitivism is a manifestation of converging utopian influences that point toward a higher degree of perfection:

> . . . when the self-satisfaction of moderns begins to weaken, as they experience urges of awakening, revitalization, and regeneration, they turn in hope and wonder both toward their own inward natures and also toward "close-to-nature" people in the outward world; for renewal is perceived to depend on contact with the primordial reservoirs of nature both within and without.[194]

The conception of primitive nature that prevailed at this time (ca. 1920) had originated in the romantic movement. Romantics tended to view primitive nature

> as fecund, spontaneous, sublime, . . . ; as "mother mysterious," a dark and amoral force from under earth, . . . ; a "blood consciousness" ranged forever against sterile rational order and efficiency, and creative of all that is lustful, much that is destructive, and all that is beautiful.[195]

Certainly this conception of primitive nature was evident in the changing attitudes of white liberals and radicals toward blacks, as the latter came to symbolize "the 'soul' which in the West had been triumphed over by the intellect." From Vachel Lindsay to Ezra Pound, whites conceived of blacks as "sensual and passionate, high-spirited and exotic."[196] Waldo Frank was no exception, as is evidenced by his novel *Holiday* (1923)—his depiction of the struggle in the South between the white and black races. To better understand the black experience, he made two trips to the South in 1920, one with the Negro poet Jean Toomer in September. (At this time he passed for black; though his dark hair and eyes made this easier, the assumption was that if Frank were with a Negro, then he, too, must be one.)[197] Yet Frank failed to grasp (perhaps because as a white man he could never really know) what it really was to be black in America. Paul Carter, in citing characterization as the novel's major weakness, explains, "The characters are either stereotypes or abstractions."[198]

The "Dionysian" conception of primitive nature was even more evident in the new attitude of white intellectuals and radicals toward Indians. And who was in the vanguard of this movement? None other than the ubiquitous Mabel Dodge, who in 1917 moved to Taos, New Mexico, to live among the Pueblo Indians, and to marry one of them, Tony Luhan. According to Christopher Lasch,

> She loved whatever was exotic and picturesque in Indian life, whatever was not white. The glory of the Indians, . . . was that they did not want progress. . . . Their living like animals was the very source of the Indian's charm. It meant (she erroneously believed) that they had not yet learned to sublimate their biological energies. If sublimation was the root of evil, the Indians still lived in an innocent Eden.[199]

For Mabel Dodge, life among the Indians was the key to her achievement of spiritual regeneration.[200]

Another who sought out the "Dionysian" Indian in Taos was

D. H. Lawrence, who was lured there in 1922 by Mabel Dodge Luhan. After Lawrence "thought he had learned a good deal about the Indians and Mexicans of New Mexico and old Mexico,"[201] he produced the novel *The Plumed Serpent*. The book has been described as

> Lawrence's answer to the cry for the resurrection of old gods. Since they had long since died out in the white consciousness, their revival should be left to the darker-skinned races—the Mexican Indian, for example. In the rhythm of ancient Indian dances, the heroine is led to abandon all of her white reserve. . . . And she senses that this is something different from the collective white consciousness which she has watched during the World War. That was mere lust; this new consciousness of strength . . . was the source of great power and happiness.[202]

But Lawrence was preceded in Taos by none other than Waldo Frank. Frank visited the Pueblo district of New Mexico in 1918 in preparation for the writing of *Our America*. There is no evidence that he set out to find the "Dionysian" Indian. More likely, following the lead of Van Wyck Brooks, he made the trip to the Southwest as part of his "search for a useable past"[203] (the phrase made famous by Brooks in "America's Coming-of-Age"). But there is some evidence that he found *something* among the Indians of the Southwest. According to Brooks, "Waldo had found in the sacred Kiva to which he was admitted 'a great incentive to new vision and stronger wisdom.'"[204] Frank notes in *Our America* that the Indian culture was "a native fact from which vast spiritual wealth might still be mined."[205]

But Frank's encounter with the Indians of the Southwest was not as important as his encounter with the Mexicans of that area. As Brooks recalls, in that "poor and exiled fragment of the world of the Spaniards" Waldo Frank "had sensed at once that it had something for him and for our people. It was something the absence of which made our proud and industrial world . . . a danger and a delusion." Thus, in Frank the lure of the primitive again reunited with the utopian vision. But what was he to do? He might have emulated Mabel Dodge, and lived among the Indians and Mexicans. Frank, however, took another route. "His intuition soon sent him to Spain . . . to find the source of strength this world possessed."[206]

2

THE ANATOMY OF A
RELATIONSHIP
Waldo Frank and Spain

In *Our America* Waldo Frank writes, "The true marriage of the Indian and the Spaniard has brought about a native culture." There is no question that he was enchanted by this culture, which he first observed in the American Southwest. The question that must be answered, before examining the relationship between Waldo Frank and Spain, is: Why did Frank choose the Spanish culture as the source of whatever it was that had moved him, and not the Indian culture? After all, Frank had written that the Indian cultures were "of a spiritual nature: tended in a degree we can measure toward spiritual greatness." Spirituality, of course, was an integral part of Frank's makeup. Furthermore, Frank perceived the Indian religion as being a faith not unlike his own:

> The Indian believes that he must live in harmony with Nature, and its Great Spirit. . . . He prays for harmony between himself and the mysterious forces that surround him: of which he is. For he has learned that from this harmony comes health.[1]

Perhaps the answer lies in Frank's belief, as expressed in *Our America*, that the Indian was unquestionably "dying" and "doomed," his world lying "maimed and buried" under the onslaught of the white man.[2] Thus it must be the Spanish culture from which the Mexicans derived their fire. Such an answer fits conveniently into the fiction that Frank had built around his reason for going to Spain in the first place. He told an Argentine audience in 1942 that as a result of his experience among the cultures of the southwestern United States his intuition led him to Spain and the study of that land's culture.[3] Then in that same year he told an interviewer for the *New York Times Book Review* that he had gone to Spain in 1921 in search of the source of whatever it was about the Mexicans of the American Southwest that had moved him.[4] Moreover, Bittner reminds us that Frank's goal had always been one America, a union of the best that both cultures, Anglo and Hispanic, had to offer. He, therefore, had to experience Spain if he would understand Latin America.[5]

Actually, the truth is not quite so clear-cut. In his *Memoirs* Frank admits that at that time in his life (1921) he was restless. With many American writers and artists crowding into Europe, the lure of Europe became irresistible. As he explains, Europe to him had always meant France, England, Italy, and Germany. He wanted to add Spain to that list. While he had been moved by the Hispanic culture that he had found in New Mexico, his interest remained superficial. He simply wanted to see the country, and after making plans to write travel articles as a way of paying for the trip, he did just that.[6] Thus, intuition was tempered by sheer adventurousness.

The Travels of the Prophet

Waldo Frank went to Spain for the first time in 1921. He recalls how upon discovering that both he and *Our America* had been given favorable mention in *El Peligro Yanqui* (the Yankee peril), a book by Luis Araquistaín who at this time was in the forefront of Spain's Socialist movement,[7] he wrote the Spaniard requesting a meeting. Araquistaín welcomed Frank to Spain and introduced him to his circle. Consequently Frank became acquainted with other writers, notably José Ortega y Gasset, Ramón Pérez de Ayala, Pío Baroja, and Azorín.[8] Ortega was one of the leading intellectuals of the so-called "generation of '98" that led the critical and reforming movement which "set itself the task of analyzing the symptoms of disease in the institutions and social framework of the nation and of prescribing remedies." This movement was strongly influenced by the writings of Angel Ganivet, whose *Ideárium español* "represented an attempt to define the racial character of Spaniards, the place in the world that naturally belonged to them and the steps that they ought to take to occupy it."[9] Significantly, Frank read this book while awaiting his first meeting with Araquistaín.[10] As for the others, Pérez de Ayala had achieved significant status in political circles for his liberalism,[11] while Baroja was "a natural intellectual anarchist who rejected all superiorities."[12] Along with Baroja, Azorín had "flirted with libertarian ideas."[13] Obviously, Frank was in his element.

Frank records in his *Memoirs*, however, that the real significance of the first visit to Spain lay in what he experienced upon seeing his first Spaniards in their native land. The sight of Spanish soldiers boarding a train at Badajoz was a spectacular revelation. These men were not like other Europeans. "They had a tone of their own, a resonant *soundness* . . . they had tension. . . ." He had to explore this further, because he knew it was something momentous.[14]

From Spain he went to Paris, where he met his first Latin American writers. Again, he felt something—an affinity with them that he could not understand. He recalls that his return to Spain was determined by his need to understand what he felt for both the Latin American writers and the soldiers at Badajoz. He had to know Spain and why he loved it—and he decided to write a book that would express his love.[15]

Late in 1923, Frank returned to Spain by way of North Africa (because, he claims, this was the organic route taken by the Arabs, Jews, and Moors, who combined with the Visigoths and Romans to produce Spaniards). Thus Frank had already placed himself on one side of the controversy on Spain's nature that raged around Ganivet's book—the side led by Miguel de Unamuno, who insisted that Spain, though it contained European, African, and Semitic elements, was unique and, therefore, "none of these."[16]

Then Frank traveled throughout the provinces and their cities, gathering his impressions and writing them down, and meeting kindred spirits along the way. In Seville he met Ramón Carande, the historian, and Pedro Salinas, the poet. In Salamanca he met Federico de Onís, head of the Spanish department of Columbia University, who was on a sabbatical. Finally, in Madrid he renewed his acquaintance with Araquistaín, Ortega y Gasset, and Pío Baroja. Also, he came to know the following notables: Victoria Kent, the lawyer who later would become the Second Republic's director of prisons and then Spain's ambassador to France during the Spanish Civil War; Ramiro de Maeztu, whom Frank characterizes as "conservative but culturally open"; the poets Juan Ramón Jiménez, Antonio Machado, and Federico García Lorca; and the writer Ramón Gómez de la Serna.[17] His circle of acquaintances came also to include Enrique Diez-Canedo, "a critical leader in Spain's cultural renascence"; Manuel Cossío, "the authority on Greco"; Alfonso Reyes, the Mexican poet and ambassador to Argentina; and Baldamiro Sanín Cano, the Colombian essayist.[18] The importance of these contacts for his future successes in Spain and Latin America should not be underestimated.

Another important aspect of this second visit was a debate that Frank carried on with Pérez de Ayala in the Madrid papers throughout February-March 1924. The exchange began when Ayala reviewed H. G. Wells's *The Future in America* (1906) and set up the United States as "a horrible example of what *laissez faire* can do to you." Frank replied with an open letter to Ayala published in *El Sol*, taking Ayala to task for following the wrong teacher. But, as often happens in such arguments, Frank and Ayala began to find that they were not as far apart as first seemed the case. The content of this debate, however, is not as important as its consequences for Frank. His impetuosity in joining the polemic won him friends. His writing in Spanish was doubly appreciated by Spaniards because it cost him some trouble. Through his confrontation with Ayala, Frank revealed qualities that some Spaniards found endearing: "being young at heart, impatient with self-righteous tradition, detesting clichés, and shaking off compromise, Waldo Frank was . . . one to communicate well with struggling reformers in any country." These qualities enabled Frank to secure allies who fit his designs perfectly.[19] No doubt, one of these ends was a favorable Spanish reception of his forthcoming book *Virgin Spain*.

Frank in 1925 was to find himself embroiled in another debate with a Spanish intellectual. Maeztu wrote that Frank was one of a dissident faction in the United States that opposed the mainstream of culture—that he belonged to an unassimilable minority, mostly Jews, who were disgruntled because they had no real power. Frank defended the "creative minority" in an article published in *La Prensa* (Madrid), written in Spanish. By the time of this exchange, Frank had already had a portion of his manuscript published in Spanish in the Madrid journal *Revista de Occidente*; and his finished book was anxiously anticipated by those who understood what he was attempting.[20] His star was definitely on the rise in Spain.

Virgin Spain: An Analysis

Published first in 1926 by Jonathan Cape of London, *Virgin Spain* is the book that carried the name of Waldo Frank throughout the Hispanic world.[21] The title is explained by an Angel Ganivet quotation on the flyleaf that reads:

Often meditating on the fervor with which Spain has ever defended and proclaimed the Doctrine of the Immaculate Conception, I have thought that in the depths of this dogma there must be a mystery akin to our national soul: that perhaps this dogma is a symbol . . . of our being.[22]

In Ganivet's *Ideárium español* (from which Frank undoubtedly obtained the above quotation), there is also the following description of Spaniards: "In our old age we have come to find ourselves still virginal in spirit."[23] This statement certainly seems more expressive of Frank's treatment of the Spaniard in *Virgin Spain* as a primitive, with the sensibility of a child—as one who had never made that crucial transition to the self-conscious phase to which Frank attached so much importance.[24] It might be suggested that Ganivet's concept of Spain as possessing a "virginal" spirit was present somewhere in Frank's unconscious, and contributed to Frank's titling of the book. Considering his makeup, Frank himself might accept this analysis.

The subtitle poses more of a problem for exposition. *Scenes from the Spiritual Drama of a Great People* leads the reader to expect scenes from a drama; yet the reader is told in the acknowledgments that the work is what the author calls a "Symphonic History." As Frank explains,

Spain is a complex integer: some of the elements which compose it are known commonly under such terms as climate, geography, historical events, literature, manners, customs, laws and art. Since I felt the Personality of Spain to hold all these *immediately*, as a body holds all its organs, . . . I have let them come, each in its measure and its turn, upon the scene: and like actors in a play, like themes in a symphony, they have spoken their parts. If I could have my way, the pages of my book would come unto my reader as a drama he sees acted in an evening, or as a work of music he hears performed in an hour.[25]

Is this synthesis—or confusion? The reader would have to know what Frank was about. Well-grounded in modern music, Frank numbered among his friends Leo Ornstein, Ernest Bloch, and Aaron Copland, contributors all to the so-called New Music that grew out of pre-World War expressionism. Furthermore, he drew an analogy between expressionistic music (meaning "expression of melodies, enriched rhythms, disintegrated lines, discordant harmonies") and the prose style of Jules Romains. Unanimism, the name by which Romains's style is identified, makes use of dissonance and discord. Unanimism was used by Romains in plays, novels,

and poems; and they were Frank's chief literary source for his
expressionistic methods.[26] Looked at in this light, the inter-
changeability of drama and symphony in Frank's case is understandable.

But even if *Virgin Spain* is to be taken as a symphony, it still
poses a problem for the uninitiated reader. Since Frank makes no
mention of his methodology ("expressionism"), one can only guess
that in his concept the symphony is not a "deliberate stately
scheme" like that of Beethoven, Haydn, or Mozart.[27] In fact,
Frank's depiction of Spain as a willful synthesis of its contradictory
activities, as exemplified by the spiritual unity sought by Isabel the
Catholic, suggests that his idea of the symphony might have been
tied to the symphony orchestra "as it . . . emerged under the
influence of giants like Berlioz, Wagner, Richard Strauss, and
Mahler, with musicians subservient to a dictatorial conductor
whose dominating will accomplished the reconciling of opposites
into harmony."[28]

As well as a symphony, however, *Virgin Spain* is meant to be a
history. Herein lies the real problem for the historian. There is no
bibliography; there are no reference footnotes. Frank's notebooks
on *Virgin Spain* reveal he used the following English texts: Anto-
nio Ballestero's *History of Spain*, Roger Merriman's *Rise of the
Spanish Empire*, William Prescott's *History of Ferdinand and
Isabella*, and finally *Arabic Spain* by Bernhard Whishaw and Ellen
M. Whishaw.[29] In the acknowledgments Frank cites the following
authorities: Onís, Ortega y Gasset, Jiménez, Araquistaín, Cossío,
Azorín, Pío Baroja, Maeztu, Diez-Canedo, Salinas, Reyes, and
Sanín Cano[30]—most of the group he associated with while in
Spain. Any other sources must be gleaned from the narrative.

The governing structure of *Virgin Spain* is Hegel's philosophy of
history; the actors in this drama, be they historical or fictional,
illustrate the dialectic, which unfolds through their psychological
development and is depicted as their real experiences.[31] Nowhere
is this more evident than in the second part, entitled "The Tragedy
of Spain." In trying to show how Spain at the end of the fifteenth
century became what it willed to become, Frank portrays Isabel of
Castile as the willful spirit who strove for a religious unity in Spain
amidst the antithetical elements of Christianity, Islam, and Judaism. Furthermore, Frank makes the realization of a "theodicy" in
Spain Isabel's *raison d'être*, and "everything that does not show
vestiges of this spiritual experiment is deleted from his account."[32]

The question remains: Is *Virgin Spain* a work of history? One
scholar writes that "in a very real sense" it is, but offers no subse-

quent explanation.[33] Frank himself reveals that his primary goal was neither factual or informational, but rather to construct a replica of the organic body within its historical context so that the reader might sense the reality symbolized by "this collective living being."[34] This is knowledge—imaginative, rational, intuitive—as Spinoza conceived it.[35] Perhaps anticipating such an explanation, John Dos Passos brands Frank's "abstract ideas" as useless. Moreover, he assigns the book's academic framework "to a reality that once may have existed but that events have relegated to the storeroom."[36] What he means will become evident as the analysis progresses. Kloucek, however, likens Frank to Nietzsche in that Frank does not obey the canons of "'historicism' practiced by the academic historian," but seeks "the universal values inherent in human experience—what Nietzsche termed the 'supra-historical'."[37] And Frank contends that his history must be seen as a "work of art."[38] In the manner of Nietzsche's aesthetic approach to history, he manipulates historical fact in order to understand "the chaos of the modern world" and to uncover "the values needed for the reconstruction of a new culture."[39] Frank's approach can only serve to blur the book's genre.

Ernest Hemingway, who knew his Spain, puts *Virgin Spain* in the same class as any of the "one-visit books," and labels it "bedside mysticism."[40] His biographer Carlos Baker, in calling it a "travelogue," writes disparagingly, "These impressionistic tours, written by observant travelers who saw the sights by day and kept diaries at night, required quick publication before the complications set in."[41]

Is the matter truly this simple? If so, why is it that reputable scholars have problems with the book's genre? Stanley T. Williams, who accepts the book's historicity, places *Virgin Spain* in the category of travel book, albeit one "with bold techniques and lofty aims" that "attempts to solve the spiritual mystery of Spain."[42] And M. J. Benardete, in his favorable analysis of the book, accepts Frank's notion of a symphonic history; but he also likens *Virgin Spain* to Voltaire's *Lettres philosophiques* and Madame de Stael's *De l'Allemagne*, and places the book in the "spiritual, didactic class of travel book, for it contains through intimations a palpitating lesson that our country may learn from despised Spain." Benardete concedes that Frank's is a "rare approach"; he attributes the book's poor American reception and the confusion as to the book's nature to the "rare background on the part of the reader" that it presupposes, "rare because Spain has been a country Western Society has not studied, visited, or understood."[43] One can only speculate how Dos Passos and Hemingway would answer such appraisals. On the basis of this sampling of review material, one might conclude that the book contains elements of both the travel book and the work of history.

What about Frank himself and his view as to the nature and purpose of his book? He, of course, did not intend *Virgin Spain* to be a travel book. Even for him, though, the book took on a life of its own. Despite his recollection that he intended to write a book expressive of his love for Spain, Frank had originally envisaged the book as a drama and a lament on the expulsion of the Jews from Spain.[44] Then, of course, came his first encounter with the country, and the subsequent rationalization by which he explained the book's genesis. As he recalls, Spain had revealed in him his own incompleteness. Intuitively, he perceived that Spain offered some quality of living that the rest of Europe and America lacked. Moreover, the Spaniard had something he and America "needed in order to live." Characteristically, Frank received the explanation for his love of Spain through a sudden insight while strolling down a Madrid street: *"The average Spaniard was an integrated person."* Unlike the other Western peoples, who had succumbed to "mechanolatry" and mechanistic science, the Spaniard had continued to live in a spiritual synthesis. This synthesis, however, while having succeeded in making the Spaniard whole, contributed to his "backwardness," at least as perceived by his European contemporaries. But for Frank, this very backwardness had saved the Spaniard from the pitfalls of rationalism and mechanism, and had prepared him to progress "toward a new 'Whole' that would be *whole.*" Frank saw in the Spaniard a spiritual outlook, a "perpendicular vigor," that all Americans, especially of the North but also of the South, lacked but needed. For this reason he dedicated *Virgin Spain* "To / those brother Americans / whose tongues are Spanish and Portuguese / whose homes are between the Rio Grande / and Tierra del Fuego / but whose America / like mine / stretches from the Arctic to the Horn."[45] Here, then, is Frank's explanation for his book. The explanation suggests Frank had a preconceived notion as to his book's purpose. In order to fulfill that purpose, the Spaniard had to be made to conform to the role Frank had chosen for him to play.

The time has come to analyze the content of *Virgin Spain*. The objective will be to determine its value as a work of history, to elucidate its controversial parts, and enlarge upon Frank's motive for writing this book.

Being a "symphony," the book begins with a prelude. This open-

ing section has been described as Frank's "poetic vision of a whole
. . . which sets the point of view for the complete work, and the
two correlatives of body-mind are readily recognized in the prominent motif of the horizontal and the vertical."[46] This is best illustrated by the final paragraph of the prelude:

> I have a vision that has not left me. I shall love this people and this
> world. For in my vision I have been born as they. . . . There is a Fun-
> nel. Its walls are the round, white sky. It is thewed together by the rays
> of the sun. And at the Funnel's mouth is the mouth of God, speaking
> the words which are the things of earth. Down this funnel, as in birth,
> we fall. Until we strike upon the land of Spain.[47]

It is precisely such a section, reeking with archetypal incarnation
mythology (the form in which a "high-spirituality person is driven
toward immersion in creatureliness in order to achieve fulfillment
for himself and for the beings of creatureliness"[48]), that opens
Frank to criticism. First, there is that of Ernest Hemingway. In
Death in the Afternoon, he dismisses this kind of writing as the

> unavoidable mysticism of a man who writes a language so badly he can-
> not make a clear statement. . . . God sent him some wonderful stuff
> about Spain . . . but it is often nonsense. . . . The whole thing is
> what . . . I call erectile writing . . . [D]ue to a certain congestion or
> other, trees for example look different to a man in that portentous
> state and a man who is not. All objects look different. They are slightly
> larger, more mysterious, and vaguely blurred. Now there has or had
> arisen in America a school of writers who . . . had . . . by conserving
> these congestions, sought to make all objects mystic through the slight
> distortion of vision that unrelieved turgidness presents. . . . [F]ull of
> pretty phallic images drawn in the manner of sentimental valentines,
> . . . it would have amounted to more if only the vision . . . had been
> a little more interesting and developed when, say, not so congested.[49]

Hemingway's "bawdy hypothesis" (as his biographer Carlos
Baker calls it)[50] is mild when compared to the indictment of
Sacheverell Sitwell, who, in his review of *Virgin Spain*, calls the
book "noisy." Chiding critics for not panning the work because that
might reflect negatively on their powers of discernment, he declares, "Any one who foams at the mouth may be gifted with
prophecy. They need not be afraid in this case. Mr. Frank is not a
writer of genius."[51]

Hemingway and Sitwell are not the only critics of Frank's style.
Even a favorable reviewer writes that Frank's language is at times

"overdrawn and over-emphatic, and at times abstruse and almost incoherent."[52]

Benardete, on the other hand, likens the prose to "highly sensuous" music whose "sheer tones" create moods. He claims the prose "yearns to engage our reasoning, it writhes to conquer our spirit with its magic."[53] Inadvertently, Benardete has exposed the problem of Frank's prose—it *does* writhe, and at times so does the reader.

Following the prelude come three parts (or movements), each with several chapters (or themes). The first part, entitled "Spain," is the longest, and is multifaceted (it contains various developments and recapitulations of different themes). For one thing, it contains Frank's descriptions of and reactions to the regions of Spain. Beginning in North Africa (here exposing the influence of Ganivet's book), moving on to Andalusia, then jumping to Aragon, and, passing through Castile, ending in Valencia, Frank gives expression to what he saw and felt on his travels. This aspect of the book shows precisely why it has been called a travel book. After all, if one cuts through the "poetic word pictures,"[54] one is left with the anecdotal renderings of a traveler who tries to impart universality to his impressions of each region's "topography, folkways, institutions, cities, pictures, buildings, peoples, [and even] skies."[55]

Frank does use history to give a background to his scenes, and, therefore, the travel aspect and history become inextricably entwined. Nowhere is this more evident than in the first chapter, which Frank begins with a description of North Africa. He stresses the role of the Oriental (Arab and Jew) in Spain's early development. By this approach, he places himself in the midst of the controversy surrounding the correct interpretation of Spain's history, throwing in his lot with the Ganivet and Unamuno school of thought, which stresses the ethnic and cultural contribution of the Semite in defining the Spaniard's racial character.[56] This stance immediately leaves Frank open to criticism from a historical standpoint. In his review of *Virgin Spain*, Thomas Walsh, using the nineteenth-century Spanish historian Marcelino Menéndez y Pelayo as his source, minimizes the Jewish element. He points out the importance of the Christian element, representative of Roman civilization, under the Moorish domination. These Christians, he says, formed "the nucleus" of those Spaniards who established a world empire and bestowed on it their culture.[57] In the same vein, Muna Lee surmises that Frank's was a conscious attempt to reveal the influences of Arabs and Jews, which are sometimes handled superficially or ignored. Lee is not pleased with the results, complaining that Spain surfaces from Frank's treatment as "predominantly Jewish and Moorish, strangely un-Latin."[58] And even Araquistaín objects to Frank's emphasis on the Oriental elements.[59]

There is, however, a respectable school of history that lends credibility to Frank's interpretation. The American historian of Spain, Stanley G. Payne, writes of the "great impact of orientalization brought by the establishment of Islam." He is also cognizant of the role played by the Jew in Spain before the Reconquista was completed.[60] And for those who attach more weight to the testimony of Spanish historians of Spain, one can cite the views of Salvador de Madariaga. He does not doubt

> that in their four hundred years of cordial intimacy in peace and war the racial intermixture must have been deep. Not only the Moor but the Jew was bound to become an important element in the Spanish people as at present constituted. The typically Oriental characteristics of the Spaniard . . . must have been reinforced by these four centuries of familiarity with two typically Oriental races.[61]

Moreover, Madariaga occupies a common ground with Frank in his assessment that Arab and Jew gave Spain their best—the Arab, in that his civilization "rose to its highest brilliancy" in Spain; and the Jew, in that "Spanish Jews were the greatest luminaries of Hebrew civilization since Biblical times."[62]

Finally, in his monumental work *The Spaniards*, Américo Castro gives convincing evidence that Arab and Jewish elements were essential in shaping Spanish history—that, in fact, Spain's "true history is inconceivable without Moors and Jews." Also, in branding Menéndez y Pelayo's history as "chauvinism," he diminishes Walsh's source and thereby the validity of his criticism.[63]

Mention of Castro raises other issues, ones on which he and Frank part company. A key question Castro attempts to answer in his book is: When did the Spaniards begin to exist? For Castro, "the Spaniard" did not come into existence until a point well along in the Middle Ages. Accordingly, Romans and Visigoths should be excluded from any true history of Spain. Especially impatient of the viewpoint that "all the inhabitants of the Iberian Peninsula had always been Spaniards," Castro can only be seen as rejecting out of hand Frank's contention that Spaniards are as old as the Celtiberians who originally peopled the peninsula. Frank's interpretation is necessary to his vision of the Spanish race as a symphony that encompasses in harmony all the parts that have, since even the most remote times, contributed their element to the Spanish "sound." To this type of biological determinism and racial psychology, the Castro thesis stands in irreconcilable conflict.[64]

Castro has been attacked for his interpretations of Spanish history. Nevertheless, he brings vast powers of persuasion to his thesis of the importance of Moorish and Jewish elements in forging "the Spaniard" and to his contention that "the Spaniard" did not emerge until the twelfth century as a consequence of the intermingling of the three "castes" of believers—Christians, Moslems, and Jews.[65] To the degree that Castro is correct in this contention, one must regard Frank's interpretation, which tends to incorporate traditional views of Spanish history, as outmoded. Nevertheless, the issue remains clouded. Some Spanish historians, including the distinguished Claudio Sánchez Albornoz (who for years engaged in a bitter polemic with Castro), trace "the Spaniard" back to the Romans and Visigoths, and thus lend credence to this facet of Frank's interpretations.[66]

As the above discussion has shown, the history in *Virgin Spain* must be gleaned from the prose, poetry, or rhetoric (only the taste of the reader can determine the correct term) that is dedicated to metahistorical, cosmological purposes. This sporadic presentation of historical fact serves to veil Frank's teleological argument. By definition, a teleology is a belief that natural phenomena are determined by an overall design or purpose in nature. And *Virgin Spain* is evidence of Frank's belief in the same. For it must be remembered that the book is foremost a "spiritual drama"; Frank represents Spain's history as a series of events involving intense conflict of forces that culminates in a spiritual synthesis. This unity, as he sees it, makes the Spaniard "whole"; and this "wholeness" helps the Spaniard meet the dual challenges of empirical rationalism and mechanolatry—those forces that had diminished the spiritual in man. The Spaniard, therefore, can serve as an example for the Americans in their striving toward a "wholeness" inclusive of the spiritual dimension. Furthermore, the demands of Frank's vision necessitate such an interpretation of Spanish history; and, in fact, his makeup predetermines it.

Tracing the outline of the argument, one begins with Frank's description of North Africa, which forms the backdrop for his discussion of Islam. Frank sees Islam as a product of Mohammed's will—the will of a practical man, not a mystic. Islam's energy, therefore, was horizontal, not vertical—dependent on the conquest of land rather than of the mind and soul. Thus when Islam's advance in the peninsula was stopped, the religion disintegrated and became subsumed into Spain's spiritual culture—which, as will be shown, Frank perceived as shaped predominantly by Catholicism.[67] According to Frank, this process of Hispanicization began as soon as the Moslem invaders settled in Andalusia, where the region's climate and fertility had a debilitating effect on the Islamic ideal. Such a postulate might be interpreted as climatic or geographical determinism. But Frank's concept of wholeness must be recalled here. Spain to Frank is more than the sum of all its parts; it is the unique product of diverse ingredients, of which climate and geography are only a portion. Thus Spain is made to have a life of its own. Spain lets in Islam, and takes from it what it needs as it pursues its destiny—the achievement of wholeness.

After tracing the route of Islam in the first three chapters, Frank jumps to the north, and traces the route of El Cid, the symbol of those who repelled the Moors, through Aragon and Castile to Valencia. Here Frank treats of Christianity and Judaism in the same manner as he does Islam. The religions, caught in the maelstrom that was Spain before the unity imposed by the Catholic kings, became Spanish so that there could be Spain. In this process, Judaism does not fare any better than Islam. Frank sees the self-centered and internationally minded Jew, like the Moslem, refusing to be absorbed completely by Spain in her cosmic quest for oneness. Christianity, on the other hand, succeeds in Spain because the Church embodies the essence of medievalism—the concept of unity, precisely what Spain is striving for.

In the second part, "The Tragedy of Spain," Frank's teleology becomes more manifest. In describing the reign of Isabel in terms of Spain's achieving her vision of spiritual unity, Frank leaves out everything else about her reign that is not involved in this spiritual quest. He depicts Isabel as leaving to her successors the achievement of religious unity beyond Spain's borders—an impossible task that becomes part of Spain's tragedy. Then he studies the lives of the real and fictional actors in Spain's spiritual drama, his aim being to illustrate how "The Will of Saint and Sinner" was directed toward oneness. Thus antithetical forces—the mystic (Ibn Gabirol, Leon Hebreo, Fray Luis de León, St. John of the Cross, St. Theresa of Avila), the Jesuit (Loyola), the jurist (Vitoria), the rogue (Lazarillo the *picaro*) and the artist (Velázquez)—combine their wills to build the structure of Spain's spiritual synthesis. Their justification is epitomized by *Don Quixote*, which serves as the ultimate expression of Spain's quest for unity. Moreover, Spain's greatest work offers a philosophy of life that the world needs.[68]

Finally, Frank sees "The Will of God" expressed in the equilibrium Spain has achieved through turning inward the energies that produced the *Siglo de Oro*. This is Spain's tragedy, for her energy is needed to maintain the equilibrium, and her vital spirit cannot be loosed upon the world again for its betterment. However, Spain is only asleep, not decadent, not dead.

In the third part, "Beyond Spain," Frank brings his argument to its obvious conclusion. He sees issuing from her a new spirit, as exemplified by her writers and artists. No longer satisfied with her own self-sufficiency, Spain needs new worlds to conquer. Spain is on the verge of discarding one whole for another, even greater whole. Frank ends with a prophecy for the Americas. Spain's spirit had once brought about a New World. Now the task of bringing about another new world has fallen to the Americas under the leadership of the United States. As Spain awakens it will pass on its spirit to the New World so that a new spiritual synthesis can be achieved there—one that might even surpass the old spiritual synthesis that Spain had achieved.

The Spain that Waldo Frank sees is basically a Spain of his own creation. Frank's use of only those historical events and facts that buttress his interpretation of Spain's history does not necessarily render *Virgin Spain* worthless as history. Surely, though, the book's claim to being a work of history is diminished by Frank's being less concerned with the exposition of the historical realities and truths about Spain than with using the country and its history as a vehicle for giving expression to the author's ideological and metaphysical aspirations. The last sentence of *Our America* again comes to mind: "In a dying world, creation is revolution." In the revolution that will transform the New World, *Virgin Spain* is Frank's opening salvo.

To round out the analysis of *Virgin Spain*, the text will be examined chapter by chapter, not only to expose the general content of each, but more importantly to point out those parts of the book that raised the most contemporary comment and criticism. What that comment and criticism were and whether or not they were justified will be considered in turn.

Frank's tracing in chapter 1 of Spain's roots to Africa's northwestern desert placed him, as already seen, in the midst of the controversy that had raged in Spain since Ganivet reopened in 1897 the question of Spain's racial character. Frank has been criticized for his "obsession of the Moor,"[69] but it has already been shown that Frank was on firm ground with this interpretation of Spain's history. Above all, the Moslem theme of this chapter allows Frank to produce a "poetic word picture"[70] of the squalor and dormancy he found in the Arab world. From an oasis to a town, down a street to a rooftop, Frank casts his gaze over scenes that elicit extremes of comment. While the writing here has been called some of the book's best,[71] it has also been singled out as containing some of the books worst sentences. As one of the "horrors" that "abound" in the work, Sitwell focuses on the following: "The male music works . . . a stomach wrench, violent as childbirth, shatters upon the mellifluous woman's body."[72]

Chapter 2, "Hinterland in Spain," is another of Frank's poetic visions. It resembles the prelude in that respect, and in a sense it is a prelude to the subsequent chapters in this part.

In chapter 3, "Andalusia," Frank follows the Moslems into Spain. The clash of the three faiths is depicted in the section subtitled "El-Andalus" (the name of the Arab kingdom in Spain).[73] Next, Frank shows how the reign of Islam can still be sensed in Andalusia in its major cities—Córdoba, Granada, and Seville. In Córdoba, Frank finds the idea of Islam living in her streets and in her mosque-made-cathedral. His Córdoba is "an eye within the face of Spain,"[74] an eye that saw the contribution of Arab and Jew, and sees the present equilibrium that exists there as the promise of the future. Suffice it to say, the first vision is true, the second is teleological. As for Frank's description of Córdoba, it has been called "penetrative";[75], his description of the Córdoban girls, however, has been labeled "pseudo-poetry."[76]

From Córdoba, Frank travels to Granada, and this section he subtitles "The Bowels." One can only guess why, for Frank never says. Perhaps he makes such a designation because digestion is completed in the bowels, and Granada was the last place in Spain where Christians in their reconquest came together with Muslims, thus culminating the "digestive" process. In any event, he relates the story of the Moors' last stand, maintaining that their situation resulted from the disintegration of Islam's ideal that set in shortly after the Muslim arrival in Spain. The ensuing atomization of Moorish Spain into small kingdoms that quarreled among themselves allowed for easy conquest by the Catholic kings. Again, his stress is on the religious aspect. The rest of this section is devoted to Frank's lament for Granada, expressed in his description of the Al-Hambra.[77] Somewhat like Dostoevsky's "underground man," who sticks out his tongue at the Crystal Palace, Frank resorts to name-calling. For him, the Al-Hambra lacks . . . the sense of being made for men to dwell in. . . . It is too far from man, too far from God. It is strong, yet it is not poetic. . . . Al-Hambra is incarnate of no warmth, no joy, no agony, no love. . . . It is a jeweled monster.[78]

Frank finds Seville more to his liking. He characterizes Seville as an "auto-erotic, self rapt goddess"[79]—in short, as providing a vision of sexual wholeness. John Dos Passos finds this description "excellent."[80] Frank's Seville is more pagan than Catholic, religion being only a pretext for her narcissism. Thus his Seville is objected to by one who knew the city to be "the home of the Isadores and the priestly martyrs of half the world." This same reviewer is aware of the similarity of Frank's Andalusia with that of his precursor, Maurice Barrès.[81] Frank was familiar with Barrès's work and cites him in a later chapter. But Frank does not acknowledge any debt to Barrès for his interpretation of Seville. Perhaps he should have. Kloucek, at any rate, draws a direct comparison between the two authors' work on Seville, including their views of Don Juan, Seville's hero.[82] It might be recalled from the first chapter, however, that Frank did not always credit those from whom he drew inspiration or by whom he was influenced.[83]

Frank concludes this chapter with a description of gypsy and Andalusian dances. The dances are art; they are, therefore, significant factors in Spain's history. Thus they are parts of the whole. Consider the following passage:

> The *bailarina* moves in a tiny square. She draws intensity from subtle signals of torso, shoulder, limb, hand; this intensity she transposes to an undulous swing carrying her now far about the platform. She is horizontal and relaxed. She turns her naked shoulders forward; the castanets click almost silently beside her hips that roll in a slow ruminance. She faces about; her caress comes full and forward. . . . Plaint and passion weave a subtle net that draws her forward. . . . Suddenly, she is held in rigor. . . . She is the drama of women giving up their sons to the Reconquest, giving the man of their marriage bed to battle with the Moor . . .[84]

Frank's description of the dances has has been called "brilliant," "excellent," and "pithy."[85] Benardete calls the section subtitled "Spain Dances" a "Dürer drawing bristling with mystical lines."[86] High praise, indeed! And just as important to Benardete is Frank's interpretation of the dances' meaningfulness. To Frank, the Andalusian dances express Spain's message—the "quickened fusion of many hostile worlds into a single Beauty."[87] So even a dance is molded into an integer of the projected whole. The same holds true for Frank's interpretation of the flamenco. This dance he sees as an expression of the Castilian will to unity.

Chapter 4 is merely a continuation of the teleological argument behind the veil of an unflattering description of the land and its people. Aragon is "The Atom" of Spain, its inhabitants aloof from the rest of Spain. But Frank sees the energy in this people most notably manifested in Aragon's role in the formation of a nation; it fused first with Catalonia and Valencia, and then joined with Castile in the formation of Spain. The role was that of a "catalyst in a solution."[88] The implication is obvious—Aragon might well play that role again when the time comes for Spain to regenerate.

From Aragon Frank moves on to Castile (chapter 5), and begins his story in Burgos at "The Castle of the Cid" (the subtitle of this first section). He briefly relates the Cid's story, mostly to illustrate how far the Cid was from possessing the traits of character that ultimately inhered in the Spaniard after all his chaotic elements became fused through unity. But the Cid's castle is another story. In its crumbling ruin, Frank sees the symbol of Castile's spirit—its will to world domination, its vision of making "a castle of the House of God."[89] More teleology.

In Salamanca, Frank characterizes the university as carrying on the spirit of the medieval synthesis. But his inclusion of those Spanish Jews and Arabs as contributors to the medieval synthesis brought the charge of "Hebraicization" down on Frank. Walsh claims Frank mentions the greatness of Spain's Arab and Jewish scholars while neglecting the contributions of their Christian contemporaries.[90] This is true. But Frank's so-called Hebraicization only comprises a paragraph in this section. Besides, Frank's paean to Spain's Jewish and Arab thinkers is warranted. Frank knows that their work nourished medieval Europe, and by implication Spain.[91] Whether or not his historical case is sound, Frank's overall vision of Spain demanded that he add the dissonant voices of Arab and Jew to the medieval synthesis that the Catholic kings adapted and molded into their model of a unified Spain.

In Segovia, Frank contrasts the chaotic landscape of the present-day town with the rational order embodied in its Roman aqueduct ("The Water Bridge" is this section's subtitle). Again his description merely serves as the vehicle for exposing those antithetical forces that "offset each other and create, once more, the complex unity of Spain."[92]

Moving on to Toledo, Frank describes its physical aspects in such a way as to make the city a living symbol of the Castilian will to unity. He includes a lament for the Jew, who for four centuries was "a master in Spain."[93] Here the charge of Hebraicization is repeated by Walsh,[94] but it is unwarranted. A reading of Castro's *The Spaniards* contains abundant evidence of the important role Jews played in Spain's history, with Toledo as their principal *situs*.[95] But Frank's treatment in this section is tarnished by his use of the Jew to show how his spirit and vision—that of the Hebrew prophets—still live in Toledo and Spain. Frank, of course, is reading into the Hebraic prophetic vision and spirit his own interpretation of the Spanish reality; for by now he clearly casts himself in the role of modern-day Hebrew prophet.

Highly suggestive is the title Frank chooses for this section: "The Miracle of El Greco." For Frank, the art of "the Greek" epitomizes the Eastern, Jewish, prophetic vision of Spain. This use of El Greco to symbolize Toledo's spiritual striving prompts another comparison with the work of Barrès.[96] Here, at least, Frank is gracious enough to mention the Frenchman, if only in conjunction with Barrès's notion that El Greco was a Jew. But Frank is less concerned with citing sources than he is with interpreting El Greco's art as the aesthetic expression of Spain's Christian synthesis ("Christianity had Jewish blood").[97]

Frank's last stop in Castile is at the Escorial, the tomb of Philip II and the "ultimate Word of Castile." The building's design is a symbol of his failure. Frank pontificates that "Unity . . . must be sought elsewhere. Not in piling up worlds but in their giving up; not in life but through death."[98]

Proceeding eastward now, Frank arrives finally at Valencia. He describes the province as the dream of Spain. Spain, well-fed by all the chaotic elements that went into her being, is now asleep. Again, the antithetical forces cancel one another, producing an equilibrium akin to sleep. This chapter is Frank at his most ambiguous, as he must be to fit Valencia, one of the many antithetical elements of Spain, into his argument.

The second part, "The Tragedy of Spain," has already been shown as the most blatant manifestation of Frank's teleological argument. Contemporary comment, however, was mostly favorable toward this part. One reviewer calls its chapters "the most powerful and creative in the book." By her other comments, however, the reviewer reveals that she is missing the creative essence of this section. She sees the second part as merely a presentation of Spain's "abstract and integral qualities as represented in the persons of her sons" who "performed the drama of their country's history."[99] The question is never asked why these particular actors were chosen to the exclusion of others. Another reviewer who finds the second part "the most creative part" at least understands Frank's effort "to reproduce the soul of Spain"—the "soul" in the spiritual sense of the word as opposed to the religious.[100]

What lies behind Spain's tragedy? According to Frank, it is the will of Spain that is responsible for her tragedy. In her will to religious unity—a medieval concept—Spain uses the apparatus of the modern state, thereby establishing a religio-political system. The demands of the state are subservient to the demands of spiritual oneness. The contradictory concepts of medieval church and modern state isolate Spain from the rest of Europe, which has resisted following Spain's lead toward religious unity and has already done away with the medieval unity. And willful Spain must accept God's will, which is that she must fail. This failure results in her turning inward; and, as a result, Spain is misunderstood—her equilibrium, her sleep, is interpreted as decadence, backwardness. Thus Spain's tragedy is twofold. Furthermore, Spain's tragedy is the world's tragedy, for the world has missed the benefits of the Spanish spirit that founded a new world, and created a synthesis that made the Spaniard an integrated, complete person.

In chapter 7, Frank poses Isabel as the symbol of Spain's will to spiritual unity. She is shown to use everything at her disposal, even the ambitions of her husband Ferdinand, to achieve religious unity, first in Spain, then Europe, and finally across the sea in the New World. One reviewer calls this study of the mood and method of the Queen "admirable," and "one of the shrewdest and most sympathetic studies of Isabella in English."[101] Even Dos Passos credits Frank with a "first-rate understanding" in his description of the queen.[102] Surely, though, there is distortion in Frank's characterization. To conform with his argument, Frank makes the will of the Catholic kings mean the will of Isabel, not Ferdinand—the same Ferdinand who served as a model for Machiavelli's *The Prince*! Since it was directed toward a kind of Mediterranean hegemony for his kingdom rather than toward religious unity, Ferdinand's will was not to Frank's liking. Hence, Frank deftly subordinates Ferdinand's will to that of his wife.

In chapter 8, "The Will of Saint and Sinner," Frank develops his contention that Spain's "will to union breaks her into extremes." Spiritual unity having been achieved, Spain desires social unity, and manifests her will to this unity in her sense of honor. According to Frank, Spain's sense of honor arises out of her need "to resist the social chaos of her land."[103] The lack of a social dimension explains the Spaniard's individualism; his need for one explains the outburst of activity issuing from the pursuit of honor that was wedded to the will of Isabel. Dos Passos is correct in calling the plan of the book "architectural,"[104] and nowhere is this more evident than in this chapter. The figures Frank chooses to study—the mystics, Loyola, Vitoria, the *picaro*, and Velázquez—are those whose lives are illustrative of the will to be one. And by being both negative and affirmative illustrations, they serve to manifest the Hegelian aspect of the synthesis that is produced by antithetical elements.

The chapter has been praised for its understanding of the Jewish mystics, for its "admirable" writing (this from an otherwise unsympathetic critic), and for its explanation of the writings of Vitoria, the founder of international law (a revelation to many).[105]

Chapter 9 deals with Cervantes's life and work. To Frank, Cervantes is a symbol of Spain's heroism and failure. His masterpiece, *Don Quixote*, is seen as an expression of the universal implications of Spain's failure. For if Spain could not achieve worldwide unity through the religious impulse or the sense of honor, perhaps unity could be achieved another way, and hence, the ultimate appeal of ideologies such as nationalism and Marxism. But *Don Quixote* also reveals to Frank the hero's prophetic solution to the world's longing for unity. Not surprisingly, Don Quixote's vision is Frank's vision. Indeed, Frank always identified with the knight. Whether or not the knight was the same as Cervantes's creation is another story. To Frank, Quixote was a reformer, and no one was as totally committed as Don Quixote "to either revolution or revelation, except Frank."[106]

This chapter evoked varying responses. Dos Passos praises Frank's description of the life of Cervantes.[107] Another reviewer, though arriving at a generally favorable view, comments that the literary expression in this chapter "becomes as involved as a twisted coil of wire."[108] Of Frank's interpretation of *Don Quixote*, Benardete says this chapter "may unblushingly vie" with the "memorable pages" on Quixote of Heine, Turgeniev, Ortega y Gasset, and Unamuno.[109] Another reviewer states that Frank's conception of Quixote "follows Unamuno closely."[110] Still another reader finds in Frank's interpretation the influence of Unamuno in both its style and its content, and suggests that Frank profited from reading the Spaniard.[111] Frank probably had read Unamuno; and, as suggested in connection with the influence of Barrès, he was not necessarily averse to unacknowledged use of any interpretation that coincided with his own intuitive insights.

The final chapter of the second part, "The Will of God," proved to be the most confusing section of the book for those unaware of Frank's aim. One reviewer admits that it is "not always easy to be positive as to the meaning of a statement."[112] Another sees this chapter as an exposition of the individualism and "true powers" of the Spaniard.[113]

There is, however, a deeper meaning to Frank's treatment of "The Will of God." In this often misunderstood chapter, Frank suggests that contemporary Spain is poised on the verge of fulfilling the prophecy that he will make in the third part, where he enlightens the reader as to Spain's role in the world's imminent transition to a higher degree of perfection. As a symbol of contemporary Spain, the bull fight is put forward by Frank. Consider Frank's way of thinking and the symbolism in the *corrida*, and his choice becomes clear. The bull fight is the drama of death and regeneration—the blood of the bull sprinkling the virgin soil from which new life springs forth. Then again, it is the male, assertive matador against the feminine, passive bull, waiting at the end to be penetrated by the sword. In well-executed passes of the encounter, matador and bull virtually freeze into one hermaphrodite form— a vision of wholeness that derives from classical Platonic mythology.[114] Moreover, in order for the bull fight to be "complete" (i.e., whole) the matador must execute passes both with the left hand and the right hand. Also, with the bull's encounter with the mounted picador, we have the encounter of dominated nature with undominated nature (horse against bull). Again, such symbolism has its origins in classical Platonic mythology; and the whole spiritualist movement, of which Frank was a part, was to a high degree injected with Neoplatonism.

The section on the bull fight evoked much comment. Dos Passos finds Frank's description of the spectacle the best he has ever read. He makes no objection to the sexual symbolism inherent in that description, although he dismisses the "psychological phraseology" as "mere ornamental verbiage."[115] Hemingway, as might be expected, rendered a negative verdict. Indeed, his overall disparagement of *Virgin Spain* may have been provoked by Frank's interpretation of the bull fight; for Hemingway's attack is contained in *Death in the Afternoon*, of which the Spanish bull fight is the subject. Baker shows in his comparison of Hemingway's and Frank's interpretations that both are "in agreement on the larger three-act outline of the typical Spanish bullfight." But, there is "nothing in Hemingway's about the bull's being cleansed for the tragedy, however, and it is apparent that he has kept his writer's eye more steadily fixed on the animal than has Frank." Like Hemingway,

Baker characterizes Frank's use of "pseudo-poetic erotic symbolism" as "erectile writing with a vengeance." He adds that Hemingway is "never guilty of Freudian fiddle-faddle."[116] Bittner explains the difference between Hemingway's and Frank's interpretations in terms of the basically different perspectives from which they view the spectacle. Hemingway sees the bull as a sportsman would, and his understanding is that of the participant. Frank sees the bull as an artist, and his understanding is that of the observer (albeit an interested one). More importantly, Bittner shows why Frank would combine what is ostensibly a Freudian interpretation of the bull fight (though it actually derives more from a classical mythological purview) with his overall aim to show the corrida as an all-encompassing symbol of Spanish life. He quotes a passage from the book that exemplifies Frank's concept of wholeness: "Gross comedy of blood; sex, dionysian and sadistic; the ancient rites of the brute and of Christ meet here in the final image of stability. Spain's warring elements reach their locked fusion—Spain's ultimate form."[117]

The section entitled "Man and Woman" has been called "the most abstract in the book and therefore highly difficult to grasp." On the surface, it is supposed to be a "deep psychological diagnosis" of the Spanish mind. But because the Spanish man and woman must meet the demands of his argument as to Spain's predestined role, Frank explains the individualism of the Spaniard, and the matriarchal principle that molds it and guides it, in favorable terms. Frank's Spaniard, in responding to his country's chaotic elements, turns his energies inward. Thus "the erstwhile life-giving impulses [that produced "one country, one king, one religion"] got leashed into equilibrium."[118] This equilibrium, though it appears to be decadence, is only sleep—a sleep willed by the Spaniard as his will mirrors the will of God. And this equilibrium, though it appears to be backwardness, is only a manifestation of the Spaniard's primitive nature. For Frank, a primitive nature is equated with an attractive, indeed enviable, child-like psyche in which there is no conflict between consciousness (the male principle) and the unconscious (the female principle); instead, the two parts coexist in wholeness.

Dos Passos, again unaware of Frank's manipulative use of material to establish preconceived conclusions, credits Frank's description of the matriarchal principle as revelatory of an understanding of the Spanish woman.[119] Sitwell, on the other hand, is critical of Frank's entire handling of "womanhood" throughout *Virgin Spain* (perhaps because of the kind of erotic symbolism inherent in

Frank's style of which Baker speaks). He wonders why Frank is driven "into such abysses" as characterize his approach to the opposite sex. He suggests that if Frank "would stop being such a He-man, . . . we should all be much happier."[120] But again, the concept of wholeness allows for such symbolism as Frank exhibits in many of his passages. Besides, such passages help to veil the teleology, making the author seem prophetically luminous and insightful.

The final section of chapter 10, "Madrid," apparently evoked no direct contemporary pointed comment, probably because it appears to be merely a description of a city to the uninitiated reader. But beneath Frank's uncomplimentary description of the city's essence, there lies symbolism and a hint of what is to come. Madrid becomes for Frank the consummate symbol both of Spain's equilibrium and of its will to be part of Europe—another aspect of Spain's tragedy. But in Madrid's rotting atmosphere, in its conservatism, Frank finds embedded an antithetical element—those liberal intellectuals who dream of awakening Spain from her sleep and bringing about a new synthesis, a new "wholeness."

The third part, "Beyond Spain" (the shortest of the three movements), predictably elicits different reactions from the critics. Ostensibly, this part is a description of present-day (ca. 1925) Spain, including a discussion of Catalonia and the Basque provinces—the uninitiated reader would find it curious that these regions are not included in the first part, which describes the other sections of Spain—and contemporary Spanish art and literature. Those who see it only in that light criticize accordingly. In a generally favorable review of *Virgin Spain* published in *La Nación* (Buenos Aires), Juan Torrendell, a "hot partisan of Catalonian nationalism," objects to the large role that Frank ascribes to Castile in national history, while ignoring "the latest developments in Catalonia."[121] Muna Lee takes issue with Frank's characterization of the Basque language as being unique, pointing out how "the kinship of Basque with Finnish, Afghan, and other Mongol tongues has been variously demonstrated."[122] Turning to another aspect of "Beyond Spain," Thomas Walsh comments on some of Frank's Spanish comrades from the contemporary literary scene. He registers approval for Valle-Inclán, Azorín, and Machado, but disparages Pérez de Ayala (a "second-class novelist"), Unamuno ("a secondary figure among Spanish thinkers"), and Jiménez ("a pathetic *comedie mystique*").[123]

One element in the assessment of *Virgin Spain* has been the contention that Frank did not so much discover Spain as mold it to

meet his needs. In his quest for a new human wholeness in a new
world that would transcend alienation, Frank *had* to find in Spain
the catalyst that would bring America into a new and higher stage
of existence. If one is aware of the prophetic element in Frank, he
or she cannot fail to perceive the element of apocalyptic vision that
suffuses the third part of *Virgin Spain*. In contrasting, for example,
the two regions (Catalonia and the Basque provinces), "where the
regional and the Spanish were at odds,"[124] Frank uses these anta-
gonistic geographic sections, as well as Spain's disparate writers, as
examples of those dissonant chords that are disrupting the country's sleep. Thus they are all part of Spain's transition to a higher
degree of perfection. Frank is aware of Catalonian nationalism—
he titles chapter 9 "The Rift in Barcelona." He is also probably
aware of the movement for autonomy among the Basques; in
chapter 12, "The Comedy of the Basque," he implies an awakening of a Basque national consciousness. But he veils these mun-
dane concepts; besides, they smack of separatism rather than
unity. The effect of these antithetical elements is more important
than their cause. That effect is an awakening of Spain's spirit
from which a new Spain will be born.[125]

Benardete mildly objects to Frank's handling of the two regions; he says "Frank does not seem to have done entire justice to
this something mercurial that is a living organism." But at least
he understands Frank's aim.

> Frank . . . disregards practically all the modern products of Spain that
> do not seem to point to the new spirit surging forth. The new Spain, to
> him, is the Spain that is beginning to lose its self-sufficiency; it is the
> Spain that, once complete, is now on the verge of becoming conscious
> that it needs new worlds to assimilate.[126]

Furthermore, because Benardete understands the prophetic nature
of the third part, i.e., the vision Frank has for Spain, he gleans the
real meaning of chapter 13 ("Two Andalusians"). Frank does not
merely describe Spain's literary scene, he "assesses the worth" of
its members. In a section entitled "The Sleepers," Frank classifies
Ramón Valle-Inclán, Azorín, Antonio Machado, and Ramón
Pérez de Ayala as symbols of Spain's sleep, "self-centered individuals," their work "too much rooted in to the complete Spain of
their ancestors." Frank ends this section with mention of the work
of Ramón Gómez de la Serna, who exemplifies Spain's transition
from sleeping to waking.[127]

Then Frank introduces "The Awakeners"—Francisco Giner de

los Ríos (founder of the *Institución Libre de Enseñanza*), Angel
Ganivet, and Miguel de Unamuno. To Frank, these creative men
are the embodiment of Spain's awakening. Each bequeathed his
spiritual vision for Spain to the next, and thus for Frank they have
been arousing Spain from sleep.

For Frank, the "Two Andalusians" who best exemplify "The
Sleepless Spirit" (the title of the last section of this chapter) of
Spain are Pablo Picasso and Juan Ramón Jiménez. They are
"dynamic because they are inchoate, unfinished."[128] Frank uses
them to announce his prophecy: "Again Spain is speaking for the
world. This painter and this lyrist, in the true sense, are *poets*.
Their word is a creation, immediate as life and as eternal: and this
conjunction of time and eternity is birth."[129]

The final chapter, "The Port of Columbus," contains Frank's
prophecy. Since the prophecy has been mentioned in the explanation of the teleological argument, only the comment it evoked will
be dealt with here. The prophecy is presented by the device of
a dramatic dialogue between Cervantes and Columbus. One reviewer cites this chapter as among the best parts of the book.[130]
Moreover, upon reading *Virgin Spain*, Unamuno translated this
chapter into Spanish and had it published in the Buenos Aires
journal *Síntesis*. As Chapman notes, "this was in itself a sumptuous
compliment to Waldo Frank and to it were annexed praises of *Virgin Spain* in the accompanying essay, '*Hispanidad*,' which honors
Frank for his accuracy and quotes him as an authority."[131] Frank
worked hard to elicit such a response from Unamuno. Not only
does he characterize Unamuno as one of Spain's awakeners, and
cast such bouquets as "Unamuno is the strongest moralist of our
day," but from the outset, in acknowledging his debt to those Spaniards who helped him to understand Spain while he was there, he
exclaims, ". . . alas! Unamuno has just been exiled."[132] Winning
Unamuno assured Frank a favorable reception for his book among
a broad intellectual circle both in Spain and Latin America.

In attempting this analysis of *Virgin Spain*, the goal has been an
objective appraisal of the work itself and of the contemporary
assessments it evoked. At the same time there has been an effort
to single out the mystical, prophetic element of the book, and also
to apply historical perspective to that part of its content that does
not reject the historical in quest of the suprahistorical. This makes
understandable the negative response of non-Hispanic readers in
the United States and England, who did not know Frank (or
Spain, for that matter), who were not sympathetic to mystical,
spiritualist, or suprarational approaches, and who could not see

that he was merely using Spain to accommodate his quest of world redemption. On the other hand, some of the enthusiastic acclaim of *Virgin Spain* in the Hispanic world can be explained by the fact that even those Hispanic readers who did not perceive Frank's ultimate purposes were at least being told some of the things they longed to hear.[133] For Spaniards, Frank had debunked the Black Legend of Spanish bigotry, cruelty, and degeneracy, sympathetically sketched Spain's decadence, and declared his optimism for Spain's future. For Latin Americans, his stress on racial psychology held the flattering message that the Latin Americans were heirs of Spain's spirit. Moreover, Frank called them brothers and dedicated the book to them, making it all the harder to reject his message.[134] Beyond this, given the spiritualist revival and a virtual explosion of the occult in Spain and Spanish America,[135] there were many readers of Frank in the Spanish-speaking world who grasped the mystical, redemptive, suprarational message—and who thrilled to it. In many instances, this same assessment would apply to admirers of *Virgin Spain* outside the Spanish-speaking world.

Vision or Revision?

Frank's career following the publication of *Virgin Spain* suggests he continued to use Spain to serve his purposes. His relationship to the country continued, in short, to be a self-serving casual affair rather than an all-consuming love. In fact, one has to look hard to find an expression of his love for Spain after 1926, or even his continuing interest in the country. A Spaniard does appear as a character in Frank's 1935 novel *The Death and Birth of David Markand*. He is a poet named Miguel Larrach who turns up at an avant-garde party in Chicago and recites a poem that is simply an artist's diatribe against American mechanolatry. Then, having engaged the reader's attention for a scant few pages, Larrach is absent for the remainder of the massive novel. Larrach is the only Spaniard in Frank's fictional works, none of which is set in Spain.[136]

On 17 July 1936, the Spanish Civil War broke out. This event should have posed a serious problem for Frank: if Spain had achieved dialectical oneness of spirit, how was a brutal civil war possible in theory? But as it was, the war elicited only passing interest from him. He had written that nothing must interfere with the writing of his novel *The Bridegroom Cometh*, begun in December 1935.[137] He did manage, however, to dash off an article for the *New Masses* that appeared on 18 August 1936, along with other opinions on the conflict by notables of the American Left. Not surprisingly, Frank's article places him among those who, as Madariaga points out, "minimized or ignored the genuine Spanish nature of the conflict and stressed its international aspect."[138] Frank had been a fellow traveler of the American Communist party since November 1931, and Frank sees the war in terms of the Marxian dialectic. Whether the war would stay localized or become worldwide, whether or not Spain and the world would go Fascist, the forces of history would determine the eventual outcome—a victory for "socialism and flowering from it toward Communism with its birth *at last* of true human beings." This last stage is Frank's own addition, his own "end of history," and his only real departure in the article from the party line,[139] but it does not diminish the fact that the Marxist of the thirties is speaking a different language from the Frank of the twenties.

Then in October 1936, having completed the first draft of his novel,[140] Frank issued an appeal to the premier of France, Léon Blum. Again, stressing the war's international aspect, Frank urges Blum to end French neutrality. He warns that this conflict, being waged by the Fascists of the world against the "people" of Spain, will soon engulf the French "People's Front" government unless Blum acts to aid Spain. If Blum fails to act, Frank concludes, he "will be betraying mankind."[141]

In December 1936, Frank headed the American Society for Technical Aid to Spanish Democracy. Then in January 1937, he delivered an address entitled "The Artist: Minister of Freedom" at the national congress of Mexican writers and artists held in Mexico City. Again, he mentions the war as part of the worldwide struggle between capitalism and "the people," making it clear to which side the artist must devote all his energies.[142]

As to going to Spain, Frank avoided such a journey until late April 1938. Why did he stay away so long, particularly if he loved Spain as much as he professed to in *Virgin Spain*? According to Bittner, Frank speculated in his notebook as to his motives in not going sooner to Spain, "attributing to himself everything from cowardice to a headache." To Bittner, it was merely a matter of Frank's tackling the revision of *The Bridegroom Cometh*; he had to shelve Spain and her "unsolvable" problems.[143]

Frank spent three weeks in Spain. Although he was attacked in the Communist press (he had not gone along with the great party line shift of 1937 in which American Communists defended the

Moscow trials as a justification of Stalinism), Spain's leaders, Communists included, treated him well.[144] Upon returning to the United States, Frank published in *The New Republic* in July a series of three articles entitled "Spain in War." The first installment, "The People," finds him discarding the Marxian dialectic and returning to the prophecy of *Virgin Spain*. And behold! Frank's "new Spain" is awake, "unfortunately reborn in a matrix of agony, treachery, and death." But Frank does not doubt the outcome of the conflict. "The Spanish people cannot . . . be beaten . . . because their will to live has become . . . *the will to struggle*." They have a spirit and a stamina that Isabel I dreamed for them, and with these qualities they stand up against the machines of the Fascists. The article contains Frank's vivid description of the quality of life in Loyalist Spain as he observed it.[145]

The second installment, "Parties and Leaders," finds Frank dealing more sympathetically with the leaders than the parties, although he obviously has doubts about the Communist leaders. Spanish acceptance of Communist leadership in conducting the war is described as mere expediency, and he predicts that following the war Spain will evolve toward what he calls "liberal-anarchism." But he reveals his naïveté in expressing his certainty that all the Soviet Union wants from its involvement in Spain is "a democratic Spain as the safest bulwark against fascism."[146]

The final installment, "The Meaning of Spain," reiterates Frank's prophecy for the country. Though the Republic may lose the war, the people will survive. According to Frank, war has purified them. Their awakening, begun twenty years before, is now virtually complete, and their "*liberal* genius . . . will . . . inform the new Spanish system."[147]

These articles are important as a proving ground for Frank. Through them he worked out the problem that a Nationalist victory would pose. The problem was this: having written a book in which he prophesied Spain's regeneration in a liberal context, Frank could not disavow his prophecy by admitting that the Fascists had won in Spain. It would mean the subsequent prophecies contained in *Re-discovery of America* (1929) and *America Hispana* (1931) would be undermined—all the more so if Fascist success spread to the American hemisphere. His reputation as a prophet and mystic would be severely questioned, if not shattered. But Frank was a resourceful man as well as a practical one. In preparing a revised edition of *Virgin Spain* (published in 1942) Frank was able to explain the Spanish Civil War as the end product of Spain's will to be Europe. While modifying the short-term optimism expressed in the articles, he left intact the prophecy offered for Spain at the end of the first edition, contenting himself merely with adding a chapter to update Spain's experience to the beginning of the 1940s. Apparently his rationalization was that Spain eventually would come to its senses, repudiate its detour down false paths, and return to the route of destiny.

The 1942 edition of *Virgin Spain* begins with an introduction by Frank's friend, Alfonso Reyes, entitled "Significance and Timeliness of *Virgin Spain*." It seems to be addressed primarily to Frank's Latin American audience, since it deals more than anything else with Frank's trips to South America. Probably he guessed, correctly as it turned out,[148] that the book would never get through the censors of Franco's Spain. Reyes underlines Frank's new message of hope: "Spain will be reborn immaculate!" For the Hispanic sense of life has never been defeated; Spain is still "this perennial soul with its still virgin strengths."[149]

Following Reyes's introduction comes the author's note. In it, Frank takes the offensive with an incredible statement that reveals his powers of rationalization and suggests something about his ego. In stating that the last chapter is entirely new, he maintains that the book

> so organically points to what has happened in Spain and in Europe since its completion that it required only the addition of a chapter whose lack, before the events it describes took place, was an eloquent flaw in the book's structure. It is as if the author had been prevented from rounding out his Symphonic History, because he wrote it ten or fifteen years before the material needed for its completion had come true.[150]

This is downright dishonest. Out of the tragedy of the Spanish Civil War, Frank is creating an entirely new teleological argument that in reality bears no relationship, organic or otherwise, to his earlier vision of Spain and its mission. Frank is manipulating the Spanish present, as he had earlier manipulated the Spanish past, to establish his credentials as a prophet.

The new chapter, "The Awakening Passion," is Frank's interpretation of the Republic's life and death. According to him, Spain's spirit, which launched the Republic, did not live in the Republic; and the Republic was not Spain. Nonetheless, Frank condemns the Western democracies for not intervening when the Republic found itself under attack from the Fascists, whom he called "the dwarfs and idiots of Velázquez . . . come to life."[151]

One intriguing aspect of this chapter is that for the first time Frank shows an understanding as to why thousands of Spain's "people" supported the Nationalist cause. They were those

> devout thousands of women who saw only that the radicals burned convents; devout thousands of men who hated the arrogant empiricism of the liberals, feeling their own intuitions somehow denied in the blueprint dimensions of the Republic. These deeply offended ones fought, they believed, for God and Spain.[152]

But then he immediately reverts to placing blame, and ascribes final responsibility for the Republic's destruction to the Republic itself for following Europe's path of empirical rationalism.[153]

Finally, he reveals the ultimate meaning of the Spanish Civil War: a democracy of man will fail if man is ignored. It was Spain's role to make this truth manifest to the world, and her ability to enact this heroic role was due to her wholeness. Frank ends his updated teleology with a reiteration of the old prophecy: "Spain went out from Spain into the whole world. In order that the world, through Spain's disaster, may become the home and the receiver, again, of Spain's spirit."[154]

In its new edition the book was not widely reviewed, and a brief sampling of the critical reaction will suffice. Benardete, obviously drawing upon his earlier analysis, reiterated his praise for the book, adding his agreement with Frank's interpretation of the Spanish Civil War.[155] Another reviewer, probably reading the book for the first time, was in sympathy with Frank's interpretation of Spain's being or essence. He refers to the book, though, as an amplification of the interpretations of Spain of Salvador de Madariaga and Havelock Ellis.[156] Such a judgment would have undoubtedly persuaded Frank that the reviewer had failed to grasp the true meaning of the book.

Thus ended Frank's relationship with Spain. He never returned to Spain, nor did he ever again write expressly on that country. Frank's relationship with Spain was on his part an unfaithful one. He used Spain and then left her—and not a virgin.

3

FROM COURTSHIP TO MARRIAGE
Waldo Frank and Latin America, 1919–1931

Waldo Frank's relationship with Spain was but a gambit in "his crusade to unite the Americas with cultural bonds."[1] As Van Wyck Brooks explains, Frank

> was drawn to Latin America because whatever were its defects, "well-being" was not considered the highest good there. It seemed to him obvious that certain values survived in the Hispanic scene that our country had forgotten. . . . [F]eeling that the mystical values flourished still in the Hispanic world, he hoped for a cultural union between the North and the South. Believing that this would restore the traditional wholeness of man, he set out to interpret these worlds to one another.[2]

Thus, with preconceived notions did Waldo Frank embark on his courtship of Latin America.

How successful was he? In the *Literary History of the United States* (1948), Frank is heralded as "the only serious North American author who exercised a direct influence" on Latin America during the 1920s.[3] More specifically,

> a good deal of what is believed in Hispanic America about the culture of the United States was planted there by him. . . . Moreover, Frank . . . gave an especially strong send-off to the literature of the United States, and opened a new era in literary relations.[4]

Frank's success in Latin America can best be understood by retracing the steps that led to his achievement of that success. Symbolic, perhaps, of the role Frank plays in his own teleology, his first contact with the Hispanic world was not a direct move in that direction. Rather, shortly after the publication of *Our America* in 1919, the favorable reactions of several Latin American writers to the book produced "the first widely circulated notice of Frank in Spanish America." Furthermore, some of the subsequent Latin American use of *Our America* enhanced Frank's chances of succeeding in his courtship (in which in 1924 he became actively involved). For example, in 1921, José Juan Tablada, writing for the newspaper *Excélsior* (Mexico City), characterized the author of *Our America* as not only the leader of those "good Yanquis" who were resisting the materialism of their country, but also as "especially pro-Mexican." Tablada's impression, based on what he interpreted to be "praise for the Hispanos" in the chapter titled "The Land of the Buried Cultures," was, of course, a misinterpretation of Frank's aim. But Arnold Chapman concludes that the mere mention of Mexico in a favorable light would have insured that nation's welcoming Frank "with open arms."[5]

Another biased use of *Our America* was made by the Argentine socialist Alfredo Palacios, who found in Frank's harsh criticism of the United States support for "his campaign-plank contention that the United States [was] too corrupt to be a fit leader for Latin Americans." By ignoring what was positive in *Our America*, Palacios presented Frank as a kindred spirit from north of the Rio Grande.[6]

The most significant use of *Our America* by a Latin American came from the Peruvian José Carlos Mariátegui. In a 1925 article entitled "Waldo Frank," Mariátegui calls the book the most original and intelligent interpretation of the United States he has seen. Moreover, Mariátegui, "the first Hispanic writer to understand Frank's concept of the creative minority," finds *Our America* a sign of a possible alliance between the "enlightened elements" of North and South America.[7] And, indeed, brought together by what Mariátegui calls "a certain similarity in our directions and in our life-experience,"[8] Mariátegui and Frank became more than allies— they became good friends and corresponded until Mariátegui's death in 1930.[9]

The aforementioned uses of *Our America* were yet to come when, in 1921, Frank had his first meeting with Latin Americans. The place was Paris, perhaps at the home of the Uruguayan poet Jules Superville. Subsequently, in his rounds about that city, Frank met many other Latin Americans—writers with whose work he was unfamiliar, but with whom he sensed "an affinity." This feeling that they were similar caused him to act unusually friendly toward them, and they, in turn, reacted favorably toward him. Moreover, he found that his book *Our America* had some common meaning for them.[10]

Frank credits the affinity with contributing to his decision shortly thereafter to write *Virgin Spain*[11]—the book he would dedicate to his Latin American "brothers."

It was in Madrid in 1924, while working on *Virgin Spain*, that Frank made his first "successful direct move" toward Latin America. He visited Mexico's ambassador to Spain, Alfonso Reyes.[12] Reyes was one of the leaders of the "cultural renascence" that Mexico was then experiencing.[13] Frank certainly knew this, and, therefore, probably expected to find in the Mexican writer-statesman a kindred spirit. Moreover, Frank must have maneuvered Reyes into taking the role of co-visionary of cultural union between the Americas. This is evidenced by Reyes's statement that he and Frank "ever understood America in the prophetic sense. America was destiny's aspiration for a new sensibility and culture." More explicitly, Reyes recalls how, during their first encounter, "seeing Waldo Frank so deep in Spain," he said to the American, "Don't forget. Spain is the road to our America."[14] Frank knew this (in his own way, of course); that was why he was in Spain in the first place. In any event, Reyes played into Frank's hands; he solicited Frank's "Mensaje a los escritores mexicanos" ("Message to the Mexican Writers"), and carried it with him on his return to Mexico shortly thereafter. Frank's "Message," which "marked the beginning of his relations" with Spanish America, first appeared, translated, "in the bulletin of the P.E.N. Club of Mexico," and was subsequently reprinted in Joaquín García Monge's *Repertorio Americano* (Costa Rica), *Atenea* (Chile), and *Valoraciones* (Argentina). As Chapman points out, the quick spread of the "Message" throughout Latin America must have given Frank the realization that not only Mexico but Hispanic America in its entirety was "in ferment," and that "a decisive moment had come that might never come again."[15]

What is the nature of the "Message?" In the form of a letter to Reyes, Frank asks the ambassador to relay to all of Latin America's intellectuals the desire of a comrade from the United States to be their friend. He cites their common ideal—to create in America a spiritual culture—and their common enemy: the materialism, imperialism, and sterile pragmatism of the modern world. In promoting the union of the creative minorities of both American continents, he argues that only through mutual understanding can these intellectuals further the course of truth in a time when the forces of exploitation and spiritual death are united throughout the world.[16] Frank flatters his audience without seeming condescending.[17] Furthermore, being a member of a creative *minority* made Frank appear to Latin Americans as a "fellow sufferer and combatant."[18]

Thus, with one brief article, Frank succeeded in getting the attention of his Latin American "brothers."

Then, in 1926 came the publication of *Virgin Spain*. Preceding the necessary Spanish translation were articles such as Luis Araquistaín's review, "Imágenes de España," carried by *La Nación* of Buenos Aires; a partial plagiarization of Araquistaín's essay by a Chilean who signed himself S., appearing in *Atenea*; and Baldamiro Sanín Cano's critique of *Virgin Spain* in *La Nación*.[19] Furthermore, parts of the book were translated and published before *España virgen* arrived late in 1927. The Latin American reviews of the Spanish edition were for the most part laudatory. For example, the Spanish critic Guillermo de Torre, living in Argentina and writing for *Síntesis* of Buenos Aires, calls the book great, and urges the young American to visit South America.[20] Another critic out of Buenos Aires, Julio Fingerit, writing for *La Vida Literaria*, praises the book's weightiness, as well as its blend of lyric and dialectic. The Chilean, Raúl Silva Castro, writing for *Atenea*, praises Frank's comprehension of Spain.[21]

With regard to Frank's Hispanic adventure, the year 1926 held a significance beyond the publication of *Virgin Spain*. In May of that year, Frank accepted the poet Hart Crane's invitation to spend a few weeks with him at his grandmother's house on the Isle of Pines off the southwest coast of Cuba. The trip there entailed a two-day layover in Havana that marked Frank's first visit (albeit unofficial) to a Latin American country. Whether or not he was recognized as someone special is not known; all that is known is that Frank and Crane spent "all their time in Cuban hotels, bars, and theaters."[22]

In any event, the ever-resourceful Frank was able to squeeze an article for the *New Republic* out of his two days in Havana. The article, entitled "Habana of the Cubans," is ostensibly an impressionistic piece that stresses the dreamlike nature of the city and its people. The article is more than a mercenary endeavor, however; Frank's purpose is to utilize Cuba to express his Platonistic faith[23]—a faith that would serve him well in a Latin America experiencing spiritual unrest.

The following year, 1927, Frank's *Re-discovery of America* appeared in serial form in the *New Republic*. The two pages on Charlie Chaplin were translated and published in *La Vida Literaria* for November 1928; and *Revista de Occidente* printed four chapters during the first half of 1929. *Re-discovery of America* was published in New York in February 1929, and *Revista* was ready with the Spanish translation by the following June. The book was "well-received" in Latin America, and, despite a verbose and often misconstrued translation by Julia Héctor de Zaballa, sales warranted another printing the following year.[24]

A companion to *Our America, Re-discovery of America* is, in short, Frank's concept of the Whole—an expression of his need to delineate man's place in the cosmos. In discussing the "death" of Europe and its implication for America, Frank examines the ways and means of survival, and finds answers in the spiritual life inherent in American culture but heretofore neglected. Moreover, with this book Frank reestablishes the theme of regeneration that would characterize the remainder of his American cultural histories. In essence, he affirms that the Americas can only become the New World if they create "new men."[25]

Latin Americans could take pride in the way Frank characterizes them in this book. He commends them for using the mystic tradition for their own salvation. Moreover, he credits them with understanding the necessity of creating a new world. Thus, he places them in a position superior to his unenlightened fellow citizens in the United States.[26]

The real importance of 1929, however, was that from July to December, Frank was on a lecture tour of Latin America that carried him through Mexico, Brazil, Uruguay, Argentina, Chile, Peru, Bolivia, Colombia, and Cuba. The idea for the tour was formed after the publication of *España virgen*, the success of which brought an invitation to lecture in Mexico. Feeling that the Mexicans were sincere,[27] Frank made arrangements with the University of Mexico to undertake the journey in the summer of 1929. Meantime, he was in correspondence during 1927 and 1928 with Enrique Espinoza (the pseudonym for Samuel Glusberg, the son of Jewish immigrants to Argentina), "the ally who more than any other individual made Frank's tour possible."[28] Espinoza, too, hoped for an intellectual rapprochement between North and South America; and in his determination to have Frank come to Argentina, he helped to find the money for the visit to Buenos Aires.[29]

Frank's purpose in making the journey was to personally bring his crusade to unite the Americas culturally to what promised to be a most receptive audience. The reaction of his fellow Americans to his tour is noteworthy. To begin with, the media of the United States ignored his trip.[30] And when the literary historians finally recognized his achievement in Latin America, they credited his influence there simply to the following: "He lectured in all the capitals from Mexico City to Buenos Aires, he spoke a fluent literary Spanish, and he attacked Yankee imperialism while defending— and introducing to a sympathetic audience—the rebel American writers."[31] Such a judgment is superficial; it ignores the real basis of Frank's influence—the spiritual note that pervades all he said and wrote. Alfonso Reyes understood the spiritual nature of Frank's journey. Furthermore, he understood the real purpose of the trip—"*to clarify America*" in terms of "the promise of a deeper synthesis of man" through hemispheric unity. That purpose, expressed in language meant to quench the religious thirst of the listener, had far more influence than Frank's speaking Spanish, or his attacks on the United States, or anything else, for that matter. As Reyes proudly states, "one might say he provoked us to fraternity in our American duty and he made us actually feel that we *are* brothers."[32]

The 1929 Lecture Tour

A brief account of Frank's six-month sojourn in Latin America is now in order. Frank arrived in Mexico in July 1929. He gave his first lecture in Spanish in the *Gran Salon de Actos* of the University of Mexico; his thesis was that the New World had yet to be created. The next day, the lead editorial of the leading morning paper was devoted to the lecture, and it took up Frank's challenge to create the New World. As Frank recalls, "The *Yanqui* was not the expected academic event; he was *news*." Evidence of this fact was that his remaining five talks were relocated to the Escuela de Segundo Enseñanza, the biggest assembly hall in the city.[33]

Some of the key men Frank met in Mexico at this time who he felt expressed in their own ways a common sense of America's destiny were: Diego Rivera, the Communist painter; José Clemente Orozco, "agonist and bitter satirist"; Alfonso Reyes, who was now ambassador to Argentina; José Vasconcelos, national minister of education and proponent of the concept that the Mexicans, by virtue of their mixed bloods, comprised *la raza cósmica*; Emilio Portes Gil, the president of the republic; and the two musicians, Carlos Chávez and Silvestre Revueltas. Of most significance, however, was Frank's meeting Moises Sáenz, the assistant minister of education who had carried the university's invitation to Frank to New York. Sáenz helped Frank by planning interviews as well as expeditions to villages and to archeological treasures. But the relationship soon produced the discordant note that was mentioned at the beginning of chapter 1. Thus was Frank confronted with the reality that while he had been received and even "loved like no other intellectual in Mexico's history," his crusade struck some of his hosts as a sham.[34]

From Mexico, Frank returned to New York, then set off for Argentina. Because he was traveling to Buenos Aires by ship, he was able to see some of Brazil on the way. He left the ship at Rio de Janeiro to wander through the city, took a train to São Paulo, and rejoined the ship three days later at Santos. When the ship reached Montevideo, the press of Buenos Aires, along with Alfonso Reyes (who had flown in from Mexico, learned of Frank's arrival, and wanted to accompany his friend on the last leg of the trip) boarded to greet Frank. Also in the boarding party were Espinoza, Coriolano Alberini, dean of the Faculty of Letters of the University of Buenos Aires (under whose aegis Frank would give his first lectures), and Eduardo Mallea, literary editor of *La Nación*.[35]

Mallea became Frank's translator for the Argentine tour; through Mallea, Frank met the famous woman of letters, Victoria Ocampo. Frank and Ocampo, in their discussions together with Mallea, discovered that they both felt like orphans in their respective countries. Understanding Ocampo's "need to make a more definitive commitment to literature and culture in Argentina," Frank challenged her to "give concrete shape to the new America in the form of a literary review." Such a review would be "a cultural bridge between the Americas, a forum for the best thinkers of both continents."[36] To this end, Frank brought her together with Espinoza. As a result of these meetings, Ocampo founded *Sur* (the first issue appeared early in 1931), and the magazine proved to be an honest expression of the best in Latin American culture. Frank considered *Sur* without a doubt the most significant consequence of his Argentine visit.[37]

Of course, meeting Ocampo was not the primary purpose of Frank's visit to Buenos Aires. He "had been invited to South America to share his messianic vision of a New America united by a spirit of hemispheric solidarity," and that he did. When he proclaimed the possibility of two American "half-worlds" becoming "one mystical organic whole, coexisting in harmony and combining the best qualities of the materialistic North and the spiritual South," he was rewarded with fêtes and cheering crowds in the streets.[38] Thus he experienced a popularity that extended to the masses. Above all, though, Frank perceived his presence in Argentina as affording opportunity for an exchange among artists. In one of his Buenos Aires speeches he declared

I am here, friends, primarily because I am an artist. . . . I have come because what interests me more than all else in the world is *creation*: aesthetic, spiritual creation. . . . America is a potential organism: a potential Whole. Actually, up to now, it has been little more than a word. And America will be created by artists. . . . Only artists can create America: and only to the extent that artists have created America, can the peoples of America experience America and enjoy it.[39]

When Frank concluded his series of talks in Buenos Aires, he proceeded to lecture in the cities of Rosario, Córdoba, Bahía Blanca, Salta, and Jujuy. He traveled by airplane (a one-prop German Junker piloted by a captain of the Argentine air force), courtesy of Argentina's liberal president Hipólito Irigoyen, whom Frank had visited in his office. When he had finished his work in Argentina, Frank embarked on a memorable flight over uncharted Andean terrain to Santiago.[40]

In Chile, Frank was greeted by José Santos Chocano, a poet in exile from his native Peru. Then, when the Peruvian dictator Augusto Leguía granted the country's intellectuals permission to invite Frank to Peru, Frank went there. At Arequipa in southern Peru, Frank was met at the train station by about forty youths who marched him into town to a rooftop where they asked him to address them. These youths, Frank learned, read *Amauta*, the magazine of José Carlos Mariátegui.[41]

Once in Lima, Frank was made an honorary doctor of the University of San Marcos.[42] More significantly, he now met Mariátegui for the first time, and soon learned the extent to which the Peruvian was being harassed by the government.[43] Frank and Mariátegui were determined to work together for realization of their shared vision. But because of Mariátegui's failing health, Frank's immediate concern was that the poet go to Buenos Aires to get revitalized. To that end, Frank wrote to Espinoza, requesting that he somehow come up with the money for Mariátegui to make the journey.[44] Departing Peru, Frank rounded out his tour in Colombia and Havana, having received invitations to lecture there while still in Argentina.[45]

On the whole, Frank's tour was "an enormous success."[46] M. J. Benardete, who edited *Waldo Frank in America Hispana* (1930), a collection of responses to the trip, writes that Frank was "first page" news, and that "he had the attention of the entire Continent—an event never equalled before." A sampling of comments from the countries he visited is indicative of the depth of the reaction his presence provoked. A Mexican editorial (in *El Universal*) exclaims, "His truth is . . . our truth." Coriolano

Alberini, in *Síntesis* (Buenos Aires), declares, "Let it not be forgotten that from our very hope, and from 'the quality of our search, the nature of the future America will be born,' and Frank is its prophet."[47]

Mariátegui, writing in *Variedades* (Lima), likens Frank to Disraeli; he rhetorically asks:

> . . . even as it was a Jew who, in the Victorian epoch, alone felt in all its magnificence, and with the luxurious fantasy of the Oriental, the Imperial role of Britain, may it not be reserved to this Jew . . . to formulate the hope and ideal of America?[48]

Finally, a Havana editorial in *Revista de Avance* states, "Men like Waldo Frank . . . can, through the uprightness of their word and the greatness of their art, tell the dissenters in their country the measure of our tragedy and force them to say *their word* to South America."[49]

On the negative side, one poignant response to Frank's message is that of Francisco Dura in *Criterio* (Buenos Aires). First, he makes the point that there is nothing new in Frank's statement that the problem of the modern world is not *economic*, but *religious* and *human*; to back up his argument, he cites Proudhon. Furthermore, he takes issue with Frank's characterization of Catholicism as an antiquated religion, and defends the church as an integral part of Latin American society. Finally, he makes the frank observation that while Frank speaks of the necessity to create a "new world," he offers no method for realizing the goal, only words.[50]

Nonetheless, Frank's tour was on the whole eminently successful, and there were a number of reasons for this. To begin with, he journeyed to Latin America during a period when the bonds of culture were almost nonexistent between the United States and the Hispanic world.[51] He came as a "self-appointed" emissary,[52] and, in sensing the need for closer relations, he was a "pioneer" (according to no less an authority than Robert Woods Bliss, the United States ambassador to Argentina at the time of the trip).[53] Moreover, Frank's trip was not one of those official acts, so rehearsed that they barely make an impression.[54]

Besides the novel circumstances of his visit, Frank's manner (as it was generally perceived) helped guarantee a warm reception. Here was a leading American intellectual who came to the Latin Americans with no condescension and openly friendly,[55] treating them as equals.[56] He spoke "a language that was quite unlike [that of] the business promoters who 'treated us as if we were Indians,' a Latin American writer said."[57] Furthermore, his "way of coming straight at people was almost irresistible, flattering while holding attention."[58] His was an "engaging passionateness" and an intimacy that "took you by the arm, so to speak, and made you look at him while he talked to you alone."[59] As Luis Alberto Sánchez, in *Letras* (the quarterly of the University of San Marcos), observes, Frank spoke with the "emotive accent of the Old Testament Prophets."[60]

Frank's message, of course, made his success. He introduced Latin America to an "unhappy America"—the creative minority to which he belonged with its positive achievements in art, philosophy, and life. "In all humility and contrition for the deeds of his government,"[61] he suggested that the Hispanic world had as much to give the United States as the other way around and, therefore, deserved to be addressed as peers. Moreover, with his recognition that Latin America not only had held onto the spiritual values bequeathed by Spain, but was in the process of adapting those values to attain a higher state of consciousness,[62] Frank "sent a religious thrill"[63] through an intelligentsia "in a feverish quest of fresh channels for heart and mind."[64]

The timing of the visit has already been alluded to. Mexico, undergoing a heralded cultural renascence, was still living through the heady days of political revolution. In Argentina, Frank found the majority of citizens to be liberal-minded, with democratic sentiments;[65] and many were deliriously optimistic about the results expected to ensue from recently established predominance of the Radical party and from the mystical, utopian university reform movement that originated in 1918. Moreover, President Hipólito Irigoyen, standard-bearer of the Radical party, was a "mystical Krausist" who symbolized the strength of an occult movement that existed throughout Latin America at this time.[66] And even though Peru was under the materialistic, bourgeois Leguía dictatorship, Frank found that many of its youth and intellectuals longed for a spiritual reawakening and rebirth.

Finally, Frank's Latin American alliances contributed to his victorious trip. In Mexico, Alfonso Reyes proved an ideal sponsor. Reyes "could disarm suspicion, which Frank had reason to apprehend" considering the sorry history of U.S.-Mexican relations. Then, there was Enrique Espinoza. As Chapman concludes, "No coadjutor could take more personal pride in Waldo Frank's triumphant sweep through Spanish America than his faithful and hardworking friend."[67] And, of course, Frank's relationship with José Carlos Mariátegui, "the most erudite and dynamic writer" on social questions in South America and whose magazine *Amauta* "came to have a continent-wide circulation among radical thinkers and leaders,"[68] helped assure a favorable reaction not only in Peru but wherever Mariátegui's name was honored.

Probably before leaving for the United States, Frank wrote an open letter to the students of Cuba, published on 15 January 1930 in Havana's *Revista de Avance.* In the full flush of his Latin American triumph, Frank, characterizing the revolutionary students' movement as a struggle to "recreate" the life of Cuba, encourages them to "go on," for only then will they "be happy." He recognizes the seeming impossibility of their task, given the presence of Yankee imperialism and the "irresponsible financial interests of the United States" aligned against them. But, with an expression of his Marxist faith, he contends they can only effectively meet their problem "from the platform of War Against Capitalism." Aligning himself with the program of action put forth by the students, he concludes:

> If I could feel that my word warmed you in the slightest degree, heartened your perseverance, it would be for me an inexpressible joy, who am alone here in this great country—alone, and unable to act for and with men like you who stand for everything I cherish.[69]

The Prophet at Home

Back in the United States in 1930, Frank set to work on his cultural history, *America Hispana.* He also found time to edit *Tales from the Argentine*, a collection of stories representative of "the native elements that have gone into the simmering process of Argentina's national birth."[70] He had begun gathering these materials in 1928 with the help of Espinoza, with whom he was in correspondence.[71] The book contained stories by the following Argentine writers: Roberto J. Payró, Leopoldo Lugones, Lucio V. López, Domingo Faustino Sarmiento, Ricardo Güiraldes, and Horacio Quiroga.[72] Significantly, Lugones was the president of the Argentine Society of Authors and had chaired the banquet welcoming Frank to Buenos Aires.[73] Since he had ideological differences with Frank, his inclusion was probably an act of diplomacy on Frank's part. As for Payró, he may have been included because in 1928 he had solicited Frank to translate into English the story that is in the book.[74] Frank included Güiraldes because while "the earlier writers *knew* they were Americans: Güiraldes *feels* he is American. And this distinction is the new note in South American letters." Furthermore, Frank notes how the Argentine writer's "sensibilities . . . had begun to touch the mystic dimensions of American life."[75]

The year 1930 also saw the publication in Madrid of Frank's Latin American lectures under the title *Primer mensaje a la América Hispana*. Based largely on a previous publication, these lectures were little more than an oral presentation of *Re-discovery of America*, with some personal anecdotes and other autobiographical information added. But this is not to say that the *Primer mensaje* is a superfluous publication; in a sense, it is a correction of the misrepresentations of Frank's thought contained in the faulty translation of *Re-discovery* published in Spanish as *El rediscubrimiento de América*. Thus, the true rendition of Frank's message finally appeared in Spanish.

Also in 1930, Frank, in his role as spokesman for better cultural relations between the Americas, took time to write two important articles in order to acquaint his fellow Americans with conditions south of the Rio Grande. In the June edition of *Scribner's Magazine* appeared the first—"What is Hispano-America to Us?" In answer to the question, Frank asserts that the basis of our relations with Latin America "must be the sense of kinship, the experience of mutual advantage" that result from "a deep mutual knowledge." He contends that such knowledge does not exist in the United States—we know *about* our southern neighbors, but we do not really *know* them. Frank then outlines the course of attaining understanding. First, "we must see . . . their cultural complexity and their cultural immaturity." Next, "by comparing their revolution to our own," we can appreciate the advantageous conditions that made the United States a reality, as well as the chaotic conditions that have retarded the realization of Latin America's destiny, i.e., the "national integration" of its peoples. Frank, predictably, announces that Hispano-America is "coming of age." But in claiming that the thought and work of Latin America's intellectuals are expressive of "the basic spirit and the creative will of the people," Frank gives his readers a subjective and distorted version of Latin American intellectual life. First, he foists his ontological vision onto the entire intelligentsia of Latin America, claiming that "all these groups are dedicated to the purpose of creating a new world." Furthermore, he repeats a theme as old as *Our America* when he writes, "They hold, indeed, what our intelligentsia have momentarily lost, because we have lost this sense of wholeness, even this will to wholeness." Thus Frank is not so much promoting better U.S.–Latin American relations as he is advancing his own claims to prophetic vision. After all, when he tells how Latin America's young intellectuals have a "common religion . . . a modern religion—an American religion," he is talking about his own belief in the necessity to create a new world! In any event, he cites the barriers to acting on this belief: the impeding force that should most concern us, he says, is "the growing interference on the part of American money and, when necessary, of American Marines, in the internal affairs of these countries." The control of Latin America by American business, Frank contends, is a situation that right-thinking persons must challenge: in "the uncontrolled dictatorship of economic forces," Frank sees a foe common to the intellectuals of both Americas. Once we recognize that together with Latin America we share a common battle as well as a common destiny, he concludes, "there rests the basis of what must be the relations between us."[76]

The second article, "Contemporary Spanish American Literature," appeared in *Publisher's Weekly* in October. Frank briefly outlines the change in the condition of Latin American letters, from an "aristocratic grade" of poetry with a limited circulation and appeal, to a prose, written by "the heirs" of the aristocratic tradition, "accessible . . . to a large reading public" and characterized by "its variety and its *vitality*." Then, after citing a few examples of those Hispanic novelists who get their material from the Latin American experience, Frank addresses the problem of introducing some of these writers to United States readers. The books, he insists, must be carefully selected; they must offer variety and appeal to a "broad general interest." Also, the translations should be above reproach. In introducing representative Latin American literature to "our cultivated public," Frank advertises his contribution: he has edited a series of Latin American books for Farrar and Rinehart.[77] Characteristically, then, Frank ends his article by promoting himself.

Sometime before the end of 1930, Frank also found time to contribute a piece on Brazil for the first issue of Victoria Ocampo's *Sur*, published early in 1931. Frank then corresponded with Ocampo during those early days when *Sur* was under attack from its critics, offering her needed support and encouragement.[78] The major focus of his attention during 1931, however, was *America Hispana*—finally published in September (by Charles Scribner's Sons), while Frank was touring the Soviet Union.

America Hispana: An Analysis

The full title of the work is *America Hispana: A Portrait and a Prospect*. The book is dedicated to Mariátegui, who died in Lima on 16 April 1930. In his dedication, Frank lists the Peruvian as having been born in Lima on 14 June 1895. Actually, Mariátegui was born in Moquegua, Peru, in 1894,[79] but Frank's error can be excused, since it reflects the common belief of the time.

As for the text, the portrait is ostensibly an attempt to trace the cultural history; the prospect is Frank's dream for America: both halves of the hemisphere integrated into one people, a new spiritual synthesis by which man will be made whole.[80] The portrait is devised according to the method of *Virgin Spain*. In other words, the governing structure of the work is the Hegelian dialectic; and yet, the approach to history is the aesthetic of Nietzsche. Although Frank justifies his selection of the particular regions or people treated in the text on the grounds that they are typical in one aspect or another of all Latin America, the selections that comprise the portrait are the threads to a pattern, i.e., Frank's new teleological argument concerning Latin America. He only depicts those people, places, and events that can be interpreted as having been determined by the destiny of Latin America to become one cultural entity with the United States. That destiny, of course, has always been Frank's vision. Thus, he casts himself in the role of a prophet, and, indeed, the prospect is meant to be prophetic. But when one understands that Frank's vision of one America is in actuality a preconceived notion (a wish, if you will), then the prospect can be seen for what it really is—a mere continuation of the teleological argument.

By means of a chapter-by-chapter examination, the ensuing analysis of *America Hispana* will expose the teleological nature of the work. Beyond this, the analysis will focus on the following purposes: to sketch the general content of each chapter; to point out those parts that raised the most contemporary comment and criticism, to document what those criticisms and comments were, and judge whether or not the critical responses were justified; and when appropriate, to suggest the motives that prompted Frank to write as he did. There is no need for a chapter-by-chapter analysis of the history contained in *America Hispana*. The factual information is correct; but its interpretation is always subordinated to the demands of the argument. Thus, *America Hispana* is history in the same sense that *Virgin Spain* is history. The historical value of both books lies in their own historicity.

The book opens with Frank's acknowledgments. Here Frank begins by calling his history "a work of art," and explaining the book's aesthetic function in terms of his Nietzschean approach to history.[81] Because, he explains, the form and substance of the book are like those of his fictional works, *America Hispana* needs to be read in the correct sequence, from cover to cover. Since most books are read that way—from beginning to end—what is Frank implying? Perhaps his implication is that mere history books, whose aims he sees as essentially to furnish factual information,[82] need not be read sequentially, as they perhaps contain only encyclopedic value. Considering Frank's aesthetic, such a conclusion is warranted.

Nonetheless, Frank recognizes that he must be uncompromising in his depiction of a people's history, because facts line the road that leads to a people's ultimate reality. In his efforts at accuracy, he notes that he had to contend with the chaotic state of the historic literature of Latin America; and he had to depend on his own intuition at times in choosing sources that were in harmony with what he knew. Moreover, he received all sorts of help from writers, artists, and scholars; foremost among those who aided him in acquiring needed material were Enrique Espinoza; Anita Brenner (who also did the English translation of the stories in *Tales from the Argentine*); Pablo Martínez del Río of Mexico; Luis Alberto Sánchez and Jorge Guillermo Leguía of Lima; Luis Valcárcel of the University of Cuzco; Baldamiro Sanín Cano; Juan Marinello of Havana; and Federico de Onís of Columbia University.[83]

One important aspect of this opening section is Frank's explanation of his inclusion of Brazil in a work titled *America Hispana*. He asserts that Hispania is a name for the *entire* Iberian Peninsula, and thus includes the culture of Portugal, despite the fact that the Portuguese are not part of the political system of Spain. Hispanic America (or America Hispana) is, therefore, that part of the Western Hemisphere that stretches from Mexico to Tierra del Fuego, inclusive of Brazil, peopled by colonists from Hispania.[84] Frank's rationalization for the inclusion of Brazil is based upon the premise that "one root have Portugal and Spain: one land. . . . And . . . one blood, one amalgam, whose single scientific name is

Spanish."[85] On this premise, Frank is in agreement with the great Portuguese historian Jaime Cortesão who writes, "Portuguese and Castilians, Galicians and Andalusians, are all branches of the same tree, grandchildren of the same fore-fathers, and those who try to deny this profound Hispanic brotherhood deny themselves a part of their own humanity."[86] On the other hand, Frank's assertions fly in the face of the convictions of most Portuguese authors who have dealt with their country's national consciousness.

Frank begins his history with a prelude that focuses, significantly, on Panama. True to his Nietzschean predilections, he finds historical truth embodied in myth—in this case, that of the two lost continents of Atlantis and Lemuria. Frank suggests that Panama is the place where the two legendary worlds intersected. Is this mythic unity in Panama, also the connecting point of the two Americas, a harbinger of the fate of the hemisphere? Such a suggestion is veiled, of course, but it nonetheless lays the groundwork for Frank's argument—and also borrows from Bolivarian analyses. This argument is advanced by the Panama Canal's history as Frank interprets it. To Frank, the Panama Canal symbolizes the potential unity of the Americas. Thus, Columbus and Cortés, who both tried to discover the waterway to the Orient, become, in Frank's treatment, "time-muddled mystics" who confused the past and the future. In other words, they were Frank's forerunners in envisaging hemispheric unity. Then, Simón Bolívar, who revived the project of the radical Cortes of Cadiz for a canal at Panama, focused on Panama *his* vision of a dual American union, a living organism, complete and autonomous. But Bolívar's spirit, which included Catholic Spain and the romantic movement, was opposed by the United States, which had no belief system other than the credo of manifest destiny. Bolívar failed because he "lacked the *tool*!"— literally and figuratively. Theodore Roosevelt, however, responding to the United States's chief drive, the desire for expansion, succeeded in building the canal. The visionary Bolívar, the willful Roosevelt—both personify the dialectic. As the spiritual vision of Latin America found its opposite in the energy and technical knowledge of the United States, so Bolívar, the heir of the Puritan prophets (Roger Williams, John Eliot, and Thomas Hooker) whose actions divined him, found his antithesis in Roosevelt, an alien to their great tradition. The reconciliation of the two, not yet accomplished, can bring about a new world. But, as Frank writes, "Bolívar and Roosevelt, meeting in Panama, premise the American drama." To establish dramatic tension, he poses an alternative to synthesis—the victory of will over spirit, embodied in the predominance of the United States.[87] But if one is aware of the teleological basis, the realization of the alternative can always be explained as being but a preliminary stage in the overall design. Hence, the vision survives.

The prelude evoked some comment. One reviewer calls Frank's mythic approach "geographical mysticism." He seems to understand, however, that Frank is merely using myth to advance his argument of a "final spiritual unity."[88] Another reviewer, Mary Austin,[89] merely finds Frank's study of the Panama Canal "concise." But, while she is not incorrect in concluding from Frank's account that the canal is one of the major reasons why people in the United States are unable to project North and South America "into one common plane of Americanism,"[90] she fails to add that Frank views the canal as a unitive rather than a divisive element.

As history, Frank's study is factual, though constructed to meet the needs of his argument and decidedly slanted. One example will suffice to illustrate Frank's orientation. In describing the conspiratorial role of the United States in bringing about the independence of Panama, he writes, "And when the dirty deed is done, Roosevelt unfurls the rhetoric of 'nationality' to make it holy; and recognizes" the new nation.[91] Thus, Frank serves what Austin calls "our need for castigation" regarding our past treatment of Latin America.[92] Moreover, he serves his own purposes. His criticism of the United States aligns him with intellectuals from Mexico to Chile; his "evocation of the philosophic Catholic acceptance of life and high value of human dignity" is designed to excite the sympathies of a Latin American audience.[93]

Following the prelude is the first book, "Portrait," comprising five chapters. The first, "The Andes," has seven sections. For the first, Frank again resorts to myth—that of the primordial Earth Mother. Thus, the rock of the Andes informs the life of those timeless Indians of the mountains of High Peru (which extends beyond Peru into Bolivia). Furthermore, the *ayllu*—the Indians' group—was bound together by earth ("softened stone"). Frank's purpose is to show how the communal mentality embodied in the *ayllu*, unlike the European concept of man as an atomistic individual,[94] is a value sprung from American soil that can contribute to the creation of the new world.

This section evoked particular comment from an expert in the field of Indian culture. Mary Austin will have none of Frank's endeavor "to derive the Indians on the spot where they are found," and claims that seventy-five years of research "demonstrate that the Indians of the Andes are very much like Indians everywhere;

that they are not markedly unlike archaic minds anywhere."[95] Austin's dismissal of Frank's mythic approach by pointing out the commonality of all Indians exhibits a total lack of understanding concerning Frank's purpose. Besides, the myth itself is a message: wholeness is a Latin American tradition, as old and timeless as the Andean Indians themselves.

The second section mixes myth with dialectic. The Incas were an *ayllu*, descendants of the rock. Yet they generated a pragmatic religion—the sun ordered their thinking and their doing. The resulting synthesis spawned "what is perhaps the first rational society." Frank then expands on the *ayllu*, depicting it as the agent of welfare. But the spirit of pragmatism that characterized the ancient South American cultures caused all forces not instrumental to the *ayllu* to be excluded. Thus, the people could not evolve beyond their communal world. The Incan empire, therefore, is posed as an example of the doom that befalls all pragmatisms. This fate is necessary to Frank's argument. For pragmatism deters a culture from going beyond those patterns that it finds essential to its endurance.[96] Thus pragmatism militates against the creation of the new world.

"The Conquistador" is Frank's version of what occurred when the Incas and the Spanish met. The narration of the coming of Pizarro and the resultant conflict between the two cultures is historically accurate. And Gardner Harding finds Frank's relation of this tale containing "an ironic relish" unsurpassed even by Prescott.[97] Frank's point of view can only be understood in terms of his teleology. The Spaniards had to be victorious. Possessed of a personal will and a transcendent imagination,[98] these sons of Spain's spiritual synthesis had to prevail over the pragmatic will of the Incan *ayllu* in order to plant Spain's spiritual values in the soil of Latin America. There, these values, transfigured, would be born anew as an element in the destined new world culture.

The fourth section concludes Frank's discussion of the fate of the *ayllu*. He maintains that the *ayllu* withdrew from the Spaniard; it did not fight back. Today, therefore, the Indian is an exile in his own mountains. And the failure of the Indian and Spaniard to understand each other has resulted in mutual degradation. But at least the Indian has gained from Christianity the guiding principle of that religion (which the Spaniards themselves never fathomed): "the secret of not wanting." Thus ennobled, the Indian embodies the survival of the *ayllu*, robbed of its formal ownership of the soil. This elaborate construct is necessary to show that the value that the *ayllu* embodies—"the organic cycle of man and group and land"[99]—has survived in Latin America. That survival, of course, is a necessary part of Frank's prophetic vision.

The fifth section is Frank's explanation of the racial psychology of the mestizo—half Spanish, half Indian, and "torn between the conflicts of his inheritances."[100] Harding finds Frank's depiction of the mestizo "a key to understanding" mestizo society and its truths, and designates this section, due to "the clarity and the penetration" therein, as one of the best in the book.[101] Ernest Gruening, on the other hand, finds the interpretation "interesting, if debatable," noting Frank's obvious bias in behalf of the mestizo or "half-breed."[102] Attempting an explanation of Frank's treatment of this theme, Mary Austin likens Frank's experience to that of D. H. Lawrence: "he has created a mask for the Amerindian Spanish populations of the countries described out of their surface differentiation from the variously derived population of the northern continent."[103]

This explanation does not go far enough. Frank characterizes the mestizo in dialectical terms; the mestizo is the chaotic result of the intermingling of two antithetical worlds. Why chaotic and not synthetic? The chaotic nature is evidence of the transition period that Latin America must experience before the new world is created. With such rationalization does Frank include the mestizo in his teleological construct.

The sixth section is Frank's concise, if slanted, account of Latin American economic history from the last days of the conquistadors to the republics of his day. His report is castigatory, but his purpose is deeper. For example, in pointing up the ancient conflict between the spiritual and the temporal that characterized the economic situation of the colonial period, Frank notes Catholicism's failure to provide a way to transform the individualism at the base of all sin. The implication is clear; Latin America needs a new religion that provides just such a method. Furthermore, Frank finds a place in his teleology for the masses, whose "tragic disinheritance" was completed by the republics. He prophesies that their plight will make them "accessible . . . to the man of truth when he comes, and when he learns to reach them."[104]

In the final section, Frank describes what he has seen in the towns of Tiahuanacu, La Paz, and Arequipa. These descriptions lead into his relation of his rooftop talk with the Peruvian students at Arequipa. This meeting falls within the prophetic framework, for he states that the students understand his message of the need to create a new world. Moreover, to bring this world about, they possess both the vision and the will, which are but the "transfigured" legacy of their ancestors.[105] Thus, from the first *ayllu* to these students, the history of the Andean region is shown to be moving toward Frank's vision of a unity based on spiritual values.

Chapter 2, "The Pampa," also has seven sections. In the first, which provides another example of "geographical mysticism," Frank defines the pampa as "a quality . . . that embraces forms." That quality is motion, and it informs the psyche of the pampa dweller. He cannot distinguish the parts from the whole; rather, he senses the continuous movement of all things in "their integral co-existence."[106] In other words, the people of the pampa instinctively understand the concept of wholeness. They are defined more in terms of interrelationships than of individual egos, and thus are rich in potential for creating the new world. Obviously, Frank's interpretation of pampa and people is tailored to meet the demands of his argument.

Furthermore, the pampa, beginning where the Andes end, *is* Argentina; the pampa's motion toward La Plata fuses the continent with the Atlantic Ocean. In turn, the shores of Europe, North America, Africa, and Spain come through the Atlantic to the pampa. These antithetical elements meet in Buenos Aires,[107] their synthesis.

Frank explains the Atlantic orientation of the pampa in the following section, "From Andes to Atlantic." Turning to history, he contends that the journey over Panama to Peru—the center of colonial life in South America—was so arduous that the Spaniards carried their exploration to Argentina in the hope of finding a water passage between oceans. The search established a "continental circulation" between Lima and Buenos Aires. Thus, settlers moved toward the Atlantic, founding cities along the way. Likewise, Spain's spiritual values, transplanted in the new world, became transfigured as they made their way down the slope from the Andes mountains to the Atlantic Ocean. The cities that he describes along the route from mountain to ocean are symbols of this step-by-step metamorphosis.[108] Either his choice of cities or his descriptions of them are made to illustrate his point; or possibly his visiting these cities generated this aspect of his argument.

The third section, "The Gaucho," is Frank's paean to Argentina's semimythic figure. The gaucho is a product of Spaniard and Indian. However, he is not a real mestizo. Why not? Because the main characteristic of the mestizo is the chaos in his mind that results from having two wills at an impasse. But the pampa's motion allows no such deadlock in the gaucho. Thus, the gaucho (thanks to the pampa) exemplifies a "new American direction." Frank completes the section with a generalized analysis of the gaucho dance in terms of its synthetic nature and by a description of the performance of the dance that he witnessed at an authentic gaucho's *estancia*.[109]

In the fourth section, Frank returns to history and explains the disappearance of the historic gaucho in terms of the epic struggle between *federales* and *unitarios*. These antithetical forces, personified by Juan Manuel de Rosas and Domingo Faustino Sarmiento, are reconciled in the Argentine nation. But both opposed the gaucho, and their opposition generated a poem, *Martin Fierro*— a synthesis that revealed the gaucho's value within the context of the life-and-death conflict. Nowhere is Frank's mystical vision clearer than in this concluding statement: "The gaucho had died in order that the land might have body; he is reborn in order that the body may have spirit."[110]

The fifth section, "Buenos Aires," is to one reviewer "a literary gem."[111] Frank's description revolves around the synthetic nature of the city. In Buenos Aires, all opposites are reconciled, even in the vanishing mestizo. To this dialectical approach, Frank adds that quality of the pampa that informs Argentine life—"the vision which, seeing things whole, *sees* life." Thus, Buenos Aires is whole and integrated. Forcing the city into the construct of his vision, Frank likens Buenos Aires to an "embryon" that is not conscious of its predestined features.[112]

"Rosario," the sixth and shortest section, is easily the most ambiguous. Frank begins by completing his dialectical and teleological interpretation of Buenos Aires. This city is still experiencing the chaos that results from the conflict between her transfigured values from Catholicism, and the spirit—individualistic, expansionist, democratic, anything but organic—that flows in from the North Atlantic. Rosario, on the other hand, which has isolated this spirit, is described as "almost as hideous as a city in Ohio." Yet Frank concludes with this judgment of the city's residents: "It is the pampa that has filled their eyes, and the Atlantic that has squared their shoulders."[113] The statement seems to indicate a synthesis (though not the final synthesis); but this contradicts his one-sided description of Rosario. In any event, the section continues Frank's observation throughout this chapter that Argentina is not really like the United States. Of course, Frank's reason for the continuous contrast between the two countries has already been examined.

The final section finds Frank fitting two of his Argentine acquaintances, Hipólito Irigoyen and Victoria Ocampo, into his dialectical mold. He correctly assesses the spiritual aspect of the former president's character, and explains Irigoyen's political life by that orientation. But then he attributes the president's failure to deal with his country's problems to his lack of a method. Like Bolívar, Irigoyen's vision was not mature enough to succeed. Furthermore, the president's career points up the "embryonic" state of his country.[114]

Finally, Frank proceeds to Ocampo and provides a vivid description of her house. A synthesis of the Old World and the New World, this house expresses the "American will" of its owner. Furthermore, the plan of the house, constructed to let in light and with all its walls white and empty, is interpreted by Frank in a teleological way: "The key of the house is *light*—a new American light in whose free moving all colors of old worlds are reborn. The theme is *structure*—a form to . . . make of light the substance of an American's living."[115] Since the construction of her house in the way she desired was a difficult task, her accomplishment stands as a symbol of Argentina's future. Thus, Frank poses Ocampo as a prophet for her people.

Chapter 3, "The Pacific," again contains seven sections. The first finds Frank expanding on his notion of the "Atlantic destiny" of Latin America. From Ecuador to central Chile, the Pacific Coast is isolated from the Atlantic life-source. Thus, geography determines the "fractional republic" of Ecuador, as well as the "common malnutrition" of every town on the Pacific seaboard. This Pacific orientation makes these regions exploitable by the "alien will" that enters the region by way of the Panama Canal. Thus, the Pacific is characterized as a barrier and made a scapegoat for the economic exploitation of the area by foreign capitalists.[116]

The content of the second section, "The Spirit of Chile," is best exposed through the comments it evoked. For example, Harding finds Frank reprimanding the Chilean man "as the truest son of the conquistador," and calls Frank's account of the War of the Pacific "rather unfriendly."[117] Another reviewer adds that "of industrial Chile, he paints a rather horrible picture—one of foreign exploitation."[118] To what purpose does Frank write as he does about Chile? First, Chile is used to typify the immoral consequences of U.S. investment throughout the whole of America Hispana.[119] This antithetical element is necessary to the dialectical structure of the book. Rendered by its mines the slave of North American capital,[120] Chile is linked to the Atlantic world through its sharing of that world's negative values. By this very fact, Chile's destiny remains the Atlantic destiny of all Latin America.

The third section, "Chuquicamata," is a narrative of the return of a young writer to his hometown, which is run by an American company that controls the area's copper mines. While it is a portrayal of the appalling poverty and corruption,[121] there is more to this story of León Hidalgo (of whom no evidence could be found to indicate whether he is a real or imagined person). Frank contrasts the mechanolatry of the North American engineers, who are spiritually dead, to the Chilean workers, who are alive because they retain some of their closeness to the earth, although their life is "vaguely inchoate." León personifies the synthesis of the two. Frank writes, "Let the machine be! and the making of copper and the desert and the church and the stars. But let man make them good by transfiguring them to his own image."[122] Such is the thinking of León Hidalgo. And León's positive completion is the embodiment of Frank's vision.

The fourth section has Frank returning to the capital of Peru. Since Lima's antithetical forces result in chaos rather than synthesis, Lima reflects its mestizo residents. Lima, in fact, is the archetype for all mestizo cities in Latin America.[123] This description of the city has no real historical value; it merely serves the dialectical nature of the overall argument. The chaos of Lima, moreover, serves the teleology, for chaos is necessary to break down the old values and prepare the way for the new world.

The fifth section is Frank's unflattering portrait of the Peruvian dictator Augusto Leguía, overthrown in 1930. The characterization of Leguía as merely the agent of foreign capitalists leads Frank to expound on the nature of dictatorship in Latin America, past and present. He is sympathetic to the classic dictators, for they symbolized their people's basic nature. But this new style of *caudillo*, exemplified by Leguía, is that of a "money dictator," whose era has yet to wane. Leguía's fall fits neatly into Frank's teleology. With the "alien current" that kept him in office "turned off," Peru now can begin to determine its own destiny.[124]

The sixth section is a brief, yet lionizing, account of the personal history of José Carlos Mariátegui.[125] Mariátegui, of course, is more than the antithesis of Leguía. Though his blood is mixed, he is no mestizo, but rather the synthesis of his dual ancestry. He is a prophet. He knows America must be recreated. Indeed, he is the projection of the "new American." Frank recalls the planned journey of Mariátegui to Buenos Aires. Though he died on the eve of his departure, his proposed crossing from the Pacific is like a portent of things to come.[126] When one recalls that it was Frank, as he tells us in his *Memoirs*, who urged Mariátegui to go to Buenos

Aires, even to the extent of asking Espinoza to make the financial arrangements, one can only wonder if Frank's urging was motivated by his desire to cast Mariátegui in the role of fulfilling the Atlantic destiny: leaving the west to reappear in the east, and thus repeating the myth of Quetzalcoatl (who was in turn associated in Indian lore with the transformation of Venus as the evening star into Venus as the morning star).

The final section is Frank's explanation of the meaning of Mariátegui's communism. He admits that the Peruvian called himself a Communist, but his was not the communism of Soviet Russia or Europe. According to Frank, Mariátegui had achieved in Europe the "mystic sense of New World destiny." He had an "organic sense of the Whole," and when he found it in Marx it caused him to value the dialectic. This is not the same as the intentional "exclusion of self-consciousness" that characterizes the doctrine of "shallow" Communists—men who are receptive to dialectical materialism because it confirms and justifies "their dislikes."[127] In essence, Frank is characterizing Mariátegui as a co-visionary. What he writes of Mariátegui, he might very well have written of himself, particularly where the mystic interpretation of Marx is concerned.[128] Considering the close friendship and correspondence of the two, one can assume that Mariátegui would concur with Frank's interpretation of him.[129]

Chapter 4 is Frank's treatment of Brazil. The first section establishes the Amazon River's (and, therefore, Brazil's) link with the Atlantic life-source, and destiny.[130] This two-page section is singled out by Ernest Gruening as characteristic of Frank's "embracing concept, of his utilization of all the senses, of his poetic license, and of the idiosyncrasies of his vocabulary."[131] This is true. Frank sees Brazil as forest, world, cosmos. The Amazon is a "blood stream" in which man is but a "micro-organism floating in the blood" of an enormous beast. Thus, the myth of the primordial Earth Mother is repeated. Furthermore, the dialectic and teleology advance, for the synthesis that is the river as bloodstream informs the life and spirit of the man of the forest. The heat, which is the forest's "soul," forces man to submit to the river. As a result, the man, like an embryo, is "timelessly submissive,"[132] poised in his role in the birth of a new world.

In the second section, Frank focuses on the Negro element in Brazil. The Negro, "the archetypical tropic forest dweller," crossed the Atlantic to Brazil, "the tropic heart of the new world." The result will be a "new world tropic culture."[133] One reviewer only considers Frank's "bio-meteorological assumption" that climate affects a culture in terms of "poetry," "lyric prose," and "symbolism."[134] The last term is the proper one, for Frank presents the Negro as a symbol of the difficulties encountered by Latin Americans in adapting to their surroundings.[135]

Having established the Negro's role in the teleology, Frank reviews Brazil's history in a scant four pages. One review finds it "interesting to note that Portugal's colony Brazil bore far more cultural and economic resemblance to our own Thirteen Colonies than to her Spanish-American neighbors."[136] Frank's approach, of course, is governed by his thinking of the Portuguese as deniers of their Spanish spirit, and, therefore, as necessarily unfit as agents of destiny. The Negro, however, inherits the blessings of both Europe and Africa, so that he will be able to make in Brazil the new world tropic culture.[137]

The third section, "São Paulo," posits the coffee man of Brazil's "real capital" as the antithesis of the Negro. As the Negro embodies the spirit of Brazil, so the coffee man embodies the forceful imposition on Brazil of the values of the United States and Europe. Frank's scheme, of course, dooms the coffee man to failure. He contends that the tropics will give birth to their own values. Thus, the climatic element in the teleology is repeated. Frank prophesies that the energy of the teeming rivers will be harnessed, "jungles will be mastered, fever will be wiped out." Then he continues the dialectic. The result of the synthesis of technological and spiritual values will be a tropic unprecedented in the history of mankind.[138]

The final section centers around Rio de Janeiro's being the fusion of all Brazil's energies. Here, the antithetical elements of geography and race are reconciled. Frank finds Rio's strength in her artists, poets, and poor. The spirit of Rio is the forest, embodied in the Negro. The Amazon, which carries the mountains to the ocean, is the symbol of the poor of Rio, who wait for the forest's will that shall make the new Brazil.[139] With such tortured reasoning does Frank repeat the Negro's role in his vision of New World destiny.

Harding notes that Brazil is only "adequately" covered in comparison to the other regions. In his view, the forest's obscuring atmosphere and Rio's beauty confused Frank.[140] Actually, the explanation is not so simple. Frank's inability to read Portuguese, except for the simple prose of newspapers,[141] obviously curtailed his access to sources. And his short stay limited his impressions. Beyond this, and more importantly, Brazil's lack of a Spanish heritage and Frank's disdain for the Portuguese necessitated his finding some elements that could legitimately place the Brazilian experience within the context of his argument. Thus, the climate and the Negro become the integral parts of the future of Brazil, linking that future tenuously to the destiny of America Hispana. Having molded Brazil to meet his needs, he moves on, no doubt, without any qualms for not having written at greater depth.

The fifth and final chapter of the first book, "The Central Sea," is divided into four sections. The first finds Frank in the Caribbean. He describes the Mayan civilization in terms of its spirituality, suggesting that its architecture expresses the sense of the immanence of God. Then, as part of the dialectic, Frank contrasts these Mayan buildings to the Gothic cathedrals of Europe and the skyscrapers of New York. They symbolize Mayan life—an experience of oneness with the cosmos. And as such, they are a model of that "cosmic sense,"[142] indigenous to the region, that the new world will need.

Frank turns next to the Aztec civilization, which also possessed the sense of oneness with all life. But Frank contends that that sense was symbolized by "human sacrifice," with the Aztec priests eating the hearts of the victims. He explains the symbol in terms of "the primordial lust of man to *eat himself*," thus partaking of the "mystic Whole." Moreover, this practice had its basis in myth; it was borrowed from the Mayas and Toltecs, who in turn received it from Atlantis. Thus, Frank returns to myth to suggest a destiny of unity with an Atlantic orientation. This interpretation is enhanced by dialectical symbolism. Since the flower was the symbol of the Aztec sense of beauty, its completeness coalesced in the Aztec mind with the end of life as symbolized by the blood that spouted from the hearts of the victims.[143]

Frank then relates in teleological terms the story of the coming of Cortés and the subsequent conquest of Mexico. Cortés, whom he characterizes as the "genius" of all the conquistadors, exemplified Spain. He understood his role in her mystery. By his triumph, he instilled his own spirit in New Spain. From that time forward, Mexico's genius has contained Cortés, Spain's genius.[144] One reviewer insightfully points out that, despite the value that Frank imputes to the Catholic legacy bequeathed by the Conquest, Frank overlooks the spiritual tragedy that occurred when the Aztec and Mayan libraries were burned, and perhaps advances the Spanish heritage while sacrificing that of the Indian.[145] In seeming answer to the second charge, Frederick Bliss Luquiens writes that Frank could not disregard the Spaniard. He could not because he knows Spain. . . . He knows, therefore, that the Spaniard has done much for Mexico, and that the spirit of Spain will yet do a great deal for Mexico and all America Hispana. He knows that while the Spaniard's descendants are not America Hispana's ethnic base nor its spiritual and aesthetic key, they are its forming factor.[146]

In any event, what is more important to Frank is that the Mexican, the product of the union of the Spaniard and Indian, is still a mestizo; baffled, like mestizos everywhere, by the clash of values inherited from his forebears, the Mexican accordingly "sank to the sole certain means of satisfaction" given him by his senses.[147]

The dialectic is personified by this Mexican and his antithesis, "the Protestant-pioneer" whom he encountered on the Rio Grande.[148] Their synthesis, of course, will bring about a new world.

Finally, Frank defines the Mexican in terms of the myth of the primordial Earth Mother. He asserts that all Mexicans are like their volcanic mountains; beneath the surface is a fire that "must some day break the mold and destroy" them.[149] One reviewer takes this "bio-geological thesis" as only one of "a hundred other symbolisms, analogies, metaphors, crypticisms."[150] The characterization, of course, is correct, but the review exhibits no understanding as to Frank's purposes.

In the second section, "The Mexican Revolution," Frank expands on a theme introduced in the previous section. The two cultures that face one another across the Rio Grande are partial, not whole. Having recourse again to the Mother Earth myth, he observes that all cultures have their roots in the earth; indeed, they are the transformation of the earth enriched by sunlight. If they lose contact with either earth or sun, they "must wither." The elements of bread, power, and religion, which comprise the whole of culture, are all sprung from the earth. The industrial culture of the United States is one of bread-and-power; the culture of Mexico is one of art-and-religion. Thus, both races are not "wholly human." This postulate is a prelude to Frank's interpretation of Mexico's history since the beginning of the Mexican war of emancipation under the lead of Father Hidalgo. The crowning event of this historical period was, of course, the Mexican Revolution, which Frank in dialectical terms calls "the essential movement of Mexico's will to complete its culture with bread and power, the Deed that synthesizes all the others." All the actors in this drama are characterized as symbols of the various intellectual elements that contributed to Mexico's chaos until 1920. From that point on, the chaos has been challenged by Mexico's politicians, intellectuals, and artists. Naturally, these men are the same who welcomed Frank to Mexico. Thus, Frank imparts to them the mystic sense that understands Mexico's need for bread and power, its need for wholeness. And Frank can then present the Mexican of his day as being in a transition from the "animal phase of unconscious participation in the Whole," which characterizes the heirs of the Aztec "cult of personal extinction," to oneness with his fellow man.[151] This transition is an apology for all of contemporary Mexico's faults and shortcomings.

Frank then turns to José Vasconcelos and Alfonso Reyes. The political defeat of the former, who possessed his people's "triune will to bread-power-religion," is passed off as only the end of a phase. More important is this Mexican's growing awareness that he requires a method with which to lead, which signals the beginning of a "more organic epoch." Frank then poses Vasconcelos as a co-visionary,[152] and implies that the Mexican needs to embrace a system obviously of Frank's devising.

Reyes, on the other hand, symbolizes the "Latin Spirit" that runs through the chaos that is Mexico. Reyes's vision joins with the message of Vasconcelos to form Mexico's future. In Reyes's poetry, Frank finds a vision of the new Mexico "rising from the blood of destiny into a transfigured day."[153]

The third section is a brief, socioeconomic history of Cuba. Frank focuses on the economic exploitation of the island throughout its history, and the spirit of the Cuban that has helped him endure. Then, he narrows his focus to José Martí, the leader of the Cuban independence movement of the late nineteenth century. He credits Martí with having "a kind of *wholeness* that only the Hispanic countries seem able to produce." Possessing a "modernly prophetic" will and "tragic consciousness," Martí saw Cuba's destiny as lying within a developed Latin America. Furthermore, his death symbolized Cuba's fate: "Cuba was shackled to the will of the Northern Power."[154]

Frank then describes Havana in terms of its Americanization. The city is the archetype of the decay that threatens to engulf Cuba. The values of the Protestant North have taken hold of Cuba; these values are personified by the American businessman. But Frank finds hope in those young Cubans who might yet justify Martí's tragedy. Why? Because they are not averse to revolutionary means. Having inherited the Spaniard's tragic sense of life, they have discovered "inner resources." They are convinced of the need for economic revolution led by "spiritual leaders."[155] Thus, Frank makes them symbols of the battle between values of North and South, and the unity that must come from that battle.

The final section finds Frank posing the Gulf of Mexico-Caribbean Sea as a symbol of the union of the two Americas. This body of water joins North America with South America, and thus could be named the American Sea or the Central Sea. He contends that the Spanish had no sense of the oneness of this water, and the two names are symbolic of Spain's failure to transfer her will to be whole to the new world. Now that the United States has established hegemony over the Central Sea, the United States's victory, partly political, wholly economic, opens the curtain on a new drama set against the backdrop of that sea. The invasion of American business corresponds to the organic integration of the Hispanic peoples just beginning. Thus, the traditional spirit of the peoples of the sea now faces the Yankee invasion with one will.[156] This opposition, of course, will lead ultimately to synthesis.

Before beginning the second book, Frank interjects an interlude in which he recreates the 1822 meeting between José San Martín and Simón Bolívar in Guayaquil. One reviewer notes that the lives of the two and "their significance in the struggle of the South American countries for freedom from Spain" are set forth "in most illuminating fashion."[157] Another declares the achievement comparable to the work of Hilaire Belloc, and finds Frank's inclusion of the meeting an "indispensable" part of the book.[158] Neither of them understands Frank's aim, however. For, after briefly outlining the military careers of the two leaders of South American independence, Frank interprets their essence according to his teleology. San Martín is a methodical man, a tactician. Unlike Bolívar, he is not a mystic. Bolívar, on the other hand, is a prophet, a poet. He is the embodiment of the continental hunger to see the birth of a new world. He had Spain in him and he was a mestizo. But he was more Spanish than a real Spaniard "in his power to live a dominant ideal and raise it to cosmic pitch," and "more American than the Indian in his love of the soil and gods of the American world."[159]

In the dialogue that Frank creates, the two men discuss the future disposition of the liberated areas. Bolívar's will prevails. He proclaims an era of chaos, which is necessary to shatter the customs and values of the Old World in preparation for the birth of the New.[160]

The second book, "Prospect," encompasses Frank's system for realizing hemispheric unity. Quite rightly, Gruening sees Frank playing here "the role of prophet." But all of the "abstractions" and "inductions" prompt him to admit that he found it difficult if not impossible at times to follow the "intricacies" of Frank's ideas and the "complexities of expression."[161]

Chapter 6, "The Atlantic World," contains three sections. In the first, Frank makes gold the symbol of the willful men who created America Hispana, while the machine is the symbol of the men who settled the thirteen colonies of the North. Focusing on the latter, Frank finds in these men the essence of their machines—discretion, aggression, tenacity. Frank then goes to the point—the dissolution of the medieval synthesis produced the atomistic individualism of Protestantism that, in turn, invented the machine.[162]

Turning to Spain, Frank briefly repeats a key interpretation set forth in *Virgin Spain*. Modern Spain is also a product of the decline of medievalism, but the values of Spain during the Reconquest were *"Catholic and medieval."* Thus, the Spaniard transported to the new world his understanding that the person who lives life as an individual apart from the whole is damned, while the person who lives life as a part of the whole is saved. Returning to North America, Frank claims that only pieces of the aforementioned values were brought to that continent as well.[163] Thus, Frank lays the groundwork for his vision of New World rebirth.

The second section, "The American Half-Worlds," is basically the same vision he shared with audiences on his tour. Behind the symbols of gold and the machine are the Hispanic and Anglo-Saxon concepts of the person. These concepts are presently fulfilled in the Americas. The Anglo-Saxon smashed what did not obey his will and so made a world that mirrored that will. The Spaniard, on the other hand, joined with his world, and so his creation, though not whole, was more intricate than that of his neighbors to the north.[164]

Turning to the North, Frank analyzes its concept of the person. He finds it derived from those three trends that emerged from the decline of the medieval Christian republic—Protestantism, capitalism, and democratism. According to his analysis, these vital viewpoints possess the traits of individualism, aggression, materialism, and rationalism. Frank goes on to analyze these tendencies in predictably negative terms,[165] since they are in opposition to the values that he obviously prefers.

In Frank's interpretation of North American history, the three elements fused in the mind of the pioneer, who created the industrial society that epitomizes the United States in this century. The religion of this culture is pragmatism, which allegedly discards the idea of the true person as the locus from which knowledge and creativity emanate. This dismissal stems from a "false concept of the person" that has its origin in Protestantism. Thus posing the negative traits of the North, Frank tries to establish dramatic tension by raising the question of the fate of the United States. While he writes that the country might be in for a tragic end if it does not keep the forces of creation from being crushed, he weakens all tension by allowing readers to share his prophetic vision of American destiny. Placing the North American in a transitional phase, he reminds the reader that "birth is transition."[166]

Turning south, Frank reiterates the Hispanic concept of the person. He asserts that the republics of America Hispana unsuspectingly express the spirit of the medieval Christian republic. Because this spirit possesses latent values, which it received from the culture of the Catholic church, it might yet be a regenerating agent.[167]

Turning then to the basic compatibility between the peoples of Latin America, Frank presents what is basically a summation of the typicalities that he sought to illustrate in the portrait. But his purpose in all this is to show that each of the Americas possesses what the other needs. The United States needs to experience the complete life, which is part of the heritage of Latin America. Conversely, America Hispana needs a social model that can contain the ethic of the people; the North has the method and the means for building a solid body.[168]

In the third section, Frank describes the true person as one who has achieved "real human consciousness." The person of today, however, is in transition from the unconscious to real human consciousness; and, therefore, his social forms are also transitional. To remedy the latter situation, Frank proposes *integral* socialism, which would transform industry according to his idea of the true person.[169] Since the true person is an inevitability, according to Frank's view of American destiny, so then is integral socialism. Thus, Frank's proposal is meant to be yet another reiteration of his tediously repeated prophecy.

Chapter 8 is Frank's three-point plan for Latin America's positive completion in its political and cultural functions. In the first part, "Vertebration," Frank posits the influx of the capitalist system as the greatest menace confronting Latin America.[170] He likens America Hispana's predicament—i.e., the great invasion of investment from the United States—to the situation faced by invertebrates when evolution demanded that they either acquire spines or perish.[171] Then Frank explains the analogy: if the ideals of Latin America are to survive this onslaught, the Latin American must win for himself "a formal, inner reconstruction," i.e., a backbone with which to resist, achieve his own body, embody his own ideals, and implant morale.[172] One reviewer takes particular offense at this section, faulting Frank for being blind to the reader's power to grasp his meaning. Moreover, he wonders how enthusiastic young Latin Americans will be when they find themselves compared to jellyfish.[173] While Frank would argue that he is clear-sighted, his clear-sightedness obviously does not always extend to the sensitivities of his readers. But his purpose in this section is, of course, larger than mere name-calling.

The second point is "Federation." Frank asserts that America Hispana (except Brazil) has a legacy of merger dating back to the colonial period. Citing the need for union, he proposes three political divisions for the Hispanic world. He bases these divisions on the premise that at present such arrangements would be mutually beneficial to all parties, particularly where self-defense and economics are concerned. The Confederation of the Central Sea would include Mexico, Cuba, Santo Domingo, Haiti, the countries of Central America, Colombia, and Venezuela. The Federation of the Andes would comprise Ecuador, Bolivia, and Peru. The United States of Austral America would encompass Argentina, Paraguay, Uruguay, and Chile. Frank contends his proposal would help create America Hispana.[174] Since the creating of America Hispana is the determinant in his vision of a redeemer continent, Frank's divisions are "prophetic" elements of transcendent wholeness.

The third point, "Integration," develops out of Frank's contention that America Hispana can only be created when Latin Americans begin to regenerate themselves. In other words, unity can only be achieved when America Hispana begins to produce men and groups whose actions will create new persons and model nations. Frank will not go so far as to put a timetable on the appearance of a unified Latin world. He will only encourage Latin Americans to dedicate their lives to the creation of the new Atlantic world that will illuminate human spirituality, for then their lives will have been meaningful.[175]

Perhaps the most cogent comment on the last two points is that of Harding, who notes that "the present anarchic basis of inter-American relations" would only be strengthened by Frank's plan.[176] On the other hand, it could be suggested that Frank is entirely logical in arguing for the necessity of a united southern front so as to ultimately impress on the United States the spiritual values of Latin America and meantime to enable Latin America to resist the values of the United States. To simplify Frank's argument, North America has the means, which South America needs; South America has the ends, which North America needs. Ferner Nuhn admits that in a theoretical sense, this is true. But Nuhn also shows real insight as to the nature of *America Hispana* when he concludes that the book "has the unfortunate effect of being all 'argument'." Finding Frank to be more interested in constructing a system, he adds: "To work out his system engages him, and throughout his book all observations, all symbols, are so quickly abstracted into the system that they lose what evocative power they might have had."[177] Had Nuhn been aware of Frank's posturing as the latest of the Hebrew prophets, he would have understood that the book itself was deed enough; and that the system is specifically a teleological argument, the determining factor of which is Frank's "prophetic" vision of one American cultural entity.

How was *America Hispana* received? The reviews in the United States were mixed, and they generally exhibited a lack of understanding for what Frank was trying to do. With Latin America it was different to an amazing degree; Frank "won their hearts."[178] Thus, to complete the metaphor introduced at the outset of this chapter, if Frank's "Message to the Mexican Writers" was the first direct move in his *courtship* of Latin America, the reception of *America Hispana* represents the consummation of a marriage.

4

KEEPING THE FAITH
Waldo Frank and Latin America, 1932–1943

Having "won" Latin America, Waldo Frank went on to exhibit throughout the 1930s and early 1940s proofs of his fidelity to the peoples of the Hispanic world. Upon closer examination, however, the proofs appear superficial. Though Frank made several visits to Latin American countries during this period and produced several articles and books, the works are less expressions of love and understanding of the Hispanics than they are evidence of the self-promotion inherent in the ever-present prophetic vision of wholeness.

In July 1932, Frank was busy revising the English translation of Ricardo Güiraldes's *Don Segundo Sombra*.[1] Published in 1935, the book tells the story of a certain gaucho who had lived on Güiraldes's father's ranch and whom the author had known and loved. Frank wrote the introduction to the book. But he used the introduction primarily as a vehicle to restate the contrast (originally drawn in *America Hispana*) between Argentina and the United States. He begins with the observation that *Don Segundo Sombra* occupies a place in Argentine letters not unlike that of *Huckleberry Finn* in the United States. He compares the books: both are histories of boys who, on their own, wander throughout the frontiers of their respective countries; "both lads are typical products of their respective worlds, . . . classic pictures of the traditions and ideas, the institutions and the folk of the two countries." Frank then draws the all-important contrast. He points out how the gaucho's world, though primitive, "kept a human quality from the culture of Spain," whereas Finn's is a "barbarous, anarchic world in which the traditions of Old England are broken up past recognition." Thus echoing themes from *Re-discovery of America* and *America Hispana*, Frank concludes with a characteristic interpretation of the land of the gaucho.

The order of Argentina is more inward, it is cultural rather than institutional. It is an order of human values, much more than of business and public affairs. But it belongs to an old agricultural world which, even in Argentina, is fast disappearing. Which explains the social and political unrest in the Latin American countries.[2]

November of 1933 found Frank heading for Argentina. At the time, he was in the midst of writing the novel *The Death and Birth of David Markand*. According to Paul Carter, Frank wanted the novel to express the synthesis of his convictions, which were three: that he was a novelist; that he was a Communist; and, that he believed in God. The difficulty of achieving this synthesis prompted him to sail for South America; perhaps, he thought, a different environment would facilitate the writing.[3] Needing several weeks of seclusion, Frank stayed at a ranch in the Sierra de la Ventana region of Argentina; the arrangements were made by Eduardo Mallea's brother Enrique. Except for some gauchos, horses, and dogs, Frank lived alone.[4] Evidently, the tactic was successful, for in three months he was back in New York, with the novel nearly finished.[5]

David Markand was finally published in October 1934. With regard to the Hispanic aspect of Frank's career, the book is important in that it contains the first Latin American character in his fiction. The role of Juan Fierro is short but significant. The protagonist David works with Juan, and lives in the Mexican's home in Chicago. The hard work of the packinghouse where both labor eventually drives David into a delirium where his past, in which he was comfortable but spiritually near death, and his present, in which he is groping toward wholeness, meet in conflict. Here, David symbolically dies and is reborn. When Juan gets a priest for David, David rejects this symbol of his Catholic wife, of his past. Instead, like a hungry baby, he clutches Juan's wife and seeks her breast. Juan tells his wife to give David anything he needs. Thus, "she gives him her breast, an obvious symbol of birth."[6]

The Fierro character as a symbol of Frank's idea of the Latin American can be variously interpreted. First, the Latin American is a Mexican. Consider Frank's designation of the Mexican as the archetypal mestizo who represents the transitional phase of man's conscious development in which most Latin Americans find themselves. Thus, Fierro calls for the priest before giving his wife to David. Then, there is the character's last name, obviously born of Frank's familiarity with *Martin Fierro*, the gaucho epic. In *America Hispana*, Frank presents the gaucho, immortalized by the poem, as one whose psyche had been impressed by the pampa's motion with the integral coexistence of things; and he makes him the symbol of the spirit of Latin America. That Juan possesses the gaucho's wholeness and spirituality is evidenced by his selfless and symbolic act. Though these interpretations might go beyond anything Frank intended the Fierro character to represent, one cannot escape the obvious symbolism in the scene described above: that the Latin American has something the American needs.

In November 1934, Frank returned to South America. Again, he needed to get away to work on his next novel;[7] and he spent the month of December at Victoria Ocampo's house.[8] He returned to the States in January 1935, after having spent his second consecutive South American summer enjoying the hospitality of his Argentine friends while engaged in projects unrelated to his Latin American work.

Frank returned to Mexico in January 1937. Since 1932 Frank had been actively involved with the Communist movement in the United States.[9] Thus, when Mexican president Lázaro Cárdenas arranged for the Communist-backed national congress of Mexican writers and artists to be held in Mexico City in January 1937, Frank was invited as delegate and speaker. While it might be assumed that he was invited because of his special relationship with Mexico and all of Latin America, Frank concedes that the invitation was sent because most Communists took it for granted that he was one of them. Anyone who observed his actions from a distance certainly would have assumed as much. As he recalls, no one paid any attention to the "*integral Communism*" that he espoused, and even though his writings exposed his deviation from the party line, the tendency was to ignore such differences.[10]

Moreover, Frank's opening address, "The Artist: Minister of Freedom," was similar to one he had read before the Soviet-financed Congress for the Defense of Culture that convened in Paris in 1935.[11] The address "once more reiterated in smoky language [e.g., "The working class, although it is to be the creator, functionally, of a free mankind, and hence contains the potential of freedom, has not the awareness of that personal link between person and cosmos, which is the true nucleus of human culture and the sole key to human freedom"[12]] his plea for an organic view of life."[13] Significantly, it also contained a line that found fault with the orthodox Communist *agitprop* view of art. Frank recalls that his criticism received a chilly reception from his youthful audience, which was composed mainly of Latin American artists. He sensed the implication of their attitude: perhaps the next generation would be coldhearted.[14] It probably never occurred to him that he had come face to face with a group whose convictions were as strong and righteous as his own.

That same month, while busy with the work of the congress, Frank found time for two long interview sessions with Leon Trotsky. The Russian had been given asylum by Cárdenas, who also furnished a detachment of soldiers to guard the Trotskys against the likelihood of Stalinist reprisals. Frank visited Trotsky at Diego Rivera's villa outside Mexico city.[15] By this time Frank had formulated a proposal for an international Trotsky trial, and this proposal had in turn embroiled him in issues both of international communism and of localized Latin American politics. When, in May of 1937, the proposal appeared in the *New Republic*, it was translated and published in *Repertorio Americano* under the title, "El proceso de Trotsky."[16] But Frank discovered through his friend Carlos Rafael Rodríguez, director of *Mediodia* of Havana, that "a most serious and dangerous falsification" of his text had occurred. Whereas he had written that Trotsky believed "the trials were a trap for him," the Spanish translation attributes that belief to Frank. In July, Frank wrote to Joaquín García Monge, the director of *Repertorio Americano*, asking for a prompt and conspicuous rectification of this "unfortunate error" that he feared would give a "wrong impression" of his stand to the magazine's Spanish-reading audience.[17]

Frank did remain in Mexico till March. Besides his work with the congress and Trotsky, he found time to deliver spontaneous talks to whatever audience he could find. Students seemed particularly receptive to his appearances. He also became the official guest of the provincial government of Jalisco during February and March. But this work remained incidental to other business. Active as he was, he also managed to complete a typewritten copy of the first two parts of *The Bridegroom Cometh*, a novel, and to go over the proofs of *In the American Jungle*, his latest compilation of essays.[18]

Actually, Frank's only activity in 1937 directly concerned with Latin America centered on the Chilean publication of a new Spanish edition of *America Hispana*, translated by Léon-Felipe. And, in truth, the only thing new about the book is the *prólogo*, which is for the most part a reiteration of his organic view of life.[19]

In 1939, Frank continued to capitalize on *America Hispana*, this time by having the book reissued in the United States under a new title, *South of Us*. But of more importance that year was his return to Mexico. During May and June, as a guest of the government,

Frank toured Mexico's provinces (ranging from Chihuahua in the north to Tehuantepec and Oaxaca in the south)[20] with Cárdenas, whom Frank tried to interest in a continental magazine.[21] There can be little doubt that Frank was in Mexico this time in his old role of prophet. For one thing, following Frank's proposal for an international Trotsky trial, Earl Browder, head of the American Communist party, made a prompt and acrimonious renunciation of all Frank stood for; and from that time forward, Frank was no longer associated with the Communists. Moreover, his relationship with Cárdenas was a personal one based on mutual admiration, replete with circumstances suggesting the Mexican's acceptance of Frank's prophetic role. For example, Cárdenas told Frank that when the doubts he had about nationalizing the oil industry overwhelmed him, his ultimate decision to go ahead with his plans was made easier by his reading of Frank's *Re-discovery of America*, from which he gained the "courage and insight to reach his verdict."[22] Furthermore, evidence of his self-conceived prophetic role during his sojourn in Mexico is to be found in Frank's literary output following the visit: a series of four articles entitled "Mexico Today" that appeared in the *Nation* in August and September, and an article on Cárdenas for the October issue of *Foreign Affairs*.

The first installment of "Mexico Today"—"The Heart of the Revolution"—begins with a description of the la Laguna region, with its complex irrigation system and collective farms (*ejidos*). Frank characterizes the region as a symbol of Mexico's revolution. Then, establishing "land" at the heart of that conflict, he contends that Mexico's history since the Aztecs has been "a tragedy of unbalance." Mexico was "a land overwhelmed with rains, yet needing water. It was a landless people wanting and loving the land." But the Cárdenas government, he explains, "begins the balance of this people" through the collectives, the dams, and the canals. These works signal the beginning of the "*act* of revolution."[23]

Presenting the schoolteacher as "the fairest incarnation of modern Mexico and of the spirit of the *ejido*," Frank goes on to record his impressions of one of them. Expanding his discussion to include Mexican education in general, as well as to current architectural trends and the new industrial centers, he implies a familiar message—that the "sober spirit" that he finds in the schools is expressive of a new sensibility and culture of community, and is destined to pervade the whole country.[24]

Finally, Frank contrasts that which he sees remaining of the "old" Mexico with the "new" Mexico exemplified by the town of Torreón, which communicates the "quality of the *ejido*." Frank's purpose is to show how the essential values of Mexico's culture are better preserved by the "*humane* socialism" of the present government than by "*inhuman* capitalism," which seems to him to have destroyed "an inestimable treasure of spirit and integrity" in the industrialized nations.[25]

The second installment, "President Cárdenas and His People," is Frank's explanation for the love affair that exists between Cárdenas and the Mexican "folk." He describes the president's methods: Cárdenas would visit a community, and, taking no precautions for his life, walk among the folk, dine with them, listen to their grievances. Frank contends that "a people not organized to articulate its wishes through the regular democratic channels of public opinion needs a chief who will come directly to the people." Not only does Cárdenas fill this need, but according to Frank the Mexican president appears "to have given the Mexican folk for the first time happiness." By this, Frank means that through Cárdenas the people have "found a channel for [their] energies."[26]

In the third installment, "Danger on the Right," Frank points out the threat of counterrevolution that exists. As evidence, he cites the incessant slander of Cárdenas and his government by the bourgeois press and the upper class; the open sabotage of the land by the rich landowners who foresaw the expropriation of their land for the *ejidos*; and the "cultural influence" of the upper classes— "more dangerous than battles." Then, he tells of the rightward drift of most of the revolution's "old generals," and of the possibility of disorder after Cárdenas leaves office. But he takes heart in the "people's army" that Cárdenas has created; and he is sure that if the forces of reaction strike, "the majority of the citizens, civil or in uniform, will make the right decision, *provided they know the facts*." Finally, he lists the political dangers facing the revolution: bureaucratism; incompetence; sloth and corruption in government, despite the greatness of Cárdenas; the "a-politicalism" of the people; the doctrinaire Marxism of Lombardo Toledano, Cárdenas's "efficient 'dialectical' partner," who would probably control Cárdenas's likely successor. Frank lays the greatest emphasis on this last point, for he sees Lombardo's leadership lacking "sufficient place for the intuitive process—not irrational but pre-rational—which gave birth to the Mexican revolution and whose neglect has given strength to all counterrevolutions."[27]

The final installment, "The Deepest Danger," finds Frank again treading familiar ground. At the heart of the country's danger, he places the Mexican people, including Cárdenas himself. Thus he notes that "many good men" regard the president's libertarianism as "quixotic and as encouraging license." Furthermore, Cárdenas's passion for "agrarian syndicalism" has resulted in an order that is "tentative, tender, subject to panic and deviation." But Frank's fears of the Mexican people are far more deeply rooted; the masses reveal to him "dangerous traits." He recalls their Aztec heritage—"the mixed cult of flowers and blood is one of the great pathologies in history." He repeats his concept of Mexico's chaos, a chaos that has left the Mexican morbid and masochistic. Then, he sees danger in imposing the white man's machine culture on the Mexican, in whom the Spaniard's personal will coexists with the Indian's group-ego, for "the Indian must reject . . . the machine's values." He also sees danger in the Mexican's inheritance of "the Spanish weakness in creating social order, in organizing social justice." Despite all this, Frank ends on a prophetic note. He labels the Cárdenas regime "an intrinsic cultural achievement for his people, for the Americas, for the world." He calls Cárdenas "a major prophet" whose vision and power are original; and declares that even if reaction prevails, the tradition of justice that Cárdenas has established "will survive—and will create."[28]

The article in *Foreign Affairs*, "Cárdenas of Mexico," is, in essence, little more than a retelling of everything Frank had written about the Mexican president in the four previous articles. Frank portrays Cárdenas as an artist, a visionary whose intuition of his country's destiny leads him to create a new tradition.[29] This is more than just a bouquet to a friend. Cárdenas is made a symbol of Frank's persistent belief that "creation is revolution." In all these articles, then, Frank remains faithful to his earliest visions of Mexican destiny, finding that the circumstances of 1939 provide ongoing confirmation.

The following year, Frank kept his name before his Latin American audience. The 1940 Spanish translation of Edward Dahlberg's *Los perros de abajo (Bottom Dogs)* carried a *prólogo* by Frank. Written prior to the outbreak of World War II, this preface gives new expression to Frank's belief that

> in an age . . . in which the accepted forms of all values have broken down and the critical field is noisily preempted by shallow and false men, every true literary artist [feels] the need of re-establishing his cultural roots, of developing and articulating his cultural values in terms of his own time. Irresistibly, he becomes a critic.[30]

In the period immediately following publication of the Cárdenas articles, Frank fulfilled his need as a true literary artist. From

November 1939 to January 1940, he wrote *Chart for Rough Water: Our Role in a New World*. The book expressed his concern over the world situation, his explanation of America's relation to the crisis in Europe, and, of course, his organic ideology. Published in April 1940, it is basically a streamlined version of his ideas, already defined in *The Re-discovery of America*, as they directly relate to the Fascist threat.[31]

Chart for Rough Water is important with regard to Frank's Hispanic adventure in that many of its ideas pervade his publications pertaining to Latin America for the next three years. Nowhere is this more evident than in his salute to *Sur* on its tenth birthday. Published in the December 1940 issue of Victoria Ocampo's magazine, the article begins with mention of how the new barbarians are destroying the liberty of Europe. *Sur*, on the other hand, represents for Frank a creative effort of the human spirit. He finds *Sur*'s origin in "the Great Tradition."[32] (It is in *Chart for Rough Water* that Frank develops his concept of the Great Tradition, identified as man's perception that the kingdom of God is within him.)[33] The origin of World War II he finds in the errors and immaturity of the Western world. Then, determining that the world crisis is one of truth, he identifies *Sur*'s function as purveyor of the knowledge of what he sees as the truth—that man's destiny is liberty and dignity. Moreover, he takes heart in *Sur*'s devotion to the values of love, human liberty, and truth. These values he regards as the primordial truths that will not die because they pertain to the essence of man, which is eternal. He concludes, therefore, that *Sur*'s birth, growth, and continued existence are strong reasons for believing that the profound latent powers of Hispanic America will not fail. Furthermore, he uses the anniversary as an occasion to call upon the readers to renew in themselves the knowledge of what Man is, in order to have the strength to continue the fight for love and truth.[34] The article, then, is both a call to arms and an expression of Frank's organic view of life, and as such it mirrors *Chart for Rough Water*.

Throughout 1941, the ideas expressed in that little book continued to appear in Frank's writing for his Latin American audience. They were the direct focus of "Sobre *Chart for Rough Water*," published in *Sur*'s February edition. Moreover, even in the article "La pintura contemporánea norteamericano," ostensibly an interpretation of North American art according to his organic philosophy, Frank gets around to a reiteration that North Americans and South Americans both live in a world in which the destiny of man—to live in the truth—is threatened. Then, interpreting the

world crisis as one in which the human desire for liberty will be resolved, he presents the artists as the enemies of fascism, the sincere singers of the destinies of the folk, and the humble priests of
liberty. Thus, he concludes that the artists of the United States are
humble men and women who fight to find in themselves the eternal
human values (love, truth, liberty), and to come to live them.[35]

For United States readers, Frank merely produced one article
in 1941 that concerned Latin America. "The Hispano-American's
World" is little more than a synthesis of elements from earlier articles and *America Hispana*. He begins by briefly pointing out the
ethnic, cultural, geographical, psychological, and political "diver-
gences" between the people of the United States and the peoples
of Latin America. Then, focusing on Hispanic writers, he repeats
his thinking on the mestizo mentality that he believes characterizes
the writing of the years since independence. He contends, however, that this period—"The Century of the Mestizo," as he calls
it—ends about 1910. What he calls "the organic century" has been
unfolding ever since, and provides evidence of the "deep common spirit" uniting the writers of America Hispana, making "of
their works a common ground." Then, he goes on to find in this
"harmony of the Hispano-American writers" a "basic harmony"
with our own creative men, and reiterates his proposal for an
alliance between the writers of the North and the South.[36]

In April 1941, Frank was offered four thousand dollars by the
State Department to go to South America on a lecture tour. Conceived as a mission to fight the rampant Nazi propaganda that por-
trayed the United States as the enemy of Latin America, the task
held no appeal for Frank, and he refused to go, choosing to con-
centrate on his next novel.[37] Letters from his South American
friends urging him to make the trip did not sway him from his
course. Yet, according to Bittner, Frank had misgivings about declining the invitation; and while he proceeded with his novel in the
summer of 1941, he nonetheless wished to illustrate how he felt
about the Hispanic world. The result was a revised edition of *Virgin
Spain*. After the Japanese attack on Pearl Harbor, however, he
knew he was needed in South America, and the novel was shelved
for the time being.[38]

Before embarking on his mission, however, Frank wrote the preface to the Spanish translation of *Chart for Rough Water*. Recalling
the world situation at the time of the book's creation, Frank tells
his Spanish audience that now the book is more timely than when
he wrote it. For, as he explains, the present fight is no more than a
symptom of what he calls "the deep war." By this new phrase, he

means the struggle that exists between the rationalistic, mechanistic, materialistic way of life that characterizes most of Western culture, and the intuitive, spiritual way of life that is the lone strength of man's future and of his essential destiny. He contends that the book's purpose is to magnify the knowledge that spirituality is the greatest strength in this "deep war" whose outcome will be a decisive moment in human history.[39]

In actuality, Frank is merely applying a new terminology to reintroduce themes presented in *Re-discovery of America* and *America Hispana*. For instance, he sees Fascists as only a present manifestation of the egocentric will to power (by reducing men to slaves) that was released with the decline of the "medieval Christian republic." Moreover, he sees victory in the deep war as dependent not only on knowledge of the necessity for spiritual awakening, but also on the creation of true "persons." Furthermore, he repeats the contrast between Latin America and the United States: they are weak in *means*, we in *ends*. Thus, while he places before the United States the immediate task of using its incomparable arsenal for the destruction of the "counterrevolution" personified by Hitler, he charges Latin America with the task of using its intuition and vision to form an arsenal of methods, ideas, and values with which man can resume his march to liberty. In other words, Frank determines that the role of the United States is to win the "simple war," the role of Latin America is to win the "deep war."[40]

Before leaving on his tour, Frank dashed off an article for *Common Ground*. Aimed at his readers north of the Rio Grande, "The Two American Half-Worlds" is merely a reiteration within the context of the current world situation of the thesis he set forth in *America Hispana*—that each world, the Protestant, machine culture of the North, and the Catholic, spiritual culture of the South, has what the other needs. Thus, he reestablishes the basis for furthering a greater understanding and cooperation between the United States and Latin America.[41]

April of 1942 saw the publication of the revised edition of *Virgin Spain*. But the book's appearance was overshadowed by the beginning of Frank's second tour of South America. His friend M. J. Benardete gives evidence of the greater importance of the latter event. He begins his review of this new edition by praising the intelligence of those U.S. government officials who sent Frank to Argentina and other countries to communicate to those nations the importance of our dedication to fascism's total destruction. Because, in his judgment, most Latin Americans, despite the official postures of their governments, do not agree with us in this duty,

Waldo Frank, therefore, "is perhaps the American best equipped to show them that they and we can create and maintain a spiritual solidarity, in spite of the many differences that appear to keep us apart."[42] In his last sentence, Benardete correctly assesses the nature and purpose of Frank's trip. He perceives it as only to an extent an official assignment. Fundamentally, Frank would lecture throughout the continent as a goodwill ambassador of the United States.[43]

The 1942 Lecture Tour

The tour, which lasted from mid-April until October, carried Frank through Brazil, Argentina, Chile, Uruguay, Peru, and Bolivia. His lectures, collected and published in Buenos Aires in September under the title *Ustedes y nosotros: Nuevo mensaje a Ibero-America*, broke little new ground. As they appear in *Ustedes y nosotros*, the lectures are seven in number. The first, "La guerra que esta debajo de la guerra," begins with Frank's demand that Latin Americans of creative force must stand up and be counted in the war against the Fascists. While he acknowledges that an Allied victory might postpone the realization of Latin American ideals, he makes a case against fascism as the greater threat to all they stand for. But this argument is only a prelude to the real point of the lecture: a new world must emerge from the struggle. He punctuates this with the certain declaration that the old thinking, e.g., empirical rationalism, is dead. He concludes by railing against the mechanolatry of the dying world, symbolized by that particular engine of destruction, the bomber[44]—an analysis he could have borrowed from his antagonist Ernest Hemingway.[45]

The second lecture, "Ustedes y nosotros," continues Frank's discussion of the new world, only in more positive language. Expanding on his idea of the new world to come, he stresses his concept of the Great Tradition. He prophesies that integration of the Great Tradition with the social life will result in an organic society. The forging of such a society he sees as the destiny of the Americas, and not even the war can impede that destiny. He concludes in regenerationist terms, reminding his listeners that death precedes birth, that darkness precedes dawn.[46]

The next two lectures, which share the common title "Los dos caminos," find Frank beginning with a political message and ending with a spiritual one. The first, "Hacia la derrota del hombre," is aimed at the youth of South America. Frank warns them against

becoming atomized individuals, and joining gangs that are probably Fascist agencies. Then, describing the Fascist mind as seeking
the humiliation of man, he cautions youth to beware of becoming
"fascisized." Concluding with an ecstatic exhortation that is more
spiritual than political, he calls on the youth to scorn both the
Right and the Left, to embrace humility, and to found the "City of
Man."[47]

In the second, "Hacia el destino humano," Frank's message becomes wholly spiritual and prophetic. He stresses the need for
organic knowledge, by which he means man's creative intuition of
the god within him. Then, after equating God with cosmos, he
prophesies that organic knowledge will be incorporated and articulated in a methodology that will become the "theology" of the new
world's religion. Moreover, he issues a call to action, not just to
fight the Fascists but to become "persons." According to Frank, by
following the "organic imperative," which is to create and serve
man at the same time, individuals become persons. Furthermore,
he declares that all men must become persons if the goal of organic
harmony is to be achieved. Concluding with an apocalyptic flourish, he asks his audience if their silence will be that of death or
birth.[48]

The title of the fifth lecture is explanatory of the content. In
"Los elementos del nuevo mundo en los Estados Unidos," Frank
engages in the same kind of selective name-dropping that characterizes works like *Our America, Re-discovery of America*, and *Primer mensaje*. Only those whose work contains elements of "wholeness" are worthy of mention. Noteworthy in this lecture is the inclusion of United States vice-president Henry Wallace. Frank relates how before leaving on the trip he received a call from Wallace; and he characterizes him as one member of the government
who has a profound interest in Latin America.[49]

In "El corazón de la literatura americana moderna," Frank gives
his views on his contemporaries. His purpose is twofold: to show
that, for all its shortcomings, American literature reflects nothing
of the Fascist mentality; and, to make the claim that great American literature follows the "Great Tradition," in accordance with
which our country is at present transforming itself. He concludes
that our adolescent literature points to our "great destiny"—a destiny we share with Latin America.[50]

The final lecture, "Llegado a Buenos Aires," is something of a
summary of Frank's relationship with the Hispanic world over the
last quarter-century. He explains how his intuitive experiences in
the southwestern United States made him study first Spain, then

Mexico and Argentina. He reiterates his feelings that the Hispanic and Indo-Hispanic world seems to possess a force for integration and essential knowledge, that this world has something his America needs, that together both worlds can form one hemisphere, one America. He contends that it is his personal conviction of the American destiny that brought him to South America in this time of peril. In calling on Latin Americans to join the battle and not remain neutral, he repeats his apocalyptic warning—that the choice is one of death or birth.[51]

In his lectures, Frank interpreted fascism in terms of his prophetic vision. The resulting anti-Fascist nature of his remarks bothered the Argentine government, and it established censorship guidelines that, according to Frank, would have rendered the lectures meaningless. Frank credits the warmth of his nonofficial reception in Argentina with allowing him to give his lectures without government interference.[52] Nonetheless, "his words were no longer so widely applauded as they had been in 1929." Then, on 1 August, he was declared *persona non grata* by the Argentine government, probably because of the "mistranslation of a crucial word critical of Argentina in his farewell article." Whatever the reason, on the morning of the next day, as he was packing to leave Buenos Aires, "five thugs forced their way into his apartment, attacked him physically while shouting anti-Semitic abuse, and threatened his life if he didn't leave Argentina immediately." His screams caused the assailants to flee, but he suffered an open head wound that required hospitalization. According to Meyer, "many of Frank's Argentine friends turned their backs on the incident for fear of reprisals. Victoria [Ocampo] and María Rose Oliver were the ones who saw to it that his injuries were treated, and twenty days later, they alone accompanied him to the airport."[53] Meanwhile, the Fascists intensified their efforts to counter Frank's message. Not only was he attacked in pro-Axis newspapers,[54] but he was rebuked in circulars that originated from the German consulate, "while painted on the walls in large letters was 'Muera el Judio Frank!' "[55]

On the positive side, the publicity the attack elicited in South America made the tour more effective than it might otherwise have been. As for the United States, the incident made the front page of the *New York Times*; and Frank kept the attack before his fellow Americans with interviews, radio talks, and a series of articles that he wrote for *Collier's* magazine.[56] The *Collier's* article for 26 September, "Argentina—Unwilling Enemy," contains his explanation of the state of affairs in Argentina that makes such attacks possible. More important, however, is how the magazine drives home the point of the article with two pictures on the opening page of the article: one, a half-page photo of Frank leaving a Buenos Aires courtroom after giving his account of the attack; the other, a smaller, but more dramatic, shot of Frank lying in a hospital bed, his head bandaged, recuperating from the beating he received at the hands of Nazi sympathizers.[57]

In October, Frank returned to New York, where he was honored for his services at a testimonial dinner sponsored by the Union for Democratic Action. But he did not let this episode in his Latin American adventure end with that. Anxious to exploit the interest generated by all the publicity the attack had received, he worked from 1 November to mid-January 1943 on turning his notes of the tour into a book.[58] The result was *South American Journey*, published on 20 May 1943, by Duell, Sloan, and Pearce.[59]

South American Journey: An Analysis

As correctly characterized by Paul Carter, *South American Journey* is no mere travel book or chronicle. Frank's trip sets the parameters for his observations on the cultures of the various nations that he called on.[60] The book does not hang together in William Bittner's judgment. He finds *South American Journey* lacking focus, because it tries to be three books in one: a study of Brazilian culture, which Frank had glossed over in *America Hispana*; the intimate account of a tour; and the story of one man's successful attempt to combat the power of Fascist propaganda.[61]

In many ways, Bittner's remarks comprise a superficial appraisal of the book, showing little comprehension of the subliminal, symbolical, mythological level on which Frank writes. In its use of a rich variety of metaphors to prophesy the coming marriage of the United States and Latin America, which will produce, at last, a truly new world inhabited by new persons, *South American Journey* actually is a singularly cohesive and consistent book. It might be misguided and pretentious, and it might not deserve a very high place in the body of mystical and occult literature trading on millenarian visions of regeneration and redemption. But no reader who is sensitive to Frank's purposes and willing to struggle to derive meaning from a text in which metaphor is consistently disguised by apparently straightforward narrative can possibly dismiss the book as lacking in what most concerned Frank: organic integration. This appraisal can best be substantiated by a chapter-by-chapter analysis of the book.

On the inside cover *South American Journey* gives a numbered list of thirty-seven names of the places Frank visited on his tour. On the fly sheet is a map of South America with numbers (that correspond to the list of names) representing the places visited. This feature of the book immediately raises a question concerning earlier works on Frank. Both Jerome Kloucek and Paul Carter in their chronologies of Frank's life list Colombia as one of the countries Frank visited on his 1942 tour (and Carter repeats this in his text *Waldo Frank*). Both omit Bolivia. Yet Frank's list contains no Colombian cities, while specifically mentioning the Bolivian cities of La Paz and Cochabamba. Furthermore, Frank makes no reference to Colombia in his book. Obviously, Frank must be cited as the authority here. Carter can probably be excused, since he leaned heavily on Kloucek for background material. As for Kloucek, his study did not go beyond mere mention of Frank's tour, and he used *South American Journey* only to the extent that it reinforced his interpretation of Frank's mind and art.[62]

The text begins with a foreword wherein Frank relates his inner struggle over whether or not to make the visit that his South American friends urged on him. He implies that his decision to go south arose out of the "organic destiny" of the Americas. Significantly, he includes *democracy* as part of that destiny; and, in equating democracy with collectivism, he establishes the challenge that he will put to Latin America: to create the collectivist world that machines have fated, "so that Man, and not slaves and not hordes, might live in it."[63]

Chapter 1, "The Face of Brazil," contains six sections. In "The Amazon," Frank describes the view from the plane that carries him to Belém. His narrative serves notice that he will continue the "poetic-scientific"[64] rhetoric that typified *Virgin Spain* and *America Hispana*. Indeed, his description of the Amazon recalls the symbolism in the latter work of the "haemal" river as bloodstream. While on the subject of the Amazon, it might be pointed out that one reviewer, "intensely excited and pleased" with the book, credits the river with inspiring "good writing," and calls Frank "our best North American writer on South America."[65] But Frank in this section is less concerned with the river and more concerned with himself. He claims that his journey is in the service of Bolívar's dream: a hemisphere united and free. Then, he credits his intuitive knowledge of his own destiny for causing him to alter his plans for going immediately to Argentina, and choosing to linger in Brazil for a while instead.[66]

The second section, "Belém do Pará . . . Natal . . . Vitoria," recounts his impressions and expressions while traveling through these cities on his way to Rio. As Ralph Bates sees it, the first page contains the best and worst of Frank's writing. Of the sentence, "Uriburú—Brazilian buzzards—wheel and dip; black, wise birds with red heads to show the carnality of their brains," Bates writes that the reader will approve of writing so "vivid, slightly overripe, and characteristically Frankian." But of Frank's description of a folk as "earth-strong, earth-sick with the languorous longing of all earth to emerge and transcend itself: whether in trees in bodies or in dreams," Bates believes the reader "will be startled by such horrible great zombies."[67]

This section is a microcosm of the themes that lend coherence and focus to a book that on superficial examination often seems to lack both. For example, Frank muses over the destiny of Brazil, and finds it in the "elemental" democracy that the folk possess. Then, after repeating the prophecy of a "new culture-birth" in Brazil as a result of the marriage of the spirits of the Negro and Amerindian, he records seeing a monkey in a tree, and, in an expression of his Spinozistic faith, writes, "Verily, God is in that monkey; and in the Brazilian man and woman is the tree lifting earth into leaf and blossoms into sky!"[68] Here, undoubtedly, he is dealing in the archetypal mythology of the tree of life that unites the opposites of soil and sky, earthly passions and celestial reason, instinct and mind, masculine and feminine principles. To add to the sexual imagery of the tree as a phallic symbol, Frank points to the presence of the monkey, an animal that since medieval times has been associated with lust and lasciviousness. By focusing on metaphors of sexuality as he returns to the concept of a new culture-birth, Frank might even be setting the stage for the sexual adventure, both real and symbolic, that befalls him in Brazil.

The importance of this section lies in Frank's new terminology, and his new outlook toward Brazil that brought it about. He now uses the term "Ibero-America" in place of "America Hispana." He contends that for the United States to be fed by Ibero-America, the region needs to be powerful, and such a condition can only be achieved through the synthesis of Brazil and the Spanish-speaking realm. Unfortunately, he senses "fissure" instead. His reason for looking at Brazil as a separate entity is that the problems of the relations between Brazil and the other republics are linked with the bond between the Brazilian and his earth. He means that just as Brazil's middle class isolates itself from the earth and her children, so Brazil steers clear of her "whole" neighbors. Whatever the validity of such a rationalization, he concludes the section by repeating his metaphor from *America Hispana*: Brazil is the forest.[69] One reviewer calls such a characterization a "pathetic fallacy" exemplifying Frank's attempts to provide easy answers to complicated questions by "flash generalizations."[70]

The third section, "Rio de Janeiro," is a pedestrian account of Frank's stay in the Brazilian capital. He tells how upon arriving he was informed that he was a guest of honor of Brazil, and how this troubled him, because the government of Getulio Vargas was a dictatorship. Then, rationalizing his acceptance of the government's hospitality, he goes on to describe street scenes, from the church where the feast of St. George is being celebrated, to the *Mangue*, "home of the cheap whores." He follows these with his impressions of various officials and journalists. Then, turning to political history, he traces Vargas's rise to power. But, unable or unwilling to label the dictator a Fascist, Frank goes on to relate a discussion he had with two Brazilians whose vision of the country's destiny differed from his. The issue hinged on the Negro, in whom Frank saw Brazil's promise of future prominence, but whom he sensed the two Brazilians would regard as a resource to be exploited. Rather than expand on this discussion, Frank rambles on, relating anecdote after anecdote. Yet these anecdotes are not without purpose. For example, Frank's description of a typical Rio day includes an interpretation of Orson Welles, then in São Christovão filming scenes for his next movie against the backdrop of the Rio *carnaval*. The positive judgment Frank presents bears repeating.

> Welles is a huge co-ordinated baby, enormous in energy and animal spirits. He may go through the "works" of life, and come out a man (his nostalgia for the truths of Ibero-America speaks well for him); or he may play safe and remain a virtuoso.[71]

Welles, in short, is personified as animalistic energy that might— or might not—ultimately achieve synthesis with discipline, rationality, and premeditated calculation so as to bring into being the complete person. Frank concludes this section with musings over Brazil's folk music. For him, its greatness lies in its lush articulation of a basic "life-rhythm."[72] In brief, Brazil's folk music arises out of the instinctual, natural part of humanity and is relatively unaffected by artificial, contrived restraints. For Frank, the music of Brazil's masses holds forth the promise of regeneration that many white enthusiasts of the Harlem Renaissance found in black jazz. For all its superficial appearances of being a rambling assembly of unrelated episodes and observations, this section reveals, if anything, a consistency that is too contrived. Frank focuses obsessively on his theme of regeneration through the marriage of art and nature, with the assumption that in Brazil one encounters the redeeming element of what is pristinely natural—precisely that element that the North American artist lacks in his own environment.

In the fourth section, "São Paulo," Frank presents the city as the result of a capitalist economy, and, therefore, a "failure." Frank spurns this middle-class municipality, this pretentious place that dominates southern Brazil. He admits his prejudice, but then excuses himself with the claim that intuition lurks in some kinds of prejudice.[73] This section is less than two pages long, and provides an example of what Lincoln Kirstein calls "a lax attitude masked by the assumption of ubiquity and omniscience."[74]

The fifth section, "Minas Geraes," begins with an impression of what Frank calls "the most blessed, the most Brazilian" of Brazil's twenty states. But the description drifts into a meditation on the mulatto leper Aleijadinho, who, in Frank's anything-but-original judgment, is the hemisphere's "greatest plastic artist" since pre-Columbian times. Then, after establishing that the primary quality of Aleijadinho's work is "tenderness," Frank makes a transition to his next anecdote with the line: "I am to find it in the flesh, in Bello Horizonte . . ." He relates how in a café he engaged in a political discussion with men at the next table. When one of them characterized Lincoln as one of our great politicians who loved his fellow man, Frank reminded his listeners that such men are rare, then offered Lenin as another lover of mankind. As a result, Frank would have us believe that they became friends, and went to another café. There, Frank became infatuated with a waitress. The rest of the section involves his conquest of the fetching Ifigenia.[75] Ralph Bates dismisses this section with words that reveal an appalling insensitivity to the symbolical level of Frank's writing; he believes the reader will skim these "inevitably sentimental pages which tell of sexual encounters, and . . . vigorous and manly things . . . embarrassing egotisms."[76]

Actually, Frank's encounter with Ifigenia can be seen as the very heart of his book. Given his mystical and occult leanings, it is not surprising that he expresses himself largely in metaphors and symbols. Beguiled by a brief glimpse of the woman in the café, Frank has subsequently to go on a long search before he can find and join together with her in ecstatic union. In Jungian terms, his search for her can be seen as the anima quest that lies at the heart of much of the world's mythology. She is archetypically feminine: passionate, instinctual, intuitive, and awaiting penetration. She is not the sophisticated woman of arts like Victoria Ocampo to whom Frank has dedicated the book, but who remains relatively less important to him because women of her stamp have no essential role to play in bringing about his prophetic vision of the union of the United States and Ibero-America. Primordial and basic, Ifigenia can make Frank complete by putting him in touch with nature again. Here we have Frank's version of the sacred marriage serving as a metaphor and microcosm for the cosmic union of the American hemisphere's *yin* and *yang* principles. In his union with Ifigenia, Frank fulfills the hint of things to come that he provided some pages earlier with his tree-of-life and monkey imagery. Mutually incited by the monkey of lust, the archetypal United States man of arts, representing the leaves that approach the sun, finds union with the woman of the Brazilian masses who has her roots in the soil.[77]

In the Ifigenia episode, Frank uses the symbolism and mythology that arose out of the United States frontier experience; only Frank now extends the setting to hemispheric rather than continental dimensions. Here is how Richard Slotkin describes the North American frontier mythology of which Frank is obviously a product:

> As the white man awakens the Indian to the light of the "social" arts and beliefs and the glories of order and cultivation, the Indian awakens the white man to undreamed of possibilities for human power and vigor. He offers . . . renewal of the imaginative powers of the mind, too long crabbed by scholastic artifices.[78]

The final section, "May Day in Rio," is Frank's impression of a Labor procession he attended. He contrasts this occasion with a similar one he observed a few years before in Cárdenas's Mexico. His purpose is to end this chapter on the hopeful note that while Brazil's folk has no political expression, neither did the Mexicans, and the latter nonetheless produced a Cárdenas government. Thus, Frank offers evidence that a folk can learn political competence.[79] In short, the natural, spontaneous masses can learn how to choose the exceptional man. He, in turn, can penetrate into the yielding, vulnerable masses, intuit their vaguely felt desires, shape their consciousness, and thereby achieve the sort of cosmic marriage between nature and reason that lies at the heart of much mythology. It is significant that Frank ends this chapter with a reference to Mexico, with its enduring and great national myth of the union of the earth goddess Tonantzin-Guadalupe with the charismatic leader Quetzlcoatl-St. Thomas.[80]

Chapter 2, "The Argentine Campaign," contains five sections. The first gives evidence of what one reviewer calls the "sympathetic understanding" of the Argentine people for which the book is "particularly notable."[81] Indeed, Frank begins by mentioning that while "nobody likes" Argentina—"a peculiar nation"—and even the Argentines don't like themselves, he likes the country and loves the people. He credits his feelings to his understanding of the people, and then attributes Argentina's peculiarity to the pampa. Expanding on the latter concept (which first appears in *America Hispana*), he briefly relates in dialectical fashion Argentina's history to date, and the pampa's role in informing Argentine life. He finds that the country's folk spirit, which is aligned against the Fascist threat, is a manifestation of the pampa's influence.[82]

The next section chronicles Frank's first days in Buenos Aires and La Plata. He misses little in the detailed account. Furthermore, he discusses Argentina's "state of seige"; his meetings with President Castillo, former president Ortiz, and Minister of Justice Rothe; his lectures and their content; the government's unsuccessful attempts to stifle his message; and, Fascist attempts to discredit him. He contends that his mission to Argentina is merely a continuation of his long-standing objective with regard to Latin America. Perceiving that Argentina's transition period has reached a climactic point, from which she either progresses toward true integration or sees her rebirth miscarry, he challenges Argentina to play her role in leading the Americas toward unity. Then, revealing the deep-seated aim of his lectures, he writes that it is no accident that Argentina has faithfully listened to him and joined him in working toward the realization of his dream for America: "If in the past she heard me when I spoke, it was because she heard herself. Now, by God, in her hour of confusion, she shall hear herself again."[83] Not only is the above passage revelatory of the consistency in Frank's message, but it hints as well at what Lewis Gannett calls "the colossal and tasteless egotism . . . almost beyond belief" with which Frank reports the continent's "reactions to the phenomenon of Waldo Frank." Indeed, this single section contains sufficient evidence to corroborate Gannett's criticism that the entire battle for democracy in South America is abridged into a chronicle of "reactions to the lectures and conversations of Waldo Frank. No other American, one gathers, has ever begun to understand" the souls of the peoples there.[84]

The third section continues the theme of equating Argentina

with the pampa amidst the chronological recounting of the lecture tour. Frank's writing continues to display what yet another reviewer refers to as the book's "incredible egotism."[85] For example, in reporting on his lectures in Bahía Blanca, he tells how the residents there turned his stay into "less a success than an ovation." The only other noteworthy aspect of this section is Frank's characterization of Victoria Ocampo.[86] As Lewis Mumford observes, "toward friends like Victoria Ocampo he is as gently ruthless as a recording angel."[87] And, indeed, amidst the praise appear words that confirm Mumford's assessment. For example, Frank asserts that Victoria Ocampo

> has lacked the will, and the gift, to explain herself. . . . Passionately, aggressively devoted to the arts, she passes for an intellectual; whereas her true domain is that of intimate, of exquisite expression. Rich and as impatient as a child princess when she is crossed in little things, her deep humility before life, her strict religiosity (that rejects the dogmas of her Church) have gone unnoticed.[88]

The next section begins with a description of Rosario. Frank makes an analogy between the city and Chicago, as he does in *America Hispana*. Indeed, his impressions of Rosario seem to have changed little with time. Next, he relates in rather pedestrian manner his travels from city to city.[89] The egotism remains, while the underlying theme of the deep war becomes more manifest. The best characterization of this section might be the one that Kirstein applies to the entire book: that Frank sees "history, geography and economics as a kind of rhapsody which is a pretext for idiosyncratic expression."[90]

The final section continues Frank's journey through the northwestern part of the country. Like previous sections, it has descriptions, impressions, racial psychology—all reminiscent of *America Hispana*. In this account of the tour, Frank brings home the theme of the deep war as he recounts a discussion he had with some University of Tucumán students on their role in the deep war. The tale concludes with Frank leaving them well after midnight, only to hear their "happy shouts" filling the silent streets.[91]

Chapter 3, "Uruguayan Interlude," exemplifies the chronological nature of the book, for at this point in the tour Frank flew to Montevideo for a few days' rest. He begins by describing the countryside as he sees it from the air, while musing over the provincial character of the capital. But the main purpose of the chapter is to register his reflections on particular problems common to all of

Latin America, and because Uruguay is so passionate and simple, it offers a "test-tube answer." He asks two questions: "What is the gaucho?" and "Why so many little countries?" To answer the first, Frank, equating gaucho with llanero, vaquero, etc., claims that to understand the gaucho traits and gaucho influence upon the nature of a country is to understand the enigma of the South American experience. Then, after briefly describing the gaucho, as he had in *America Hispana*, he concludes that the prevailing gaucho spirit— anarchy—is the reason for Latin America's continuous coups and ubiquitous *caudillos*.[92]

The answer to the second question involves Frank in a defense of small countries. Using his own interpretation of Uruguay's history to make his case, he credits the gaucho spirit with everything from Uruguay's achieving independence to creating a country abundant in "human values." Then, he praises all small countries, not only because they allow the creative person to emerge promptly, but because they provide the most useful immunity to the "leveling process" intrinsic to the collective system with its machine production, the foremost guard of both the people and the individual.[93] Thus, this chapter provides a framework in which Frank can reiterate a familiar message.

Chapter 4, "Argentine Campaign (Concluded)," contains five sections. The first presents more descriptions and impressions of Buenos Aires and its inhabitants as they appear to Frank on his return. Noteworthy is a brief sketch of General Justo, former Argentine president. As Mumford notes, "toward his enemies he [Frank] tempers his ruthlessness with magnanimity." Such sketches, Mumford contends, would in themselves make a "distinguished book."[94] There follows a penetrating, but predictably jaundiced, characterization of Argentina's elite.

> Under their elegance, I feel their crass will; under their courtesy, a bravado that must vaguely point, far beyond their consciousness, to a hate and a fear. I prefer the class, as it is in my own country and England: openly philistine and illiterate. These men have a veneer of culture that is more dangerous. . . .[95]

The next section, "Patagonia . . . Tierra del Fuego," traces Frank's steps to the southern part of Argentina. Again, the pages are filled by descriptions of the land, its towns and its inhabitants, as well as Frank's almost minute-to-minute account of his movements. More important, perhaps, are his impressions; he analyzes the Argentine people and labels them "the only normally *human* people on earth!"[96] Equating "human" with "whole," "organic," Frank remains true to his interpretation in *America Hispana* of Argentina's folk.

Then, Frank muses on why the government did not object to his blatant call for revolution within the context of the deep war. He mentions that a friend attributes the government's noninterference to Frank's solid hold on the Argentine public; but Frank questions such an explanation. Lest one think that Frank has tempered his egotism, however, consider his description of the reactions of his audience: "The rough-hewn and sensitive folk are interested in *me*. That's what they had me there for: to look at me, and to look again." He concludes with an anecdote about a young man who asked him to autograph a copy of his (Frank's) *Dawn in Russia*. He explains that although autographing is routine in South America, this incident was different, for it illustrated how his writing had made an empathetic connection with one Latin American.[97]

In "Sortie to Chile," the narrative continues with Frank describing his visit to Punta Arenas, the world's "southernmost city." Characterizing the city as a microcosm of Chile, he finds this nation a land still under the control of large landowners and foreign investors. Although learning that large numbers of citizens of German descent in this city are Nazis to the core, Frank seems unperturbed because he regards them as atypical. He is more interested in those Chileans who perceive their fate, rooted as they are in the virgin soil. With echoes of *America Hispana*, he finds within these people the Spanish heritage as well as that of their Native American ancestors.[98]

"Patagonian Oil" begins with Frank's vivid description of social conditions in the oil town of Comodoro Rivadavia. His point is to present this city as a good example of what happens when the restyling of a nation's economy is not paralleled by a similar transformation of that people's human values. As a result, the working class becomes rigidly controlled, and so is rendered powerless. This discussion goes off on a tangent, however, with Frank defending the South American prostitute. Finding her occupation more honest than careers in the legal profession, the business world, the political realm, or the graphic and performing arts, Frank, keeping to his theme of wholeness, credits her with feeling the benevolent function of her calling.[99]

Finally, he ends this section by describing a discussion he had with a Communist woman. According to Frank, the woman was all set to hate him because a Party member said he was a Fascist. Relating their talk, in which he defends himself against the charge, he tells how the woman responded to his message—she became less hostile, yet she remained unconvinced, her thinking bound by a rigid dogma. The entire episode seems contrived when Frank concludes by expressing his need for a methodology by means of which to convey his vision.[100]

The final section tells the story of the beating he received in Buenos Aires. Lewis Mumford, who understands Frank's purpose in making the tour—to point out to Latin America its role in the deep war—characterizes the Fascist attack as "only a minor episode" in the journey.[101] And yet, in Bittner's judgment, the sensational assault can be seen as a symbol not only of his South American crusade but of the entire Second World War.[102] The assessment of Lewis Gannett also stresses the importance of the incident; he believes that the Fascists' cruelty toward Frank generated more support for the United States in Argentina than any other event involving one of our goodwill ambassadors.[103]

Frank begins by singling out his farewell message as the cause of both the *persona non grata* declaration and the ensuing beating. Persuasive and logical in this appraisal, Frank departs from reality in his account of what followed the attack. After castigating the groups who did not stand by him, he maintains that the common folk, instinctively aware that the assault on him was a direct result of the government's declaration, tried every means imaginable to separate themselves from their government and to communicate their unity with Frank. Then, he goes on to say that throughout the country, the provincial press as well as many localized organizations expressed their feelings in opposition to the attack. Allegedly, moreover, a few hundred people came in person to the sanitarium where he had been taken.[104]

Frank's account seems to contradict Doris Meyer's characterization of the incident and its aftermath. According to her, "many of Frank's Argentine friends turned their backs on the incident for fear of reprisals."[105] Outside of Frank's reminiscences there are no accounts to indicate that the average citizen was any less fearful of manifesting his sympathy for him, assuming he felt such sympathy. Undoubtedly Frank exaggerated the outpouring of Argentine support, thereby furthering his consistent objective of self-aggrandizement. Besides, his partisan account tends to validate everything positive he has written of the Argentine people, thereby promoting the idea of the acceptance of his righteous message.

Chapter 5 contains four sections that relate Frank's movements through Chile. The first begins with his stop at Mendoza before flying across the Andes to Chile. He describes an enthusiastic reaction in Mendoza, and this leads to the conclusion that Argentina was hardly dominated by the Fascists. Here, then, is justification for his belief that Argentina had not rejected his prophetic voice. Resuming his flight over the Andes, he focuses henceforth on Chile. As he had done in greater detail in *America Hispana*, he attributes Chile's history, geography, and psychology to the determining influence of the country's symbol, the Andes. (In dealing with the Andes, Frank's language often smacks of sacred mountain metaphors that, as with the world or cosmic tree, pertain to the union of opposites.) Next, he presents his observations on Chile's political and economic situation.[106] In assessing the Popular Front government, he is guardedly favorable. Ralph Bates credits him with not being blind to the reality that most reformers and revolutionaries, as a rule, "betray their followers."[107] And yet Frank's explanation for endemic betrayal is almost apologetic. He sees it as a ramification of the paradox that freedom in the political sphere has fostered an underdeveloped economy. Meanwhile, Chile's leaders do little to solve economic problems because they sense no urgency from the people who have selected them expressly for their faith in freedom. This rationalization is quickly followed by the Frankian interpretation of Chile's potential for prosperity as a symbol of spiritual strength.[108]

In "Santiago," Frank tells how the Popular Front parties of Chile, in their resolve to force the Chilean president Juan Antonio Ríos and the foreign minister Ernesto Barros Jarpa into a break with the Axis, capitalized on the beating Frank received: "I had become a flag for democracy; they intended to wave it." Moreover, despite Fascist attempts to discredit him, he assures the reader that following his first lecture entitled the "War Beneath the War," he had captured the hearts of Santiago's populace; "the applause was heavy and enduring."[109] In this appraisal, Frank might be exaggerating almost as blatantly as he does in suggesting that his beating in Buenos Aires served significantly to increase pressure on the Chilean government to break relations with the Axis.

In this section Frank's penchant for grandiose thought is once more revealed as he describes a deal he advised President Ríos to strike with the Roosevelt administration. Under it Chile would sever its ties with the Axis powers, while the United States would offer a loan so that Chile could get back her mines, now owned by American capitalists. Frank has to admit, though, that Ríos was unresponsive.[110] Nor is there any reason to assume Roosevelt would have been responsive. Certainly there is no evidence that Frank had official authorization to make this proposal. As usual, he was engaging in wishful thinking, arising in this instance out of his published views concerning Chile's exploitation by foreign (particularly United States) investors and his conviction that the new order of hemispheric harmony and wholeness would banish such exploitation.

The third section proposes that the above deal might serve as an example of how we in the United States could demonstrate our understanding of our neighbors' needs and thereby truly lead the hemisphere, which remains faithful to our democratic ideals.[111] Of course, his argument is within the framework of the deep war.

Then, altering his view of Chile (from *America Hispana*) as a country turned toward the Pacific, Frank finds Chile to be as aware of the Atlantic world as Argentina. He credits this awareness to the Panama Canal. This strained analysis arises out of Frank's contention that the original animating spark came to America Hispana across the Atlantic, from Spain. And, if the Hispanic New World is to remain true to itself and its destiny of balancing the United States so as to achieve hemispheric wholeness, then the Atlantic connection must be kept intact. However, the new-world regeneration that Frank envisions is threatened by the manner in which the United States utilizes the canal in furthering its economic exploitation of Chile and the rest of Ibero-America. Only with the ending of the commercial exploitation associated with the U.S. use of the canal will come the sort of unencumbered access to its Atlantic inheritance that Chile requires, together with the possibility of North-South synthesis in the American hemisphere. The problem with Frank's analysis is that the canal was operational in 1929 when he interpreted Chile as turned toward the Pacific. In crediting the canal with Chile's awareness now of the Atlantic world, he might have explained why he did not see the canal then as an agent for making Chile aware of its Atlantic destiny. Instead, he simply describes the time of his first visit as those "abnormal days of 1929."[112]

The final section recounts Frank's days in Concepción, Valdivia, and Temuco—cities with considerable German populations. He is decidedly negative in his characterization of these Germans who, he says, are probably not more than 85 percent pro-Nazi. He does include, however, a favorable sketch of the German but militantly anti-Nazi bishop Guido Beck de Ramberga. Then, with an abrupt change of topic, he concludes with a description of the squalid living conditions of Chile's Indian and creole inhabitants. His purpose is to make the contrast between the negative physical aspects of their lives and their positive spiritual qualities. For he finds the

Indians to be "earth-men," and he describes the creoles as people "luminous with spirit."[113]

Chapter 6 is a mix of experiences and observations. Frank tells how he was urged by twenty-eight Peruvian congressmen to visit the capital city of Lima as their guest in the name of democracy; and how he was soon dismayed by the political and economic situation he found. Though this section contains familiar interpretations of Peru's history based on racial psychology and the like, Frank makes several interesting points. First, he judges the Incan empire to have been whole, "the last true unity of South Pacific America." With its democratic base, it points to the importance of democracy in achieving a new wholeness.[114] His subsequent interpretation of Peru is based on his conviction that the great war underway is of no concern to that nation's starving Indians as long as the United States collaborates with the dictatorship, thereby consolidating its control.[115] Yet, is Frank indulging in fantasy when he asserts that without our help the government would collapse and the people's will would prevail? What, in any event, is the people's will? Frank finds it in *Aprismo*, a "continent-wide movement of political redemption."[116] The personification of this movement is Víctor Raúl Haya de la Torre, leader of the outlawed APRA (Alianza Popular Revolucionaria Americana), the most prominent force for democracy in Peru. (Haya allegedly was Mariátegui's successor, and Frank characterizes them both as a couple of the age's great Latin American revolutionaries.) According to Frank, APRA affirms Bolívar's goal of a unified Latin America. He relates his clandestine meeting with Haya at which this ideal was discussed, along with what the United States ought to do with the Peruvian government, which backed the Allied war effort against democracy's Fascist foes, and yet checked the advance of democracy on the home front. For Frank, the answer to the latter is simple: support Haya and his friends, the finest political partners we could ask for in helping us create the new world following the war.[117]

Evidence suggests a closer bond between Frank and Haya than the sharing of the ideals of democracy and Ibero-American unity. Fredrick Pike, in his study of the spiritualist facet of Haya de la Torre, depicts a man who felt himself a prophet, a mystic. A man who considered himself a person of superior sensibility and insight, Haya typified the spiritualist, immanence-of-God school in his quest to be reborn in wholeness. His was an apocalyptic faith that included a glorious destiny for Latin America. Significantly, one of the greatest influences on him was Romain Rolland.[118] Needless to say, such a man would seem a kindred spirit to Waldo Frank.

Chapter 7 puts forth a proposal for Paraguay and Bolivia. Making an exception to his defense of small nations, Frank suggests a merger between the two countries. After interpreting the two countries, he concludes, characteristically and predictably, that the mentalities of each nation are complementary to one another, as are their economies. And just as the warfare that has raged between them over the years gives proof of their proximity to each other, so fusion between them might usher in a new era of peace for the continent.[119] Commenting on the plausibility of such a proposal, one reviewer not only suggests that the respective governments of the two countries would react unfavorably to the idea, but wonders whether the foreign offices of both Argentina and Peru would see the proposal as "a trial balloon from an admirer of Sumner Welles or one more ineptitude from the ineffable Yanqui."[120] Actually, Frank considers the proposal a "poet's dream," adding that both countries have flowered when they have heeded their poets' wisdom.[121] Hubert Herring assures us that rather than a poet "it was as a prophet that his disciples [in the United States] received him," poignantly adding that "one of the less reverent was heard to remark that the Prophets of Israel invariably began their sentences with 'Thus saith the Lord,' while Waldo Frank begins with a simple I."[122]

Chapter 8 continues the journey as Frank returns to Brazil. In the first section, "The Thick Wood (Mato Grosso)," he presents this forest province as a prototype. Then, he expands on a theme he introduced in *America Hispana*—that Brazil is the forest from which a new world culture will arise. Briefly recounting Brazil's history, he shows the country's development standing in marked contrast to that of Spanish America, not to mention the United States. But his real purpose is to justify a metaphor that fits the demands of his teleology. For, following his interpretation of Brazil's history, he points out that for four hundred years the forest symbolized the slow, organic growth of the country, rooted as it was in the earth, obedient to its inevitable fate. In *America Hispana*, he presented the Negro as the formative element in Brazil's racial makeup and called the Negro the archetypal forest-dweller; now, saying that perhaps as many as 85 percent of Brazil's people have African blood, he repeats the earlier claim in terms of the people of Mato Grosso. Though they have little African blood in them, they possess conspicuous attributes that are associated with the African, and, therefore, the forest.[123]

In the forest-African analogy, Frank is obviously trading on the common stereotype according to which blacks are people in intimate contact with the psychic foundation, the unconscious with its passions and instincts, just as trees are rooted in the spontaneous, life-giving source of nature, the soil.

The next section is Frank's account of his travel through the Amazon region. He finds the river system comparable to the Mediterranean Sea in its dynamism, as evidenced by its turbulent current. Then, he goes on to give his descriptions of the geography of the region. Included are typical Frankian observations: "Manaus has the odor of decay. It smells of greed, exploitation and shrinkage"; or, "the folk, which is all *caboclo* (Portuguese and Indian) is low-keyed, languid, silent, ugly with its struggle."[124] Ralph Bates specifies this section as "one of the best accounts of that land of heavy rainfall, brown forest rivers, and will-less derelicts" that he has ever found.[125] Indeed, in this section Frank reveals himself to be less the preacher and more the poet. There is a purpose, though, that underlies Frank's poetic descriptions. By stressing the river, associated through the years with the psyche's unconscious, Frank makes the point that Brazil represents a Jungian anima figure, a goddess of nature who awaits the questing male in the recesses of the unconscious. For him, Brazil serves the same purpose that North American Indians, with their legends and myths of sacred water, have served for many United States seekers of wholeness—including Frank himself at one point of his development.

Frank follows with a treatment of the next phase of his journey—his travels to Brazil's Sertão region. It is similar to the previous section in that he describes the region and its inhabitants in terms of how the latter reflects the qualities of the former. In this case, the people mirror the toughness, the anger, of the land. His theme is that while the *sertanejos* resemble their land in that both differ from the rest of the country, these folk are nonetheless indispensable to Brazil's nature as well as her economy. Like the forest dweller and the Amazonian, the *sertanejo* is close to nature with all its telluric, extrarational determinants. As an example, Frank relates the story of Antonio Conselheiro, the mystical, misogynistic herald of the "Second Kingdom." In the 1890s he fathered a movement that eventually led to a clash with the government and ended with the death of all of his followers.[126]

"The Luminous Land" continues the pattern of previous sections. Here Frank presents descriptions, impressions, and observations as he moves from Belém to the state of Pernambuco, then on to the city of Bahía. As usual, there is a theme that runs through this section: the African strain is the dominant one in Brazil, since

Brazil is forest and the Negro belongs to the race that peoples the forest. Furthermore, the major strain within the forest is wholeness. In this section, Frank includes a short description of the harmonious race relations in Brazil based on the studies of Gilberto Freyre. He concludes that racial democracy, for which Brazil has set an example for the world, must form the basis for any society that would truly be democratic. Then, he defends the African religious rites, legally banned by the government in all states except Bahía. To Frank, these rites express a deep awareness of the organic nature of life, and they sustain Brazil's artistic and intellectual growth toward maturity. But these rites, like racial democracy, are credited by Frank to Brazil's intuition. In his role of prophet, he warns against intuition as a guide to action, for it has its dark side: sloth, naïveté, pride, and unthinking behavior. Then, with his own ontology in mind, he prophesies that Brazil will be secure only when she attains an ordered consciousness.[127]

The final section finds Frank at the last stop on his journey, Rio de Janeiro. Rather than record his impressions of the city, he devotes the section to sketches of Brazil's dictator Getulio Vargas; Vargas's daughter; and Oswaldo Aranha, Brazil's chancellor and foreign minister. Frank manages to integrate this treatment into the overarching scheme of his book by interpreting the two men in terms of his vision of the world (the deep war), as well as his vision of Brazil and its destiny. According to Frank, both men are symbols of the major malady of our age—the false simplification that divides the world between fascism and nazism on the one hand, and dialectical materialism on the other. Priding himself on his ability to transcend this simplification, Frank judges neither Vargas nor Aranha to be Fascists. The shrewd Vargas he finds more like the archetypal Latin dictator. Furthermore, he presents Vargas as an instrument of Brazil's destiny. He characterizes Aranha as "a fisher in troubled waters" who feels comfortable with both imperialists like the English and the Americans, and Fascists like the Portuguese, Spanish, and Italians. He says he is a leftist, not so much on principle but because it is the intelligent and tasteful thing to be. Fitting both men into his teleology concerning Brazil, he declares them to be politicians playing a role in their country's unconscious desire to become unified and solidified, men who have appeared because Brazil's vast population has yet to mature politically, economically, and intellectually. That this development must occur, Frank is certain.[128]

Chapter 9 contains Frank's conclusions drawn from the journey. The first section begins with his musings while in Miami. They include observations (derived from Jung) on the racial psychology of the inhabitants of the Americas.[129] Characterized as "geo-sexual" by one reviewer,[130] these observations provide a framework for Frank's case for racial democracy in the United States. He finds racial democracy necessary not only for the establishment of a new worldwide society, but also necessary for us to be true to the ideals for which we are fighting the war.[131]

The rest of the section exposes Frank's purpose in devoting a third of the book to Brazil. In an about-face from his former case for the inclusion of Brazil as part of America Hispana, he flatly states that Brazil is a distinct entity. Then, after declaring the need to think about America in terms of the three Americas—the United States and Canada; the Spanish-American countries; and Brazil—he calls for better relations between each America and the other two, based upon knowledge and mutual understanding.[132]

The final section presents Frank's vision of the future of the Americas. As the title indicates, "One America" must combine the functioning principle of each America, since each has what the others need to grow to maturity. Basically, then, his vision has not changed from its earlier formulations. The only new element is Frank's stress on democracy as an integral part of hemispheric destiny. Indeed, he proceeds to make a religion of democracy—an American religion whose heart is the person, *"the whole man."* Thus, Frank defines democracy in terms of his concept of organic wholeness, exposing thereby the spiritual aspect of his message. Then, he reiterates his concept of the deep war as he restates his case for hemispheric unity: each has what the others need to be made whole and to win. As he does in *America Hispana*, he submits a program. This one, if followed, will fulfill the United States's destiny of hemispheric leadership. The program includes taking control of Latin America's resources away from American capitalists and giving it back to the peoples; supporting democracy throughout the region by refusing to give recognition to apparent dictators; facing our negligence in racial democracy; and fostering an intellectual and cultural dialogue between Anglo- and Ibero-America beginning in the schools.[133] This program, ranging from the farfetched to the prosaic, contains nothing new; it only reiterates earlier proposals. It is offered in the hope of awakening in the United States an understanding of its destiny of leadership so that it will begin to act in accordance with destiny.

Frank includes in the appendices his "Address on Arrival in Buenos Aires" and his "Farewell to Argentina." It has already been pointed out that the volatility of the latter contributed to

Frank's being declared *persona non grata* by the government and being beaten by pro-Nazi sympathizers. As for the former, which is primarily concerned with the deep war, it moved one reviewer to exclaim: "Argentinians well deserve their reputation for courtesy if they manifested no impatience or distaste at hearing it."[134]

Judged on the basis of the canons of historical methodology, *South American Journey*, like the Frank books analyzed in the preceding chapters, simply does not measure up. This is scarcely surprising. Works, after all, predicated on belief in the forging of new worlds and new human occupants must obviously and inevitably be ahistorical. Still, Frank might be justified in designating the book as cultural history—assuming culture is concerned with, and in part shaped by, mythological stereotypes and images rather than by the sort of material determinants subject to scientific, empirical probing. In his mystical, apocalyptical approach to hemispheric relations, Frank provides deep insights into the sort of stereotypes and images that North Americans apply to South Americans, and they to us. These stereotypes and images are as subject to change and as permeated by ambiguity as shifting perspectives and evaluations of cowboys and Indians, settlers and the wilderness, cities and frontier in North American lore. But, no North American can understand the forging of his own tentative and paradox-ridden identity without at least some subliminal grasp of the meaning and significance of his country's frontier mythology. And it might be fair to say that no person can hope to feel truly at home in the setting of the American hemisphere without some comprehension of the myths and images that have shaped the respective cultural contexts out of which the people of the northern and southern continents face each other with the hope for wholeness and the fear of contamination.

5

A DREAM DEFERRED

Waldo Frank and Latin America, 1943–1967

After the publication of *South American Journey*, Waldo Frank kept up his relationship with Latin America in much the same way he had after the publication of *America Hispana*. That is, he visited several Latin American countries, and wrote a few articles and two books on Latin American topics. For the most part, all of his writings exhibited his overriding concern with the organic view of life—that vision of wholeness that he had expounded from the beginning of his Hispanic adventure. However, while his message remained the same, his audience in both Latin America and the United States began to diminish as the kind of thinking he had characterized as the enemy in the deep war seemed to be prevailing throughout the hemisphere. But the charge might be leveled at Frank that after his 1942 tour he began to take for granted his following in Latin America—and perhaps for a time lost interest in them altogether.

Frank's literary output for the five years following the publication of *South American Journey* contained only three articles with any relation to Latin America. The first, "Rubén Darío and the Jews," appeared in the August issue of *Contemporary Jewish Record* and is simply a short introduction to a reprint of an 1896 article by Darío entitled, "On Israel." Calling the Nicaraguan writer America Hispana's greatest poet, Frank characterizes Darío's poetry as "apocalyptic" and "intuitive," and he finds Darío's article—a defense of the Jews—valuable in that it is "instinctive" and "spontaneous." Moreover, he makes the article a prophetic symbol of "the generous soul of America Hispana."[1]

The second article, written and published in 1943, reappeared in the August 1944 publication, *The Jew in Our Day*—a collection of essays on Jewish problems. (The article is really one-half of "Israel in the Western Hemisphere," which is divided into "A. In

America Hispana" and "B. In the United States.") Frank concerns himself with the place of the Jews in Latin America. He begins by defining the Jews as a people who have "made the spirit of their great men into the body of their common conduct" and "whose culture is based on knowledge of man and on a way of life which humbly serves man's reality and destiny." (Since he considers himself to be a Jew, it is not surprising that his interpretation of the Jews should mirror his personal ideal.) Then, after dispelling the "fallacies" that the Jews are Orientals and "a people of the city," he states, "The essentially Western spirit of the Jew and his at-homeness in an agricultural world will serve to situate him in America Hispana and to illuminate his potential fitness to play a part in Latin America's preponderantly non-industrial economy."[2]

Then, after noting the promise of America Hispana, he points to the Jewish presence in South America, underscoring the great influx of Jews that has occurred since World War I, and finds this presence prophetic: "In respect to the values, ideas and needs of Ibero-America, the Jews, if latecomers, are timely. Their convergence upon Hispano-American life appears to be destiny."[3]

The article's importance lies chiefly in Frank's placing the Jews (and, therefore, himself) into his teleological construct. But perhaps as important is the clue this article offers to the true basis of Frank's affinity to the Hispanic world. In a brief paragraph, he reasons:

The very name of Ibero-America suggests the fitness of Israel within it. For Iberia is Spain and Portugal; Iberia is the European part of Ibero-America (which is far more Indian and African than it is Latin). And it is not necessary here to insist on the great part played by the Jews in the formation of the Iberian cultures. It is true that most of the Jews today who have come to live in Mexico, Brazil, Peru, Bolivia, Chile and Argentina, are not of Spanish or Portuguese descent. But they are Jews; they partake of the same ethos as the Iberian Jews who saturated the Hispanic world with Semitic values. Only insofar as they deny themselves are they separate from fundamental strains in the Hispanic tradition.[4]

The third article appeared in 1944 in the 21 October issue of the *Nation*. "A Policy for Argentina" is little more than an expansion of the program for Latin America that he originally proposed in *South American Journey*, updated now to meet contemporary conditions.[5]

There followed a hiatus in Frank's Hispanic adventure until 1948, at which time he was invited to attend the inauguration of

Rómulo Gallegos, the Venezuelan novelist, as president of Venezuela. Frank was happy to accept, aware that he was being honored as a kind of "godfather" to the progressive administration about to take control in Caracas.[6] As it turned out, the inauguration was a cultural affair. In celebration of the event, the paintings of various American artists were put on display, and in the giant *corrida* there were nightly tournaments of song and dance representative of the best in Latin American folk music. A few days later, at the home of Rómulo Betancourt, provisional president of the junta that had overthrown the military dictatorship, a conversation between Frank and Betancourt turned to the inadequacy of the many books on Simón Bolívar. Betancourt suggested that Frank write a book on Bolívar, and a few days later the book was commissioned.[7] According to Bittner, the Venezuelans understood that Frank and Bolívar shared the same dream for America. The new government, therefore, believed that Frank was the perfect choice to clarify the life of the Liberator, and accordingly they proposed a handsome subsidy for the project. In other words, the offer was one that Frank could not refuse.[8]

Frank became totally absorbed in the writing of the biography. For three years, he poured over the voluminous documents relating to Bolívar and also traveled to the various locales of Bolívar's life: Venezuela, Colombia, Panama, Ecuador, Peru, and Bolivia. And even though in November of 1948—on the very day, in fact, that Frank returned to Venezuela to begin his research—the Gallegos government was overthrown by the military, the generals, despite Frank's objection to the coup, respected the book deal. Bittner offers this as evidence of the unique bond between Latin America and Waldo Frank.[9] Perhaps, as Carter notes, the government simply did not want to look "anti-cultural."[10] Whatever the case, *Birth of a World: Bolívar in Terms of His Peoples*, though published in the United States and England in 1951, was not issued in its Spanish translation for several years—the Venezuelan government controlling some of the Spanish-language rights.[11]

On 14 January 1949, shortly after Frank had arrived in Bogotá from Venezuela, his "manifesto" entitled "To the Youth of Latin America" appeared on the front page of *El Espectador*, the city's leading liberal newspaper. According to the editors of the *Nation*, who reprinted the article in their 19 March issue, "the message received wide attention in the few Latin American republics which still have a free government." Basically, Frank proposed yet another program for Latin America.[12]

The following year, while in the midst of his work on *Birth of a*

World, Frank found time to go to Havana and deliver a message before the Interamerican Conference for Democracy and Liberty on 13 May 1950. "Necesitamos crear un mundo nuevo" is Frank's oft-stated, apocalyptic warning; he says that without a cure for the illness that afflicts democracy, our civilization will founder and die. His cure is a familiar one: an economy of peace, based on socialism and freedom; and schools, universities, workers' syndicates, and churches transformed to awaken the workers' innate love of life. He contends that with such techniques of production and knowledge, America Hispana, which is better equipped than any other part of the world to begin this work, can create a society of free men.[13]

Birth of a World: An Analysis

Finally, in September 1951, *Birth of a World: Bolívar in Terms of His Peoples* was published by Houghton Mifflin Company of Boston. Ostensibly, the book is a scholarly biography of the great South American liberator. In his foreword, Frank describes his historical methodology. After noting the enormity of the literature on Bolívar and the plight of the historian in assimilating this vast amount of source material, he claims that every episode presented as fact can be documented. Nonetheless, he announces that he will not adhere to the academic style of biography, for to fill the book with footnotes, to interrupt the flow of the narrative, would defeat the book's primary aim—it is intended for a general audience. Then, after mentioning some of the primary sources on which he relied, he goes on to add the further "unchallengeable" sources: the people, the art, the towns, the legends, and the land, all of which played parts in Bolívar's "American drama." He explains that no biography can get to the reality of its subject without offering the background of the "telluric, demotic, economic and spiritual forces by which he lived" and he expresses his belief that rarely in history have such "subliminal and collective elements play[ed] so dominant a role" as they did in the life of Bolívar. Finally, after expressing gratitude to those who helped him in his research and in his visits to the sites of Bolívar's tale—he names the most important of them—he adds as a source his close connection with the people of Latin America for more than two decades.[14]

Then, defining biography as "portraiture," which "*is* always a transaction of *the present*," he gives his *motive* for writing the book. He says his realization that Bolívar personifies many of the values of the Hispanic world—values so timely "that he and his world are ours"—convinced him that "Bolívar, if we *experience* him, may signify today as much to the United States as to America Hispana. The meaning of this for the world, if it is true, given the strategic place and potential creative power of the United States, is manifest."[15]

In a letter to Frank dated 24 September 1951, Edmund Wilson expresses his approval of Frank's method and motive. He writes:

> You have . . . compensated for your faults of style by the broad range of vision and the long perspective you have been able to bring to the subject—which make you . . . unique in the field. I feel that I have not only learned a lot from the historical point of view . . . but that the book enables me to estimate Bolívar's career in relation to the rest of the world in a way that the ordinary biography would not. You are in general . . . at your best when you are lighting up the cultural and moral role of some figure or nation or race.[16]

Most reviews, however, paid little attention to Frank's method or stated motive, and merely rendered superficial judgments on the book. For example, *Kirkus Reviews* simply summarizes the content and concludes that the work is "a sympathetic, understanding portrait."[17] Likewise, Milton Byam concludes his summary by designating the biography "unqualifiedly recommended to all."[18]

Those who concerned themselves primarily with Frank's methodology proved equally superficial. For example, Claude G. Bowers, United States ambassador to Chile and historian of sorts, praises Frank's scholarship and declares that of all Frank's books, this one is to him "the most exciting." He concludes that the biography—of both a man and a continent—is one that people in the United States "would do well to read." Significantly, in Bowers's view Frank has subjected Bolívar to "cold clinical analysis" and, therefore, the Bolívar he presents "is not all white or black."[19] This perception is similar to Hubert Herring's. After stating that Frank's tale is insightful, well-researched, and sensitive, he claims that the typical Latin American biographer either overlooks "his hero's clay feet" or "sheathes them in satin slippers," whereas Frank's account is authentic. Herring does point out, however, that Frank's partiality toward Bolívar vis-à-vis his depiction of San Martín will provoke dissent, as will his mystical interpretation of Bolívar. Indeed, the latter prompts Herring to write that Frank's poetry and prophecy, which Latin Americans find charming, lead him down "mystical paths in which a dull-witted northern critic finds himself tangled and tripped."[20]

At least two reviewers, while favorably evaluating Frank's scholarship in view of his not departing "far from the facts," touch upon motives for writing that correctly go beyond Frank's stated motive. Yet, they do not go far enough. J. Fred Rippy finds Frank contributing to the legend of Bolívar by evaluating the Liberator in terms of his (Frank's) own values. For example, the depiction of Bolívar as a champion of racial equality and world confederation corresponds to Frank's goals, but not to the truth. Rippy registers the suspicion that Frank is a "socialist"; and he concludes with a warning that "propaganda, fancy, and social philosofy [sic], when mixed with history, are likely to distort and mislead."[21] Similarly, Richard H. Dillon insightfully finds the book pervaded with a "philosophical mood." Yet Dillon exhibits no understanding of what that mood is. He has a hard time believing that Bolívar was as "consistently right" as Frank makes him appear; and then concludes that Frank's total identification with his subject exposes his "real weakness" as a biographer.[22]

Actually, Frank's biography is another teleological construct, designed to show this period of Latin American history as prelude to the future he has prophesied for that part of the world. Furthermore, Frank presents the life of Bolívar in a way as to make the Liberator his predecessor in envisioning hemispheric unity. As Arturo Uslar Pietri, a long-term student of Bolívar as well as a professor and former Venezuelan cabinet member—two of his novels and one short-story collection by him are cited by Frank in the bibliography—makes clear, Frank errs when he oversimplifies history and then presents it from an "arbitrary perspective." Thus, his book becomes "a hymn to the hero of his own vision of America."[23] When Erna Fergusson wrongly writes that *Birth of a World* does not seem warranted as a title "because the world Bolívar envisioned has not come to birth,"[24] she not only overlooks the chaotic world to which Bolívar's actions gave birth, but she fails to see that Frank's book is, in reality, an instrument of his own teleology. Bolívar, hampered by the Enlightenment influence on his thought, was unable to bring his new world beyond the state of chaos. But Frank is now ready to carry on the work of his precursor. With his new American religion, his own methodology—the tool that in *America Hispana* he found Bolívar lacking—he will point the way toward completion of the task that Bolívar began.

An analysis of selected sections of *Birth of a World* will serve to illustrate how Frank used episodes of Bolívar's life as vehicles for expressing his favorite themes, as well as to illuminate his purpose. The first chapter of the first book, "The Heart," begins with an unidentified quote: "My soul is beautiful with the presence of primitive nature." This establishes Frank's point of view. He not only recognizes the presence of the primitive nature within man, but evaluates that presence as positive. He sees Venezuela as the source of primitiveness. Shaped like a heart, it pumps the basic blood to the rest of the continent. And from this heart Bolívar emerged. The man, like his land, personified the heart of the revolution.[25]

Next, Frank poses the violent, vibrant Orinoco River as equivalent to the "main artery" of the heart. He means to show that as the Orinoco streams from its source in the jungle to the Atlantic, its spirit fills the land and its inhabitants, from the Indians to the Spaniards, with its primitive, violent nature. Not until the Spaniards began to feel the presence of the Orinoco's spirit, as the river was exposed in their own heartbeats, and "in the blood on their hands," could they fulfill their role as leaders of the revolution.[26]

It is with chapter 2, "Education of a Provincial Prince," that Frank begins the historical approach to his subject, tracing Bolívar's roots back to the first family member to leave the Basque land for the new world. Bolívar's father is characterized as an intellectual and rebel of the Spanish tradition who disdained the "outlandish" liberal ideas of the French and English, who were cultural inferiors.[27] Such an interpretation is important, for Frank, obviously believing these traits to have been inherited by the son, is again stressing the preeminence of the values of Spain over those of the rest of Western Europe.

Later in the chapter, Bolívar, while in Madrid, married a Spanish woman, only to have her die six months later. So he went to Paris and took a mistress; but he called her *Teresa*, the name of his first wife. Frank says that Teresa was a symbol to Bolívar of the "eternal feminine" that promises wholeness. But deprivation of Teresa caused him intuitively to sense some fulfilling destiny for himself. This resulted in his promise to never marry again,[28] as Bolívar in effect wed himself to destiny.

Chapter 3, "Miranda and the Rationalist Revolution," points up the skill with which Frank has worked events surrounding Bolívar's life into his construct. For Frank needs to show that the old thinking, e.g., empirical rationalism, failed to bring about a revolution in the new world. The chapter begins with "The Technician"—Frank's interpretation of Francisco Miranda. At the outset he hints at the reason for Miranda's failure: Miranda left his native Caracas at the age of twenty-one, never having viewed either the Orinoco or the jungle, and did not touch Venezuelan soil for thirty-five years thereafter. Moreover, he read the revolutionary books of the French Enlightenment, while the spirit of Christian Spain was unknown to him. A child of his time, Miranda saw the problem of freeing his country from Spain as one of method. But that method was mechanistic. As Frank explains Miranda's method, all that was needed was simply "to build a *machine*, and when it was ready, *to apply it to the people*." It is obvious to anyone familiar with Frank's vision that such a method, based on rationalistic, mechanistic, individualistic thinking, would be doomed to failure, as was Spain's similarly inspired eighteenth-century striving to become a modern European state. Thus, Miranda is a symbol of the failure of Enlightenment thought to solve the problems of the modern world. Like the secular thought he personified, Miranda lacked "the organic principle of integration."[29]

The final section of this chapter, "Birth of Bolívar," shows Bolívar, having sustained defeat at the hands of the royalists, sailing to Cartagena in New Granada, hoping to offer his services to the patriots who held the city. Frank sees the journey as climactic in Bolívar's life—the point where Bolívar becomes Bolívar. He writes,

> The intense forced pause gripped the energy of each impulse, fused it with the others . . . whereas each impulse in turn had overwhelmed him, now *he* contained them all, and this gave him detachment: the matrix of creative power. No other process within the limits of psychology can explain the transfigured man. . . .[30]

Since from this point Bolívar is not only the leader of the cause but more successful than Miranda, who had been captured by the royalists, this explanation is needed to separate the rationalistic revolutionary from the integrated liberator.

Also noteworthy is Frank's mentioning of Mordecai Ricardo, the Dutch Sephardic Jew of Curaçao who extended both his hand and his purse to the penniless Bolívar so he could proceed with his plans.[31] Ricardo can be seen as the generous spirit of the Jew whose destined place in America Hispana Frank had spelled out in an earlier article.

In the final section ("Nadir") of chapter 4, Frank describes Bolívar's situation at its lowest point. Returning to Cartagena, Bolívar is forced because of the jealousy of others to leave the continent for Jamaica—in essence, leaving all of New Granada and Venezuela to fall into Spanish hands. Again, Frank's Bolívar is magnanimous, stoical; and his decision to leave his army in order to save it, so that "the soldiers of American independence would fight again . . . not each other, but for American independence"[32] establishes him as a sacrificial lamb, a messianic hero. Like Christ, he must sacrifice himself to bring about the redemption of his world.

In "Manuel Piar" (the sixth section of chapter 5), Frank presents the man whom Bolívar made general of the forces of Guayana as a symbol of the spirit of the Negro. For Frank sees the Negro as a symbol of the soul—of the instinctual forces, blood and the unconscious that must be fused with consciousness and awareness. Piar was always uneasy in the Liberator's company, and shunned the great man whenever he could,[33] and Bolívar's noting of this is seen by Frank as prophetic. It anticipated the ultimate fate of Piar— execution as a traitor, with Bolívar signing the death sentence— and the racial tensions that continued to exist in Latin America long after Bolívar was gone.

The title of the final section of the same chapter, "Casacoima," refers to the lagoon that is situated before the small fortified town of Guyana la Antigua. The place had to be taken before Bolívar's next objective, Angostura, could be approached. On their advance to the town, the patriots were surprised by Spanish soldiers; Bolívar, trapped, plunged into the lagoon, filled with crocodiles and poisonous snakes. Bolívar's escape from the Spaniards' bullets and the crocodiles' teeth revealed more clearly his destiny. Beyond this, Frank uses Bolívar's swimming under water while in the lagoon to convey the idea that Bolívar's immersion into the jungle world of the Orinoco (a metaphor for his own unconscious) has finally clarified his vision. As the prophet returning from his plunge into the netherworld, Bolívar can tell his men that he foresees their taking Angostura, and Peru as well.[34]

The third section of chapter 8, "Manuela Sáenz," is Frank's portrait of the forging of a rebel. Manuela Sáenz, by her early experiences, became a woman who with her hatred of Spain, contempt for the Church, and free, though shocking, behavior, can be seen as a symbol of Frank's ideal of the Latin American woman. Also, in a Jungian sense she is the archetypal woman. And in organic terms, Frank finds her like the Andean world from whence she came—"brash, restless, free-thinking, and chaste." Furthermore, although she was married, Frank sees the marriage as having been rationally determined,[35] that is, a kind of settlement between daughter and mother; and this is his way of hinting at a reason for the marriage's failure from the start.

The following section, "Two Men and a Woman," refers to Sucre, San Martín, and Sáenz. Frank writes that upon meeting

Bolívar, "Manuela had found her career. She possessed Bolívar." Thus, Frank provides a parallel with the story of his liaison with Ifigenia in *South American Journey*. Frank is implying that through their sexual relationship, Manuela's "whole nature—impetuous, generous, strong," like that of America Hispana—connects with Bolívar's "seed," his dream of the creating of "a free, united America Hispana." That the seed is planted is found in Frank's relation of how Bolívar's dream "became her own passionate assignment." Thus, she is a symbol of Latin America's acceptance of Bolívar's idea, as yet unborn. Furthermore, Frank's contention that Bolívar was able to "enter and possess her only in so far as *he* was in her"[36] again points up Bolívar's destined role, if Manuela is a symbol of their world.

As for Sucre, whom Bolívar loved, Frank characterizes him as "the *ideal* Christian knight." Thus, Sucre can be seen as a symbol of Bolívar's longing for the medieval synthesis, since to Frank it is part of the Liberator's makeup. That Sucre's virtue and zeal infuriated[37] Bolívar can symbolize the need for a new methodology, a new religion of man for the new world, since Sucre's ascetic, otherworldly qualities are the same ones that failed to sustain the "Christian Republic."

Finally, Frank's characterization of San Martín recalls the characterization made in *America Hispana*. A soldier, a rationalist, a man of Europe, San Martín was to Frank a man of order who, unhappy in his immersion in the chaos of this land, desired to quit it as soon as possible. Because San Martín was of a traditional, realistic nature,[38] he was unable to bring order out of chaos. Frank means to diminish him in comparison to Bolívar, who of course chose to create from chaos.

The fourth and final section of chapter 11, "Night," refers to Bolívar's last days. With his health steadily declining, he learned of Sucre's assassination. Then, he spent October and November of his last year in a place called Soledad (solitude). It is a symbol of wholeness: "all of it was lost in the plain of grey grass and sparse grey trees fusing with the river into sky and ocean." This recalling of the all-encompassing Earth Mother is meant to prophesy the impending death of Bolívar, and to point up his being but an integer of the Whole. But Frank begins the section with a prophecy as well. His relation of Bolívar's journey on the Magdalena River through the jungle to the sea[39] symbolizes the Atlantic destiny of the values represented by the jungle and embodied in Bolívar.

Chapter 12, "Mountain and Sea," contains another Christ metaphor. Frank portrays Bolívar's life as a suspension; "this was the Cross of life on which he had hung." Also, Frank equates suspension with transition; thus, he repeats the regenerationist thinking that "of the unresolved transition, he was dying." Finally, Frank pounds home the idea of the organic destiny of Bolívar and the man's own sense of it with the following: ". . . the peace of his last days . . . reveals that Bolívar had a sense of himself which may be likened to the organic knowledge of the grain of corn that it must die in the earth in order to live."[40] But all in all, the effect of this chapter remains that Bolívar's vision was unfulfilled due to its coming in the transitional phase of man's move to a higher consciousness, at a point in that transition too premature for realization.

Chapter 13, "The Hundred Years," is Frank's interpretation of the century following Bolívar's death. In the section entitled "The Inheritors," Frank begins by making the case for Bolívar as prophet of a vision that mirrors Frank's (thus making Frank one of the inheritors). He interprets the Panama Congress as being revelatory of Bolívar's vision of a hemisphere of united nations; and he sees Bolívar's "Federal Union" as a global realization of his organic vision. Yet Frank goes further, suggesting that perhaps Bolívar foresaw the day when there would be the fusion of American values, north and south, rekindled from the gravity of an ominous new era. Thus Bolívar is made a prophet for the United States as well as Latin America. This, of course, is Frank's vision rather than Bolívar's. Frank says, ". . . Bolívar was geared to the American reality; in his will to free America and to make it the City of Man, not more than in the tragic collapse of the methods and tools with which he strove to build it."[41] That phrase—"to make it the City of Man"—was used by Frank in *Ustedes y nosotros* to express his dream of an America to be.

"Legend and Myth" (the third section of the final chapter) can be seen as Frank's admission that what he has presented as biography is really an exercise in mythmaking. First, he defines legend as expressive of the "self-love" of a people. After allowing that legend sometimes makes use of facts, and then briefly listing some aspects of Bolívar's "white" and "black" legends, he defines myth: "Myth is legend (and history) transfigured; it is born when the collective spirit of the folk know its relation with the universal." In other words, myth goes beyond mere storytelling and becomes prophecy. Thus, Frank will make a myth of Bolívar: Bolívar lived within a conflict whose outcome he knew to be a foregone conclusion, and thus was doomed. Within the chaos of his people he voiced their chief demand: "order and unity." And though he presented the chaos and it damned him, Bolívar embodies the legacy of "his culture, its challenge and its potential in America to create a new world from chaos."[42] Thus, the myth does more than point to the organic destiny of the new world; the birth of the myth sounds the end of the transition stage of man's consciousness, and the beginning of the integration of the parts of the Whole—truly the birth of a world.

Finally, "The Atlantic World in Bolívar" is Frank's interpretation of Bolívar's relevance to the contemporary world. Bolívar sacrificed himself for the vision of a "new world for Man" (Frank's vision, of course), because he needed other means—again, the tool of which Frank spoke in *America Hispana*. Bolívar's unconsciousness of Asia and Africa is explained in terms of his "ecumenical vision" that was indifferent to race. Thus, Frank extends Bolívar's vision to include the prophecy that is really his own. With the contention that Bolívar's acceptance of blacks and Indians symbolized the great man's acceptance of Africa and Asia, he predicts: "Nothing less complete, now that the West's imperialism wanes, must be the spirit of the West in order to be accepted by Africa and Asia; must be the spirit of the United States to be accepted by America Hispana."[43]

Frank concludes with an old theme: In a world in deep crisis, we in the United States know we are in a minority in the world and we need Latin America on our side. What can we do to bring about the Bolivarian unity, the American design that, believing that all men are created equal, will be firmly established among all men? Bolívar knew; but not knowing enough to bring it about, he sacrificed himself. Frank knows; the "tool," the "weapon" with which we can begin to create one America is none other than the Great Tradition, which teaches the idea that all men are brothers in the eyes of a god who is potentially present in every one of them. Faith in this tradition, which created both Europe and America, must engender faith in its inherent strength. But faith can only go so far; people must "strive to *enact*" the Great Tradition by changing their economies, their political systems, their values, and their arts.[44]

Thus Bolívar's successor in a sense reiterates his earlier spiritual message from *Chart for Rough Water*—to be creative, revolution must be religion.

Prophet or Profit?

While the Bolívar biography did not hasten the creation of the new world, the undaunted Frank continued to inject his organic message in his writings for or about Latin America. For example, in

1953, in his introduction to Joaquím María Machado de Assís's novel, *Dom Casmurro*, he explains the achievement of this "epileptic son of a poor mulatto" in terms of his land, Brazil, where "all bloods circulated freely in the nation's body, each element contributing to the whole what it had to give and receiving . . . culturally, spiritually . . . what it needed." Frank concludes, "Brazil let the elements of his nature live, and grow into a literary art of unsurpassed precision."[45]

Then, on 13 March 1954, Frank's article, "Puerto Rico and Psychosis," appeared in the *Nation*. In this piece he assesses the "fantastic lunacy" of the Puerto Ricans who the week before entered the House of Representatives and began shooting. Believing that "madness can be as revealing as creative genius," he concludes that the actions of the Puerto Ricans exposed their truth: that they are suspicious of our offer of freedom, especially if we define freedom according to our own values, which do not allow "men to become wholly human."[46]

The following month, Frank began a monthly, syndicated column entitled "Voz de América" for thirty Latin American papers. Thanks to the latitude his position as columnist gave him, he was able to travel to Israel (in 1956) at the expense of the syndicate to write a series of articles on that young nation, and these writings formed the basis of his next book, *Bridgehead: The Drama of Israel* (1957).[47] This work gives evidence of Frank's aim of making his subject matter relevant to his Hispanic audience while at the same time expounding "wholeness." For example, in comparing the town of Beersheba with towns in Venezuela, Mexico, and Spain, Frank finds "the glowing amalgam of blue sky and golden dust, the same clarity of air making each man, beast and tree an isolate entity before the thought of God joins them."[48]

Indeed, the unity of all things was Frank's chief preoccupation where Latin America was concerned. Even his obituary for Gabriela Mistral interprets the Chilean and her work in organic terms. He writes that Gabriela reminded him of the Andes, which were "miraculously" present in her "warm, spontaneous" verse.[49]

Finally, in the summer of 1959, the Havana newspapers noted their approval of "one of his *Voz* articles, a fanciful piece on the conference of the Organization of American States in Chile," and this resulted in an invitation for the "friend of the revolution" to come to Cuba. Frank visited the island that fall, at which time he was urged by Amando Hart Dávalos, minister of education, and Raúl Roa, chancellor and chairman of the office of cultural relations, to write a book about the Cuban experience. Without making a definitive commitment, he returned to the United States, and in 1960 he became temporary chairman of the Fair Play for Cuba Committee. Even so, Frank began to doubt Castro's motives. "'His hysterical speeches sicken me,' he admitted in his journal; and then he wondered: 'If he opposed an action would he inevitably modulate from opposition to violence?'" Nevertheless, he returned to Cuba in April 1960 to get a contract to do the book for his price of twenty-five thousand dollars.[50]

Frank spent the summer working on the book. Because of his growing apprehension over Castro's "dictatorial" performance, he found the writing difficult. Furthermore, he resigned his committee chairmanship. Yet he stayed on as a member of that committee, and even returned to Cuba in October to interview the leaders of the revolution, including Castro.[51]

Following the Bay of Pigs incident, Frank's published criticism of the failed invasion served the perception in the United States that he was in the enemy camp. Thus, when in June 1961, congressional hearings were held on the Fair Play for Cuba Committee, considerable mention was made of Frank's political associations and actions. Frank was not called to testify, however, and luckily a newly formed publisher, Marzani and Munsell, gladly accepted his otherwise unwanted manuscript.[52]

Cuba: Prophetic Island: An Analysis

Published in October 1961, *Cuba: Prophetic Island* is Frank's last teleological argument for the organic destiny of the Americas. In characteristic fashion, he uses Cuba and its history as the basis for this final exposition of his apocalyptic vision. For example, in describing the circumstances of Castro's speech before the United Nations, he contrasts the U.N.'s fragile-looking buildings with the slums—survivors of the industrial age—that surround them. He finds that the U.N. buildings forecast the new world—and an omen.[53] While the idea of the United Nations is the dream of the future, this future is threatened by the tenacity of the old world values.

In addition to fragility, the U.N. as perceived by Frank exudes coolness. He differentiates the coolness from the heat that Castro brings to the rostrum. According to Frank, Castro's heat is the heat of birth; Castro personifies the birth process of the Cuban nation, begun on 26 July 1953, and continuing with the current revolution. The purpose of this contrast is to explain the lack of rapport between Castro and the assembly he was addressing. The major obstacle to profound intercourse between Castro and the delegates was then, and is still, the distinction between a heat that causes a physical metamorphosis and a coolness that has to persist in its present state "to resist the molecular changes of incandescence."[54]

Unlike the U.N., Havana, in Frank's view, has responded to Castro. This proves that Castro's transcendent vision has met the deep need that the gaiety of Havana reveals to Frank: Havana is possessed of the tragic sense of life that knows that if the new Cuba is not born now, it never will be. "Cuba must live as a mature republic *now*"; it must seek relations with similar republics both in Latin America and throughout the world. Cuba realizes that to procrastinate in its development can only cause misery; this explains the "hysterical hurry of Castro and his colleagues, which is practical wisdom."[55]

Frank finds other parts of Cuba intuitively exhibiting signs of birth. For example, Cienfuegos, a product of nineteenth-century Spain, has "darkness" as its chief physical trait; the city becomes a symbol of the old, alien values of Europe. But Frank claims that while the people reside in ordinary-looking homes that were built during the last century, "they *live* in a different matrix." That matrix is the Hispanic tradition—Spain's church and culture—which informed their minds until the spiritual values of that tradition became transfigured and burst forth in revolution. Thus, the history of the island, despite all the chaos, was all part of the maturation process. Frank finds further evidence of Cuba's birth in the valley of Viñales. To him, birth is a transition, and he interprets the plight of the people in the valley as changing from resignation to innovation. In his judgment, such a progression is, in the realm of "social energy," as sudden as the shift to atomic energy—"and as significant to man."[56]

A major aspect of this work is Frank's fitting Cuba and its history into his teleology. He begins by establishing the island's organic destiny through a characteristic construct. He contends that because Cuba is surrounded by water, the island people were molded by "this aqueous land." Moreover, he explains, all life originated in the sea, and man intuitively understands that it is the sea from whence he came. "He beholds his past destiny in the sea, and loves it; beholds it in his threatful present and future, and fears it."[57]

Then, mixing racial psychology with "geographical mysticism," Frank interprets the mind of the Cuban in terms of the traits of the island's history. The Cuban has within him the kindness of the

Taino, the savagery of the Carib, and the greed of the Spaniard, as well as the qualities of the alligator (Cuba's shape has suggested the alligator to the Cubans) and the hurricane. But Frank finds an even deeper prophetic meaning in the island's shape, a meaning that also informs the mind of the Cuban. He sees Cuba in the shape of a phallus pointing north and west,

> penetrating the widely open vulva of Florida and Yucutan toward the immense womb of the Gulf, whose north shore represents Anglo-Saxondom, with Mexico—Amerindia—closing in upon the west and south. These are the mother organs. Cuba's thrust into them symbolizes the new impetus of revolution from the east . . . upon the mother Americas, both old, both superseded, which nevertheless must shape, as the mother shapes, the unborn, the newcomer.[58]

Frank uses this incestuous metaphor as an explanation of his own symbolism as well as a prelude to his interpretation of Cuba's history. He then proceeds to show Cuba as a product of the economic and political failure of Spain's development during the sixteenth and seventeenth centuries—those years after the decline of the medieval Christian republic when Spain willed to be Europe. Thus, Cuba's backwardness formed the basis for its present maturity as a society and a state.[59]

In Cuba's prophetic poets, recent singers, generals of the Thirty Years War with Spain, and political leaders and soldiers of the current revolution, Frank hears the prophetic strain of the Semite. Cuba received it from Spain, which in turn, of course, received it from its Arab and Jewish populations—both shaped by prophetic cultures—and through the Jewish, Christian, and Moslem schoolmen and the great literary mystics. The implication is that the new Cuba, born of revolution, has retained the quality of the medieval synthesis. Its creators are prophets like Don Quixote—the knight who resisted the rationalism and individualism of the modern world—who continue the struggle for truth, justice, and, above all else, love.[60]

Posing José Martí as an heir of the Semitic theme of prophecy, Frank not only makes the Cuban a symbol of the spiritual values of Latin America, but claims that any Anglo-Saxon American who would compare favorably to him would have to combine the careers of Thomas Jefferson, Abraham Lincoln, and Walt Whitman. Calling Martí a "saint with a sword," Frank explains the metaphor by characterizing Martí's program of "ideals" (upon which the renewed war of 1895 was waged) as so incredibly lofty that it reads "more like an epistle of a modern Paul than like the working orders of a revolution."[61]

Frank is primarily concerned with Martí's career as it reveals a prophet of the organic destiny of the Americas, and he uses Martí's writing as support for such a characterization. In describing a piece of Martí's prose, he finds that "something of cosmos has been infused into the base statement, making it an experience: organic, human." As for Martí's poetry, he finds its chief trait to be "*springlike* energy and fragrance," thus conveying the message of regeneration. And significantly, Martí's time in the United States, as interpreted by Frank, provides him the knowledge of what is good and evil in that country; thus, Martí's vision of hemispheric unity is in terms of the good of *both* worlds.[62]

Of course, Martí was a prophet whose vision went beyond his own lifetime. Thus, Frank interprets Martí's death in terms of the teleology. Martí and Cuba were as one. When he articulated Cuba's need for regeneration, this was Cuba speaking. His demise symbolizes Cuba's sleep during the long years leading up to the present revolution. The island, like Martí, had been "neglected, exploited, and violated until it [had to] die or be reborn—in a new body. This culture-spirit was too vital to die. And it was not ready to live."[63] At least not until Fidel Castro called forth the new Cuba by recasting the vision of José Martí.

Not surprisingly, then, Frank submits Castro as another heir to the Semitic theme of prophecy. Indeed, Frank's characterization of Castro is another important aspect of the book—and the most misinterpreted. Frank describes the deeds of Castro as guided by a deep understanding of Cuba and all of Latin America, yet liberated by a genuine "innocence" that caused him to act impetuously when a more savvy politician might hesitate. This is more than just an explanation or an apology. According to Frank, the spiritual harmony of an "organic birth" was present in Castro's deeds. Frank's purpose becomes evident: he means to show the Cuban leader as a mere instrument of destiny. Castro is the product of over four hundred years of history and a culture that predates Cuba. He and his comrades were produced by their culture and in turn they are the producers of the new revolutionary culture. Casting the Cuban in a prophet's role, Frank contends that Castro is aware of this but speaks in simpler terms to better reach his people. Obviously, Frank finds Castro a kindred spirit. This is especially evident when he quotes Castro as having said in Chile, "this is a *humanist* revolution, because it does not deprive man of his essence, but holds the *whole man* as its fundamental aim."[64] Frank himself could not have phrased a better description.

Much of Frank's characterization of Castro hints at the author's mythological indoctrination. For example, his description of Castro's mid-afternoon meeting with the director of the Institute of Agrarian Reform suggests Vulcan: Castro makes a point with his colleagues much like "an iron worker, having heated the metal, hammers it to shape." In the same section, his description of Castro wading through the crowd in the city of Matanzas suggests Narcissus: the people who surrounded Castro "had somehow the shape of Castro. And what was the shape of Castro? Was it not Cuba itself? Was it not *itself*, that the folk loved in Castro? Was it not this presence which *his* presence gave, of a deeper community between each Cuban and his world" beyond the city limits of Matanzas?[65]

Finally, in dealing with Castro's inclination not to have a triumphal entry into Havana, Frank tells how the people, in a spontaneous act, go to Havana and issue a command for Castro to appear. He likens them to the sun, for they rise and set at the right moment.[66] Thus, Castro's going to them in a helicopter suggests Phaëthon going to the sun in his chariot.

The implications of these mythological suggestions are obvious. Castro as Vulcan is the creator; and to Frank, creation is revolution. As for the myth of Narcissus, it supports Frank's contention that the feeling the Cuban people have for Castro is love. Finally, the myth of Phaëthon suggests the hazardous road Castro must travel. And, like Phaëthon, Castro is oblivious to the dangers, and proceeds recklessly on his course. Furthermore, Phaëthon's quest set the world aflame, and Castro's heat, the heat of Cuba's birth, has done the same.

Frank's characterization of Castro is not limited to mythological suggestions. In relating the arrival of Castro in Matanzas and the subsequent reception of the Cuban leader by his people, Frank explicitly likens Castro to the sun. Because a sunrise gives all who view it a spiritual lift, the people gravitate toward Castro. In another instance, Frank sees Castro's rejection of gradualism as making him a disciple of the nineteenth-century Venezuelan socialist Daniel DeLeón; they are both prophets who share a natural perception of the evolutionary "leaps" that can occur, which is not surprising insofar as they are heirs of the Semitic strain within their culture.[67]

Frank's most telling comparison follows his explanation that Castro's biggest blunders (of which Frank has not seen many) appear to stem from absentmindedness. With such a characterization, Frank can then liken Castro to Don Quixote, who was also good, but whose achievements became outrageous because of his mistaken or incomplete understanding of the world in which he lived, because his intellect was not equal to his plans.[68]

Frank implies this comparison between Castro and Cervantes's hero throughout the book. In one instance, he credits to intuitive knowledge Castro's naming the revolution "movimiento 26 de julio"—for that day when his 168 youths unsuccessfully assaulted the Moncada barracks—explaining that Castro knew that the people of Cuba grasped the meaning of his action: it was the same as the moral of Don Quixote's failed quest, "the message of the mystery that human life, under all its joys, is tragic."[69]

Finally, because Frank interprets the Cuban revolution as the moment of Cuba's birth, he poses Castro as the artist who is creating this child. This explains Castro's dictatorial behavior, for aren't all artists dictators? They gather their material, "ruthlessly rejecting, selecting, finally shaping it to form."[70]

Frank's representation of the revolution is in the same vein as that of his characterization of Castro. For example, in describing the political situation that eventually led to the assault on the Moncada barracks, Frank means to show the organic origins of the revolution. The suicide of Eduardo Chibás, idealistic leader of the liberal Ortodoxo party, showed Castro and young Cuba that reform would not come about through any system of laws grounded in the old order. What was required was a totally new environment within which Cuba's birth would be complete. Their revolution, therefore, with its attendant coercion, was their way of connecting with Cuba's soil. "If they touched Cuba, they would touch the peasants and the workers of Cuba, and in a modern myth of Antaeus, strength would issue: Cuba would at last come to be. . . ."[71]

Also, the republic sprouted from the rich wilderness of the Sierra Maestra, the district of Cuba where the revolutionaries spent the first days of the revolution. This suggests the organic nature of the movement. Frank furthers this idea by explaining that the process by which the revolution grew was largely an unconscious one, "for much of it took place in the reticent minds of the peasants." Next, Frank reverts to a biblical theme as he depicts the forging of the revolution in the wilderness. He compares the time spent by the revolutionaries in the Sierra Maestra to the experience of the Jews in the Sinai. As God's chosen people designed the structure of their future homeland in the desert, living only on the manna provided by the Lord, so the Cubans, whose manna "was sugar and *malanga*," worked out their program of agrarian reform in the Sierra.[72]

Frank's interpretation of contemporary Cuba and its leaders is predictable, but nonetheless noteworthy. For example, of the Cuba he has found, he praises the agrarian reform, for it put into production fields that under the old order had never been cultivated. Thus, despite all the "dislocations" that were wrought by the new economic system, despite all the mistakes that arose from on-the-job training, the statistics show that the land immediately increased its yield.[73]

Frank examines the complexity of reform, turning at last to practical considerations, and for the need to synthesize technology with humanism in order to attain *completeness*, wholeness. Because reform is causing problems for the revolution and its leaders, Cuba must turn to the Soviet Union for help. Frank, of course, is sympathetic, for Cuba's economy has problems that she does not have the technical know-how to handle. Castro understood that in order to effectively rid his country of Batista and the circumstances that spawned him, which is what the people want, he must supply his people with some way that they can enjoy the fruits of their labors.[74]

Furthermore, Frank finds Cuba's leaders certain that technology can create prosperity for all. He concludes, "they are *good men* and what they are attempting in their imperiled world is *good*." And the key to their goodness is that "they are in love with Cuba's incompleteness, and with the task . . . of Cuba's self-fulfillment as a people."[75] In other words, their vision, like Frank's, is the creation of a world that will be whole, and in which the whole man can live.

Individually, Frank interprets the important leaders. One example will suffice to show how Frank's perception is influenced by his presuppositions. Raúl Castro, Fidel's brother, is supposed to be a Communist. According to Frank, however, Raúl does not accept communism because the nationalism and the Hispanic Americanism of Martí provide him with all the dogma he needs.[76]

The interpretations lead into a prophecy: world opinion, especially that of Hispanic America and the entire hemisphere, about the Cuban revolution will tell a lot about the future that men want for themselves. But Frank is sure of what that future will be for Cuba. He concludes that the destiny of Cuba within Latin America, within the hemisphere it shares with Anglo-America, and within the world that now sees Cuba's rebirth paralleled by similar developments in Africa, Asia, and Europe, "rests with the character of the Cubans as it will emerge, made articulate by its leaders."[77]

Frank uses his final chapter to wax didactic. After relating how the Organization of American States condemned Cuba because of her relations with Communist countries, he implies that Castro's answer to the condemnation—an assertion of Cuban independence and the acceptance of Russia's missiles—was due to his intuitive knowledge of how Cuba's long road to salvation must be traversed. For, as Frank imagines, Castro might have told the Russians he accepted their friendship and business, but not their rockets. But Castro, who Frank calls a "true tribune," knows that "no crowd could spontaneously compose such a reply." Nonetheless, Frank states that the peoples of the world "must learn to find such a reply within themselves—or man must vanish." The way, of course, is his methodology, which he finds, though inarticulate, in Cuba. He writes, "Cuba's strength is in its fresh attitude toward individual man and public power." But he contends that Cuba must, like the Jews, obey and incorporate its prophets. Yet even though Frank sees Castro as a prophet, as revealed by what he has done to carry Cuba along the true road to salvation, he will not label Castro's reforms as perfect.[78] The implication is that the Cubans must become Frankian *persons* for the reforms to last and for true salvation to be achieved.

Frank discusses the ideal of the New World, of hemispheric unity, and how it came to mean domination by the United States. Because Castro has now marked the end of the era of United States domination, now that empathy with Cuba "cuts across hemispheric lines, dissolving them," Frank must reaffirm his belief in the destiny of hemispheric unity. He writes, "Only a rediscovered value in viable, contemporary terms—valid in the United States no less than in America Hispana—would re-endow the hemisphere with meaning."[79]

Not surprisingly, Frank finds that value to be *our value of the person*. After all, he contends, only the nations of America, from the time of their birth, "were consciously and deliberately rooted in the democratic Judaeo-Christian vision of the whole man." Not surprisingly, he finds this the key ingredient to a new apocalypse and the awakening of the hemisphere. Even though we lack the method to achieve this dream and this "love," we must persevere; for if we forsake that objective, then all is lost.[80]

The world stands in urgent need, Frank believes, of his method for achieving the realization of the whole man, which is mankind's only hope. Citing the nuclear threat, Frank warns that science has produced machines of mass destruction. Thus, man must obtain the wisdom to keep from being annihilated. This challenge is something of an evolutionary turning point. Either man changes to meet the demands of a new environment, or he becomes extinct. Threatened by the very juggernaut he has created, man must now "leap to safety."[81]

As for Castro and his men, Frank sees them on the true path to salvation, and thus they have to be embraced just as they are. He knows that for the realization of his vision they and their actions have an everlasting significance.[82]

Finally, Frank points up the spiritual nature of both the Cuban situation and his message. For the United States to suppress the Cuban revolution and thus delude Latin America would be a sin. Likewise, for the other nations of Hispanic America to desert Cuba in its time of need would be a sin. Finally, for the Cubans to forget that social justice must be tempered with love (without which justice can become arbitrary) would be a sin. (He uses the word *sin* because included in its meaning is the "profound truth" that man is one with the cosmos.) The lesson is that an understanding of the true nature of the Cuban revolution must translate into American cooperation with Cuba's efforts.[83] Then, of course, the realization of Frank's vision of hemispheric unity and of a world of, by, and for the whole man will be enhanced.

Frank's book received scant attention. Those reviews that went beyond brief, objective sketches of the book's contents concentrated on the fact that Castro had admitted to being a Communist shortly after the book's publication. Thus, one reviewer sympathetically offers that Frank's passion for the "downtrodden and exploited masses of Latin America . . . made him an easy prey for Fidel Castro."[84] Another reviewer is less kind. In noting that Castro himself has made Frank's "intended apologia for him" virtually worthless, Daniel James finds the book damaging to Frank's reputation as a political writer as well as an expert on Latin America; and he contemptuously concludes that Frank's "infatuation" with Castro's Cuba is "perhaps the most acute case on record, and should be of some clinical interest."[85]

Of course, neither reviewer understood Frank's purpose. And unhappily, neither did the United States government. The House Committee on Un-American Activities summoned Frank in 1962 to appear before an executive session; he was questioned for over three hours. Also, in March 1963, he was called to testify before the Senate Internal Security Committee.[86]

Cuba: Prophetic Island was Frank's last published book. That his interest in the Hispanic world was maintained to the very last is evidenced by the generous amount of space given over to the Hispanic adventure in the *Memoirs*. Toward the end of that text, he could still write of America Hispana that while it still lacked the design, it maintained the spirit necessary for organic growth. Thus, the people of Latin America were much wealthier in human terms than their capitalistic neighbors to the north.[87] Furthermore, there is nothing in the *Memoirs* to suggest that he had repudiated his vision of one America. When he died on 9 January 1967, his vision remained unrealized. And so it still remains to this day—a dream deferred.

Assessing the Man and His Message

"A prophet is not without honor except in his native land." Such was the fate of Waldo Frank and his message. William Bittner wrote in 1958 that Frank's "work has been applauded more outside his own country than in," and states boldly: "To Latin America he is the personification of the American dream."[88] Jerome Kloucek, in that same year, admitted that Frank was most successful in Latin America, where enthusiasm for his work was greatest.[89] In 1967 Paul Carter asserted that while Frank's writing was largely unknown in the United States, he "continue[d] to be read and admired" in Latin America.[90] Finally, in his introduction to Frank's *Memoirs*, published in 1973, Lewis Mumford echoed Carter in his contention that Frank had lost his U.S. audience but kept his readership in Latin America.[91]

As proof of Frank's popularity in the Hispanic world, both Kloucek and Bittner point to the acclaim of *Virgin Spain* and the publication of *Waldo Frank in America Hispana*, M. J. Benardete's compilation of the laudatory reactions of Latin Americans to Frank's 1929 lecture tour. Bittner cites the latter book as evidence of the "respect and admiration" that Latin Americans hold for Frank.[92] The book was published in 1930, however. What proof exists as to Frank's enduring appeal? Carter offers the following: a 1941 survey of catalogues of Hispanic publishers, found in the *Literary History of the United States* (1948), which lists more translations of Frank's work than that of any other North American author; Van Wyck Brooks's 1957 comment in *Days of the Phoenix* that a knowledgeable source told him Frank had influenced "a whole school" of Argentine novelists; and, finally, the reprint of six of Frank's novels in *Waldo Frank: Obras escogidas* by Aguilar of Madrid in 1961, and a follow-up volume by the same press in 1963 entitled *Waldo Frank: Retratos culturales*, which contained *Virgin Spain, Re-discovery of America, America Hispana*, and *Birth of a World*.[93]

Beyond Frank's lifetime, however, there is only the word of Lewis Mumford—and that in 1973—that Frank is still read in Latin America. Today, there is no evidence that any of his books are in print in the Spanish-speaking world. It would be even more difficult to prove that he has readers there. Considering the current Americanization of Latin America, a seeming triumph of the very capitalist culture that Frank so abhorred, it is doubtful that his writings are still valued by any but a small minority of our neighbors to the south.

If Waldo Frank's books are no longer influential in Latin America, admittedly the last bastion of his readership, of what significance then is the life and work of Waldo Frank? With regard to the Hispanic adventure, one must consider that Frank went to Latin America at a time (1929) when a huge cultural gap existed between Anglo-America and Hispanic America, and became an important bridge between North and South. At first glance, this reputation seems based on subjective perceptions more than on reality. For example, upon his return to New York, he was honored with a testimonial dinner at the Hotel Roosevelt on 17 February 1930. There Professor Federico de Onís of Columbia University gave a speech entitled "Waldo Frank as an Interpreter of Spanish Culture," while Frank himself spoke on the subject "What is Hispano-America to us?" The event was attended by such notables as Franz Boas, Herbert Croly, Charlie Chaplin, John Dewey, Lewis Mumford, Maxwell Perkins, and Alfred Stieglitz, to name but a few.[94] No doubt, these influential people helped to spread the impression that Frank was an expert on Latin America. Certainly subsequent commentary on his writing on Hispanic themes never questions his authority.

As for Latin Americans, they had Frank presented to them from the outset as a leading U.S. intellectual, and it was as such that they embraced him.[95] This understanding became a constant during Frank's subsequent trips to America Hispana. Even a shrewd, practical politician like Víctor Raúl Haya de la Torre mistook Frank in 1942 "for a genuine spokesman of North American thought, rather than as a fringe figure whose narrowly circumscribed influence would quickly ebb."[96] Finally, would the Cuban government, strapped for cash by the end of 1959,[97] have given twenty-five thousand dollars to someone it deemed to be without any influence in the United States? More than likely, Castro believed Frank to be well-respected throughout the hemisphere and, therefore, the perfect choice to make the revolution more palatable to other observers.

Benardete's book, however, stands as the best evidence that Frank had an importance for Latin Americans beyond their belief that he was a major U.S. thinker. In the foreword is the statement: "The value of his [Frank's] ideas and his personality does not come from the fact that they are representative of all North Americans or many of them, but, on the contrary, because they are his own, because of their originality." Indeed, the entries all focus on the man and his message rather than any reputation he brought with him from home. This was particularly the case in Argentina, where his lectures enjoyed a "unique success" in that country's leading universities. According to the reporting of *El Mundo* of Lima, which covered Frank's stay in Buenos Aires, his success was due to "the wave of sympathy which the man aroused by virtue of the congruence of his thoughts with the most subtle intuitions of his public."[98]

Why was Latin America so receptive to his message? Blessed with an innate spirituality and a formidable intellect (and an enormous ego, as I have pointed out), Waldo Frank appeared on the scene at a propitious moment when the world was experiencing one of its periodic outbursts of "utopian longing." The temper of the times guaranteed the enthusiastic reception of his early apocalyptic works; indeed, Frank was a product of the very influences that made the 1920s and 1930s decades wherein man's achievement of perfection appeared to many to be imminent. With the counterculture in the United States finding new gods like Freud and Marx, and with its Latin American counterpart renewing its search for truth through the old one, Frank's writing on Hispanic themes during those years found eager audiences.

Frank called these works "history," but his approach was Nietzschean, i.e., history with a purpose. In *Virgin Spain* and *America Hispana*, he offered teleological constructs that confirmed his prophecy: the eventual union of Anglo-American and Hispanic America, incorporating the best elements of each, which would usher in a true New World peopled by new "persons" aware of their oneness with all things. While these books were factually correct, his aim was always suprahistorical. Only that which furthered his argument was included.

Not surprisingly, he was not original in his interpretations. In preparation for his writing, he read his predecessors on the various aspects of history that he chose to illuminate, and made their ideas his own. Where there was some disagreement between schools of thought, he came down on the side that best suited his purposes. Nonetheless, he achieved a reputation as a keen interpreter of Hispanic culture. In the United States, where ignorance of the Spanish-speaking realm was the rule, his explanations were taken at face value. Besides, his U.S. readers were more interested in his castigation of his government's policy, his chastisement of his fellow countrymen's attitudes toward Spain and Latin America, and his championing of collectivism vis-à-vis capitalism, which they applauded. Meanwhile, in the Hispanic world, because his representation of those lands and peoples mirrored Spanish and Latin American self-evaluations, he insured a warm reception for himself and an acceptance of his message. Add to that the respect he showed for the Spanish-speaking peoples, and it is no wonder that he was welcomed with a fervor that was only superseded by the zeal with which his disciples there trumpeted the spirituality of his message.

The respect he displayed toward Spaniards as well as to the peoples south of the Rio Grande seems to be the key to his success. By all accounts he treated them as equals, without condescension, in all humility. One might wonder how Frank could have made such an impression on Hispanics when his main personality trait appeared to many to have been his monumental egotism. He certainly didn't disguise it in his writings. It is unlikely that he could have done so in any event. Might not Hispanics have found such conceit as objectionable as many of his U.S. critics did? Perhaps an answer can be found in the writings of Miguel de Unamuno, whom Frank read in preparation for *Virgin Spain*. In *El individualismo español* the Spaniard writes:

> It is hard to understand how a person, without speaking, without writing, without painting anything, without chiseling a piece of sculpture, without playing any music, without transacting any kind of business, *without doing anything at all*, can expect that by the single act of being present he will be regarded as a man of extraordinary merit and outstanding talent. Nevertheless, here in Spain—I do not know whether such is the case elsewhere—more than a few examples of this extremely old phenomenon are known.[99]

It is not hard to assume that Frank knew he could present himself to these people just as he was and in all likelihood be accepted as one of them. If Unamuno's characterization is correct, such people would be unphased by Frank's ego, while others would probably allow it, for Frank at least had *done something* to merit it. This also might explain the affinity that he claims he felt for the first Latin Americans he met as well as those first Spanish soldiers he saw.

While one can only speculate as to the origin of his "affinity," it can be easily demonstrated that beyond his personal success, Frank's greatest contribution to history was in his role as goodwill ambassador (even if goodwill was a by-product of a more self-serving purpose). One needs only to look at the state of U.S.-Latin American relations at the time of the 1929 lecture tour. Less than a year earlier, President-elect Herbert Hoover visited half of the Latin American republics. As the historian of U.S. foreign policy, Alexander DeConde, characterizes that trip: "In some places, particularly Argentina, Hoover received chilly receptions. Some skeptics there feared that his words might not be 'more than wind blowing across the Pampas.'"[100] The atmosphere was unchanged when Frank appeared on the scene the following year. As Luis Alberto Sánchez noted in his speech introducing Frank at the National University of San Marcos, "We have suffered from a plague of messages," which usually "turned out to be a churchly pastoral or a military proclamation." Of course, by the end of his speech, Sánchez concluded: "By his insistent refusal of the chaos of his country . . . we recognize Frank as ours, and of our race; of that race which he defined so well—the race of discontent and disconformity, but, as well, of hope."[101] Thus, it is clear that Frank at least contributed to a feeling in Latin America—no matter how ephemeral—that it was empathetically understood in the United States. And such a feeling was no insignificant ingredient in contributing to the success of the Good Neighbor policy. Consider again the testimony of Robert Woods Bliss, U.S. ambassador to Argentina at the time of Frank's tour. He told Jerome Kloucek in 1954 that Frank was a "pioneer" in recognizing the need for improved relations between the United States and its neighbors to the south.[102] Then, on the heels of Frank's triumphant tour and the publication of *America Hispana* (1931) came the Roosevelt administration and its Good Neighbor policy. FDR, of course, had his own reasons for wanting better relations with Latin America, but at least the new president showed Latin Americans that Frank wasn't the only Yankee critical of his country. Speaking in many of the same accents as Frank, Roosevelt was personally attractive to Latin Americans; they liked his New Deal program of social and economic reform, his emphasis on anti-imperialism, and his championing of the "oppressed."[103] And so the claim can be made that Frank prepared the way for the acceptance of Roosevelt and his Good Neighbor policy, and thus did serve a purpose in hemispheric relations, contributing to a fleeting moment of hemispheric wholeness at a time when such wholeness was of vital, strategic importance to the United States.

Just as Frank's appearance on the literary and intellectual scene fortunately coincided with the reappearance of utopian longing, so the timing of his tour and the message he brought with him were fortunate. This corresponded to the Great Depression and the respectable school of thought in the United States that wholeness could be achieved by a return to the land. Frank was not alone in his pursuit of wholeness. While he saw Latin America's organic destiny tied to its return to the soil (to which it had always been close), men like John Collier, FDR's commissioner of Indian affairs, and Vice-President Henry Wallace were among the many who saw the land as the answer to the needs of their fellow Americans for self-respect and survival.

Of course, things did not turn out the way Frank had foretold or any of the other dreamers had wished. By the 1940s, Frank appeared to be, for the most part, a false prophet. Still, his stature was such that Vice-President Henry Wallace himself and the U.S. State Department recognized him as an important link to Latin America. Thus they chose Frank, despite all the quirkiness of his visionary message, to be the one to speak to the whole of South America against fascism and for democracy.

Frank never admitted that his prophecies had missed the mark. Just as he shamelessly worked the Spanish Civil War into the revised edition of *Virgin Spain*, so he persisted in adapting his teleology to changing hemispheric conditions in his later works. He found "democratism" alien to the unity he predicted in *America Hispana*; he made democracy a necessary ingredient for wholeness in *South American Journey*. In his latter works he foresaw Latin America progressing toward "racial democracy"; one can only imagine how he would explain away the racism in the southern part of this hemisphere that, if anything, has hardened over the last couple of generations.

As for his ultimate prophecy, his end of history—the realization of his vision of hemispheric unity—it has not been (and will probably never be) fulfilled. Certainly Castro was no instrument of destiny. Indeed, one has to look hard for any of his predictions that has come to pass. There is, in *The Rediscovery of Man* (1958), the warning: "If, within a generation, Washington has not learned the

facts of American life, the Americas will have balanced their mis-
trust with contacts in the other hemisphere."[104] Then along came
Fidel Castro, not to mention Salvador Allende and Daniel Ortega.
This isn't earthshaking prophecy, however; any insightful observer
could have predicted as much. Add all the recent developments
that Frank did not foretell—the forces of reaction in Central
America, the Americanization of Latin America, the drug-based
economies of Colombia, Bolivia, Peru, etc., the specter of
Pinochet in Chile, and on and on—and he appears to have been
not much of a prophet at all

In the final analysis, Frank's importance lies in his historicity, a
historicity like that of his books. He needs to be looked at as a
period piece, an actor who graced the world stage at a time when
other Americans began to credit Hispanics with having something
worth emulating. For Frank, that something was spirituality, and
his message excited audiences throughout the Spanish-speaking
world who knew what he was about. But times changed, and Frank
did not. From the onset of the Second World War to the time of
his death, the kind of thinking that contributed to his success either
declined precipitously, as was the case with the "romance of American communism," or seemingly disappeared, as was the case with
Latin America's "mystical underground." Meanwhile, the very
thinking that Frank had denigrated to the point of proclaiming
its demise—individualistic, rationalistic, mechanistic thinking—
seemed to be ascendant throughout this period. Yet Frank persisted in his thinking—collectivist, intuitive, organic. Certainly,
with his later work he was going against the tide. As a result, he
paid the price of seeing his audience diminish, first in the United
States, and eventually even in Latin America. And he had to experience the disappointment of being unable to get his last two
novels published.

Frank, however, could hardly have changed his message. For, as
Luis Alberto Sánchez understood early on, Frank's message was
"in reality himself—his person and his life."[105] He had always seen
himself as carrying on Bolívar's work, i.e., the goal of hemispheric
unity. Moreover, to achieve that end, he lived his beliefs that in
seeking the new world, we create her and that creation is revolution. One can conclude that Frank believed that his message (and,
therefore, his life) was all that was necessary to realize his concept
of the new world. To again quote Sánchez: "His faith *acts*; his ideal
becomes incarnate in a method. . . ."[106] In other words, Frank
found the "tool" that Bolívar lacked. That tool was his own methodology, spelled out in *The Rediscovery of Man*. To put it simply, it

called for personal conversion to the belief that God is within man, then spreading that word through all existing institutions that forward communication, e.g., schools, churches, unions. Thus, the word becomes the act. He was the way, the truth, and the life— Waldean to the end.

Of course, Frank's "act," as Moises Sáenz predicted back in 1929, achieved nothing lasting. To recall the verdict that John Dos Passos reached on *Virgin Spain*: Do Frank and his message, then, belong "to a reality that once may have existed but that events have relegated to the storeroom?" Perhaps in a historical sense. But his life must be interpreted in symbolic terms. Frank, in striving to see his vision realized, in expounding his message, perhaps unwittingly gave us here in the United States the real "tool" for achieving harmony, if not unity, with our neighbors to the south: the way that he approached Hispanics with respect, as equals, aware of their history and their plight. He set an example that since has been followed all too infrequently. Surely more could be accomplished in hemispheric relations his way than with acts such as the mining of the harbor at Corinto or the invasion of Panama.

NOTES

Chapter 1. The Making of a Prophet: An Introduction

1. Waldo Frank, *Memoirs of Waldo Frank*, ed. Alan Trachtenberg (Amherst: University of Massachusetts Press, 1973), p. 157.
2. Ibid., pp. 157–60.
3. Ibid., pp. 157, 159–60, 166.
4. William Bittner, *The Novels of Waldo Frank* (Philadelphia: University of Pennsylvania Press, 1958), p. 20.
5. Lewis Mumford, introduction to *Memoirs of Waldo Frank*, p. xvii.
6. Paul J. Carter, *Waldo Frank*, Twayne's United States Authors Series (New Haven, Conn.: Twayne Publishers, Inc., 1967), p. 22.
7. Bittner, *Novels of Waldo Frank*, p. 20.
8. Waldo Frank, *In the American Jungle (1925–1936)* (New York: Farrar & Rinehart, 1937), p. 7.
9. Jerome W. Kloucek, "Waldo Frank: The Ground of His Mind and Art" (Ph.D. diss., Northwestern University, 1958; Ann Arbor, Michigan: University Microfilms, Inc., 1981), p. 13.
10. Frank, *In the American Jungle*, p. 7.
11. Bittner, *Novels of Waldo Frank*, p. 21.
12. Frank, *Memoirs*, pp. 7, 12.
13. Kloucek, "Waldo Frank," p. 16.
14. Ibid.
15. Bittner, *Novels of Waldo Frank*, pp. 20–21.
16. Frank, *Memoirs*, p. 15.
17. Kloucek, "Waldo Frank," p. 15.
18. Ibid.
19. Carter, *Waldo Frank*, p. 22.
20. Frank, *Memoirs*, p. 6.
21. Casey Nelson Blake, *Beloved Community: The Cultural Criticism of Randolph Bourne, Van Wyck Brooks, Waldo Frank & Lewis Mumford* (Chapel Hill and London: The University of North Carolina Press, 1990), p. 38. Blake sees this episode as well as the incidents of spiritual awakening that follow as evidence of Frank's feminine ideal (pp. 38–39). He writes: "Frank was very clear about the psychological connection between mystical consciousness and buried memories of maternal love" (p. 35).
22. Waldo Frank, *The Rediscovery of Man: A Memoir and a Methodology of Modern Life* (New York: George Braziller, 1958), p. 257.
23. Ibid., pp. 256–57.
24. Bittner, *Novels of Waldo Frank*, pp. 24–25.
25. Mumford, introduction to *Memoirs*, p. xix.

26. Frank, *Memoirs*, p. 8.

27. Kloucek, "Waldo Frank," p. 11.

28. Frank, *Memoirs*, pp. 6– 7.

29. Ibid., pp. 19–20.

30. Ibid., pp. 6–7.

31. Kloucek, "Waldo Frank," p. 16.

32. Frank, *Memoirs*, pp. 10–11, 18, 24–25. According to Bittner, Putnam's perhaps planned "to exploit Frank as a prodigy," and therefore his father pulled it from publication "as something Waldo might later regret" (p. 25).

33. Kloucek, "Waldo Frank," p. 538.

34. Frank, *Memoirs*, pp. 18, 21–22.

35. With his father's affair over and forgotten (at least by Julius Frank) by autumn of that same year, Frank confesses in his *Memoirs* that at that time he became aware of a love for his father that he hadn't known before. That does not mean, however, that the rebellion was over. Beyond his refusal to take the Shakespeare course, Frank seems to have continued the revolt well into his adulthood. In *Our America* (1919) he attacked the Society for Ethical Culture to which his father belonged. Julius Frank, for his part, had no comment on his son's criticism. Ibid., pp. 15, 22.

36. Carter, *Waldo Frank*, p. 23.

37. Frank, *Memoirs*, pp. 29–30, 34.

38. Bittner, *Novels of Waldo Frank*, p. 27.

39. Carter, *Waldo Frank*, p. 24.

40. Frank, *Memoirs*, pp. 46, 48, 49.

41. Kloucek, "Waldo Frank," p. 538.

42. Frank, *Memoirs*, p. 49, 58, 60.

43. Carter, *Waldo Frank*, p. 26.

44. Frank, *Memoirs*, p. 49.

45. Kloucek, "Waldo Frank," p. 538.

46. Bittner, *Novels of Waldo Frank*, pp. 31–32.

47. Kloucek, "Waldo Frank," p. 254.

48. Two recent works that explain this belief and show that it was a recurrent phenomenon with deep roots are: James H. Billington, *Fire in the Minds of Men: Origins of the Revolutionary Faith* (New York: Basic Books, Inc., 1980); and Melvin J. Lasky, *Utopia and Revolution: On the Origins of a Metaphor, or Some Illustrations of the Problem of Political Temperament and Intellectual Climate and How Ideas, Ideals and Ideologies Have Been Historically Related* (Chicago: The University of Chicago Press, 1976).

49. Frank, *Memoirs*, pp. 107–8.

50. Henry F. May, *The End of American Innocence: A Study of the First Years of Our Time, 1912–1917* (New York: Alfred A. Knopf, 1959), pp. ix, xiii.

51. Ibid., pp. 168–69.

52. Ibid., pp. 228–29.

53. Kloucek, "Waldo Frank," pp. 68–70. While Kloucek admits that Frank certainly must have been cognizant of Bergson's ideas and would have found support in the Frenchman for those concepts of his that coincided with the thought of Bergson, he only credits Bergson as an indirect influence. He notes that intuition and creativity are notions too easily attributed to Bergson who, in fact, did not originate them.

54. May, *End of American Innocence*, pp. 195, 206.

55. Ibid., pp. 207–8. It must be noted that "in his long and tortured search for

a new god to replace the old one, Nietzsche considered and rejected art as well as science" (p. 195).

56. Kloucek, "Waldo Frank," p. 128.

57. Carter, *Waldo Frank*, p. 26.

58. Kloucek, "Waldo Frank," pp. 128n, 131, 137.

59. Ibid., p. 128.

60. Waldo Frank, *Our America* (New York: Boni & Liveright, 1919), p. 232.

61. May, *End of American Innocence*, p. 243. For evidence that this fashionable Russophilia was not confined to America, see Martin Green, *Children of the Sun: A Narrative of "Decadence" in England after 1918* (New York: Basic Books, Inc., 1976), pp. 26–35 passim.

62. Bittner, *Novels of Waldo Frank*, pp. 23–24.

63. Kloucek, "Waldo Frank," p. 334–35.

64. May, *End of American Innocence*, pp. 197, 203.

65. Kloucek, "Waldo Frank," p. 342–43.

66. Ibid., p. 348.

67. May, *End of American Innocence*, p. 240. Howard Mumford Jones, on the other hand, writes that the poetry of "the French Symbolists enjoyed a new vogue," associated with the movement in literature known as the "New Spirit." See Howard Mumford Jones, *Guide to American Literature and Its Backgrounds Since 1890* (Cambridge: Harvard University Press, 1953), p. 125.

68. Kloucek, "Waldo Frank," pp. 338, 348–51.

69. May, *End of American Innocence*, p. 49.

70. Kloucek, "Waldo Frank," pp. 364–68.

71. Bittner, *Novels of Waldo Frank*, p. 23.

72. In November 1916, the first number of the magazine *Seven Arts* was issued. Its editor James Oppenheim believed that America "could be regenerated by art," and his conviction became the magazine's *raison d'être*. Oppenheim credits himself with having "had a definite idea as to how America was to become more human. It was the dream so many have had: a magazine, *the* magazine which should evoke and mobilize all our native talent, both creative and critical, give it freedom of expression and so scatter broadcast the new Americanism which would naturally have the response of America." See James Oppenheim, "The Story of the *Seven Arts*," *American Mercury* 20 (1930): 156.

The "call to arms" that appeared in that first number, stressing the importance of art to civilization, opened, however, with an expression of an even broader editorial faith. It began: "It is our faith and the faith of many that we are living in the first days of a renascent period, a time which means for America the coming of that national self-consciousness which is the beginning of greatness" (ibid., p. 157). According to Van Wyck Brooks, this "manifesto" was written by his fellow associate editor, Waldo Frank. Brooks recalls that Frank was the "real creator" of the magazine. See Van Wyck Brooks, *Days of the Phoenix: The Nineteen-Twenties I Remember* (New York: E. P. Dutton and Company, 1957), p. 17.

Actually, it seems that both Oppenheim and Frank had arrived at the idea for a magazine (such as the *Seven Arts* came to be) independently of each other. Frank recalls that he told Oppenheim upon first meeting him, "We need a magazine." When Oppenheim heard him speak, it was as if Frank were "answering a cue" (Frank, *Memoirs*, pp. 83–84). As for Brooks's contention, suffice it to say that Oppenheim and Frank were the cofounders of the magazine, although "Frank was to a large extent responsible for the form and direction of the magazine." See Frederick J. Hoffman, Charles Allen, and Carolyn F. Ulrich, *The Little Maga-*

zine: A History and a Bibliography (Princeton: Princeton University Press, 1947), p. 88.

73. Kloucek, "Waldo Frank," p. 333.

74. Alfred Kazin, *On Native Grounds: An Interpretation of Modern American Prose Literature* (New York: Reynal & Hitchcock, 1942), p. 172.

75. Daniel Aaron, *Writers on the Left: Episodes in American Literary Communism* (New York: Harcourt, Brace and World, 1961), p. 6.

76. John R. Willingham, "The Achievement of Waldo Frank," *Literary Review* 1 (Summer, 1958): 472.

77. Kloucek, "Waldo Frank," p. 332.

78. Willingham, "Achievement of Waldo Frank," pp. 476–77.

79. May, *End of American Innocence*, p. 237.

80. Kazin, *On Native Grounds*, p. 168.

81. Hoffman et al., *The Little Magazine*, p. 184.

82. Kloucek, "Waldo Frank," p. 330.

83. Paul Rosenfeld, *Men Seen: Twenty-Four Modern Authors* (New York: The Dial Press, 1925), pp. 89–91.

84. Hoffman et al., *The Little Magazine*, p. 89.

85. Frank, *Memoirs*, p. 201.

86. Christopher Lasch, *The New Radicalism in America, 1889–1963: The Intellectual as a Social Type* (New York: Alfred A. Knopf, 1965), p. 132.

87. Frederick J. Hoffman, *Freudianism and the Literary Mind* (Baton Rouge: Louisiana State University Press, 1945), pp. 47, 49. According to Hoffman, "The importance of translation cannot be overestimated. Brill's role, therefore, is significant."

88. May, *End of American Innocence*, p. 233.

89. Oppenheim, "Story of the *Seven Arts*," p. 157.

90. Gorham Munson, "The Fledgling Years, 1916–1924," *Sewanee Review* 40 (1932): 24–25.

91. Hoffman, *Freudianism*, pp. 52, 55–57.

92. May, *End of American Innocence*, p. 233.

93. Hoffman, *Freudianism*, pp. 2, 3, 28–30.

94. Ibid., pp. 30, 32.

95. Ibid., pp. 32–33.

96. May, *End of American Innocence*, pp. 232, 235.

97. Hoffman, *Freudianism*, p. 53.

98. Hoffman et al., *The Little Magazine*, p. 69.

99. Frank, *Memoirs*, p. 248n.

100. Hoffman, *Freudianism*, p. 256.

101. Kloucek, "Waldo Frank," p. 177.

102. Frank, *Memoirs*, pp. 200–201.

103. Waldo Frank, *America Hispana: A Portrait and a Prospect* (New York: Charles Scribner's Sons, 1931), p. 350.

104. Frank, *Memoirs*, p. 201.

105. Kloucek, "Waldo Frank," p. 182.

106. Hoffman, *Freudianism*, p. 255.

107. Frank, *Memoirs*, pp. 200–201, 203.

108. Ibid., p. 208.

109. Hoffman, *Freudianism*, p. 263.

110. E. L. Doctorow, *Ragtime* (New York: Random House, 1975; Bantam edition, 1976), pp. 165–75.

111. James Webb, *The Harmonious Circle: The Lives and Work of G. I. Gurd-jieff, P. D. Ouspensky, and Their Followers* (New York: G. P. Putnam's Sons, 1980), p. 501.

112. Ibid., p. 502.

113. Alfred Braunthal, *Salvation and the Perfect Society: The Eternal Quest* (Amherst: University of Massachusetts Press, 1979), p. 73.

114. Bruce F. Campbell, *Ancient Wisdom Revived: A History of the Theosophical Movement* (Berkeley and Los Angeles: University of California Press, 1980), p. 11.

115. Webb, *Harmonious Circle*, p. 524.

116. Braunthal, *Salvation*, pp. 88–89.

117. Campbell, *Ancient Wisdom Revived*, pp. 10, 11.

118. Webb, *Harmonious Circle*, p. 513.

119. Campbell, *Ancient Wisdom Revived*, pp. 9, 10, 12, 15.

120. Ibid., pp. 31, 36, 51.

121. Webb, *Harmonious Circle*, pp. 103, 109–12, 116, 121.

122. Ibid., pp. 92, 162, 266.

123. Bittner, *Novels of Waldo Frank*, pp. 25, 27, 31.

124. Kloucek, "Waldo Frank," p. 221.

125. Ibid., pp. 220–21.

126. Ibid., pp. 54–55.

127. Ibid., pp. 58, 66, 129. Frank began his study of Spinoza during the years 1913–14.

128. Ibid., pp. 73–74.

129. Ibid., pp. 125–26.

130. Frank, *In the American Jungle*, pp. 249–50.

131. Kloucek, "Waldo Frank," p. 127.

132. Bittner, *Novels of Waldo Frank*, p. 59.

133. Frank, *The Rediscovery of Man*, pp. 110, 336.

134. Kloucek, "Waldo Frank," pp. 226, 229, 235. Frank became associated with the Menorah Movement, a branch of Reform Judaism, which sought the meaning of Jewishness in order to adapt it to present circumstances. One of the Movement's leaders, Adolph Oko—a Spinoza scholar—was Frank's mentor on Jewish subjects. Oko accompanied Frank on his trip to Palestine in 1926, at which time they became intimate friends (p. 247).

135. Ibid., p. 234.

136. Bittner, *Novels of Waldo Frank*, p. 58.

137. Webb, *Harmonious Circle*, pp. 271–72.

138. Kloucek, "Waldo Frank," p. 225.

139. Webb, *Harmonious Circle*, pp. 276, 286, 302, 303.

140. To Gurdjieff's followers, this was simply plagiarism of the Master. Ibid., pp. 345–47.

141. Lasky, pp. 9, 17, 67. For the entire explanation of how utopian longing develops into revolutionary commitment, see Lasky, *Utopia and Revolution*, pp. 2–96.

142. Billington, *Fire in the Minds*, pp. 414–15.

143. Ibid., pp. 417, 436.

144. Ibid., p. 440.

145. Oppenheim, "Story of the *Seven Arts*," p. 157.

146. Aaron, *Writers on the Left*, p. 12.

147. Kazin, *On Native Grounds*, p. 167.

148. Aaron, *Writers on the Left*, p. 13.

149. Lasky, *Utopia and Revolution*, p. 152.

150. Ibid., p. 153.

151. Munson, "Fledgling Years," p. 24.

152. Mumford, introduction to *Memoirs*, p. xvii.

153. Bittner, *Novels of Waldo Frank*, p. 24.

154. Frank, *Memoirs*, pp. 142, 202.

155. Kloucek, "Waldo Frank," pp. 427, 430. John Reed should be identified. "A romantic poet from Oregon, correspondent for the radical *Masses*, and a sometime lover of Mabel Dodge, Reed was an enthusiast in search of a cause." He wrote "the most single influential account of the Bolshevik Revolution of 1917: *Ten Days That Shook the World*" (Billington, *Fire in the Minds*, p. 440). Reed was also interested in the Mexican Revolution of 1910 and wrote an account of that event (*Insurgent Mexico*). His interest could have helped turn Frank's attention to Latin America.

156. Frank, *Memoirs*, pp. 81–82. Ironically, in 1914 Frank almost enlisted to fight for France, due to the sentimental attachment he felt to that country. When Margaret Naumburg threatened to break off their relationship if he did, however, he acceded to her wishes (p. 78).

157. Carter, *Waldo Frank*, p. 31; Kloucek, "Waldo Frank," p. 539.

158. Carter, *Waldo Frank*, p. 38.

159. Kloucek, "Waldo Frank," p. 540.

160. For other examples of those who viewed communism in this light, see Vivian Gornick, *The Romance of American Communism* (New York: Basic Books, 1978).

161. Frank, *Memoirs*, pp. 184–85.

162. Kloucek, "Waldo Frank," p. 541.

163. Frank, *Memoirs*, pp. 181–82.

164. Kloucek, "Waldo Frank," p. 541.

165. Ibid. The friendship between Frank and Anderson began when on the advice of Edna Kenton, a member of the advisory board of the *Seven Arts*, Frank wrote Anderson and asked to see some of his stories. Anderson answered the request, after which Frank wrote a glowing article on Anderson's writing for the first issue of the magazine. Frank, *Memoirs*, p. 86. Their correspondence continued until February 1917 when Anderson visited New York, at which time the friendship was sealed. By the early 1920s, however, Frank's mysticism alienated Anderson, and their relationship was never the same. Kloucek, "Waldo Frank," pp. 268, 539.

166. Ibid., p. 541.

167. Carter, *Waldo Frank*, p. 17.

168. Aaron, *Writers on the Left*, pp. 2–4.

169. Ibid., p. 4.

170. Ibid., p. 5.

171. May, *End of American Innocence*, pp. 222–23.

172. Douglas L. Wilson, introduction to *The Genteel Tradition: Nine Essays by George Santayana* (Cambridge: Harvard University Press, 1967), pp. 4–6.

173. Ibid., p. 20. Wilson draws the parallels between the writings of Santayana and Brooks, pp. 20–23.

174. Richard H. Pells, *Radical Visions and American Dreams: Culture and Social Thought in the Depression Years* (New York: Harper & Row, 1973), p. 7.

175. Ibid., p. 8.

176. Van Wyck Brooks, *Scenes and Portraits: Memories of Childhood and Youth* (New York: E. P. Dutton & Company, Inc., 1954), pp. 242–43.

177. Paul Rosenfeld, *Port of New York: Essays on Fourteen American Moderns* (New York: Harcourt, Brace and Company, 1924), p. 49.

178. Frank, *Memoirs*, p. 217.

179. Hoffman et al., *The Little Magazine*, pp. 86–87.

180. Frank, *Memoirs*, p. 85.

181. Oppenheim, "Story of the *Seven Arts*," p. 157.

182. Frank, *Memoirs*, pp. 87–88.

183. Ibid., p. 95.

184. Hoffman et al., *The Little Magazine*, p. 92.

185. Alan Trachtenberg, preface to *Memoirs of Waldo Frank*, p. xiii.

186. Rosenfeld, *Port of New York*, p. 47.

187. Frank, *Memoirs*, p. 87.

188. Bittner, *Novels of Waldo Frank*, p. 57.

189. Brooks, *Days of the Phoenix*, p. 159.

190. Henri Baudet, *Paradise on Earth: Some Thoughts on European Images of Non-European Man*, trans. Elizabeth Wentholt (New Haven: Yale University Press, 1965), pp. 34–35.

191. Robert F. Berkhofer, *The White Man's Indian: Images of the American Indian from Columbus to the Present* (New York: Alfred A. Knopf, 1978), p. 72.

192. Hayden White, "The Forms of Wildness: Archaeology of an Idea," in *The Wild Man Within: An Image in Western Thought from the Renaissance to Romanticism*, ed. Edward Dudley and Maximilian E. Novak (Pittsburgh: University of Pittsburgh Press, 1972), p. 3.

193. Berkhofer, *White Man's Indian*, p. 178.

194. Fredrick B. Pike, "Dabbling in Psychohistory: A Look at United States-Spanish Mutual Images from the 1920s to the 1970s," *Red River Valley Historical Journal* 4 (Summer 1980): 383.

195. Peter L. Thorsley, Jr., "The Wild Man's Revenge," in *The Wild Man Within*, pp. 285–86.

196. Wilson J. Moses, *The Golden Age of Black Nationalism, 1850–1925* (Hamden, Conn.: The Shoe String Press, Inc., 1978), pp. 255–57, 262.

197. Frank, *Memoirs*, p. 104.

198. Carter, *Waldo Frank*, p. 54, 58.

199. Lasch, *New Redicalism*, pp. 130–31.

200. Ibid., p. 119.

201. Richard Aldington, introduction to *The Plumed Serpent*, by D. H. Lawrence (London: William Heinemann Ltd., 1955), pp. vii–viii. Between 1922 and 1924, Lawrence split his time between Taos and Mexico, experiencing what Aldington calls a "soul-adventure" (p. ix).

202. Hoffman, *Freudianism*, p. 169.

203. The paradox presented by the phrase "the search for a useable past" is similar to that presented by Baudet in his comparison of primitivism and utopianism. Howard Mumford Jones writes this explanation of the meaning of Brooks's phrase: "It was insufficient to find fault with the present state of American culture because of a supposedly bad tradition; it was necessary, paradoxically enough, to find a new tradition, or to reinterpret an old one so that it could lend support to the new valuations, hazy as these valuations might be." (*Guide to American Literature*, p. 174).

204. Brooks, *Days of the Phoenix*, p. 160.

205. Frank, *Our America*, p. 116.
206. Brooks, *Days of the Phoenix*, p. 28.

Chapter 2. The Anatomy of a Relationship: Waldo Frank and Spain

1. Waldo Frank, *Our America*, pp. 96–97, 107, 113.
2. Ibid., p. 115.
3. Waldo Frank, *Ustedes y nosotros: Nuevo mensaje a Ibero-América* (Buenos Aires: Editorial Losada, 1942), p. 205.
4. Jerome Kloucek, "Waldo Frank," p. 509.
5. William Bittner, *The Novels of Waldo Frank*, p. 115.
6. Waldo Frank, *Memoirs*, pp. 108–10.
7. Gerald Brenan, *The Spanish Labyrinth: An Account of the Social and Political Background of the Spanish Civil War* (Cambridge: Cambridge University Press, 1943; reprint ed., New York: The Syndics of the Cambridge University Press, 1976), p. 222.
8. Frank, *Memoirs*, pp. 111–12.
9. Gerald Brenan, *The Literature of the Spanish People: From Roman Times to the Present Day* (Cambridge: Cambridge University Press, 1951), p. 418.
10. Frank, *Memoirs*, p. 111.
11. Arnold Chapman, "Waldo Frank in the Hispanic World: The First Phase," *Hispania* 44 (December, 1961): 627.
12. Raymond Carr, *Spain 1808–1939* (Oxford: Oxford University Press, 1966), p. 529.
13. Brenan, *The Spanish Labyrinth*, p. 166.
14. Frank, *Memoirs*, pp. 110–11.
15. Ibid., pp. 122–23. Before he got around to doing so, however, other projects intervened. Firstly, he needed to complete two novels begun in 1920. Both *Rahab* and *City Block* were published in 1922. Secondly, in May of that same year, he celebrated the birth of his first child, his son Thomas. See Kloucek, "Waldo Frank," p. 539.
16. Ibid., pp. 111, 127.
17. Ibid., pp. 129–32.
18. Waldo Frank, *Virgin Spain: Scenes from the Spiritual Drama of a Great People* (London: Jonathan Cape, 1926), pp. 1–2.
19. Chapman, "Waldo Frank in the Hispanic World," pp. 630–33.
20. Arnold Chapman, "Waldo Frank in Spanish America: Between Journeys, 1924–1929," *Hispania* 47 (September, 1964): 511, 515.
21. If the publication of *Virgin Spain* was the high point of 1926, the low point had to be his divorce from Margaret Naumburg, made final that year. Frank admits that he undermined the marriage by shirking his responsibilities as a husband because he was more engrossed in his writing career. Frank, *Memoirs*, p. 140.
22. Frank, *Virgin Spain*, n.p.
23. Américo Castro, *The Spaniards: An Introduction to their History*, trans. Willard F. King and Selma Margaretten (Berkeley: University of California Press, 1971), p. 37.

24. Kloucek, "Waldo Frank," p. 172.

25. Frank, *Virgin Spain*, p. 2.

26. Kloucek, "Waldo Frank," pp. 373, 383.

27. Thomas Walsh, review of *Virgin Spain*, by Waldo Frank, *Commonweal* 4 (9 June 1926): 134.

28. Fredrick B. Pike, "Dabbling in Psychohistory," pp. 385–86.

29. Kloucek, "Waldo Frank," p. 514.

30. Frank, *Virgin Spain*, pp. 1–2.

31. Kloucek, "Waldo Frank," pp. 30, 35.

32. M. J. Benardete, "Spiritual Spain—A Synthesis," *Hispania* 10 (February 1927): 10.

33. Stanley T. Williams, *The Spanish Background of American Literature*, vol. 1 (New Haven: Yale University Press; London: Oxford University Press, 1955), p. 81.

34. Waldo Frank, *America Hispana*, p. ix.

35. Kloucek, "Waldo Frank," pp. 99–100.

36. John Dos Passos, "Spain on a Monument," *New Masses* 1 (July 1926): 27.

37. Kloucek, "Waldo Frank," p. 157.

38. Frank, *America Hispana*, p. ix.

39. Kloucek, "Waldo Frank," p. 158.

40. Ernest Hemingway, *Death in the Afternoon* (New York and London: Charles Scribner's Sons, 1932), pp. 52–53.

41. Carlos Baker, *Hemingway: The Writer as Artist* (Princeton: Princeton University Press, 1952), pp. 147, 150.

42. Williams, *Spanish Background*, pp. 81–82.

43. Benardete, "Spiritual Spain," pp. 3, 20.

44. Kloucek, "Waldo Frank," p. 269.

45. Frank, *Memoirs*, pp. 128–34. Cf. Benardete, "Spiritual Spain," pp. 17–18. He discerns that the reason for the dedication is Frank's belief that there can be no spiritual autonomy in the United States "unless we rhythm up harmoniously with South America."

46. Kloucek, "Waldo Frank," p. 87.

47. Frank, *Virgin Spain*, p. 9.

48. Fredrick B. Pike, *The Politics of the Miraculous in Peru: Haya de la Torre and the Spiritualist Tradition* (Lincoln and London: University of Nebraska Press, 1986), p. 90.

49. Hemingway, *Death in the Afternoon*, pp. 53–54.

50. Baker, *Hemingway*, p. 150.

51. Sacheverell Sitwell, "Virgin Spain," *Dial* 82 (January 1927): 64. Kloucek disregards Hemingway's criticism because "his invective with its anti-Semitic slant indicates a purpose other than critical" ("Waldo Frank," p. 512n). A reading of Hemingway's criticism, however, reveals no anti-Semitic slant whatsoever. Because Frank is Jewish, does poking fun at his writing constitute anti-Semitism? Or is it anti-Semitism when one criticizes another for an affectation of mysticism or for the use of Freudian psychology in writing? Kloucek no doubt is aware of Frank's earlier criticism of Hemingway's work; but even if Hemingway is merely returning in kind, that might mean that his criticism of Frank is personal, but not anti-Semitic. Perhaps Hemingway himself refutes Kloucek's argument in a letter he wrote to Edmund Wilson dated 10 September 1951. Wilson had wanted to print in his *The Shores of Light* (New York, 1952) three letters Hemingway had sent him in 1923–24. Hemingway gave his permission, but asked Wilson to change

"Jews" to "New York people" in a reference to Paul Rosenfeld and Waldo Frank, claiming that he "did not mean to give any derogatory or anti-Semitic meaning as it would be read today." See *Ernest Hemingway, Selected Letters 1917–1961*, ed. Carlos Baker (New York: Charles Scribner's Sons, 1981), pp. 732, 733n. Suffice it to say that Hemingway's criticism is the judgment of a writer with an established reputation as a stylist on another whose prose he found turgid.

As for Sitwell, Kloucek maintains that the Englishman simply did not understand or sympathize with Frank's purpose ("Waldo Frank," p. 384n). Sitwell, like Hemingway, is generally critical of Frank's writing style. He does label one chapter "admirable," however, and calls Frank a "writer of talent"—a talent, though, that must be developed.

52. Ernest Peixotto, "The Soul of Spain," *Saturday Review of Literature* 2 (17 April 1926): 720.

53. Benardete, "Spiritual Spain," p. 5.

54. Carter, *Waldo Frank*, p. 70.

55. Benardete, "Spiritual Spain," p. 7.

56. Ibid., p. 5.

57. Walsh, review of *Virgin Spain*, p. 134.

58. Muna Lee, "Speaking of Spain, Here Is Waldo Frank," *New York Times Book Review* (18 April 1926): 7.

59. Chapman, "Waldo Frank in Spanish America," p. 517.

60. Stanley G. Payne, *Spain & Portugal*, vol. 1 (Madison: The University of Wisconsin Press, 1973), pp. 26, 78.

61. Salvador de Madariaga, *Spain: A Modern History* (New York: Frederick A. Praeger, 1958; second printing, 1960), p. 18.

62. Ibid.

63. Castro, *The Spaniards*, pp. 3, 565.

64. Ibid., chap. 6, passim; pp. vii, 24–29. Payne, in rejecting Castro's contention that Spanish society absorbed the exotic psychology of Moslem and Jew directly, echoes Frank in allowing for an interaction of different racial psychologies that produced a "unique culture and psychology" (*Spain and Portugal*, I: 136).

65. Castro, chap. 3, in particular.

66. Sánchez Albornoz, in fact, views the Castile of the Reconquest "as the heir of classical antiquity and the Visigothic tradition." See Claudio Sánchez Albornoz, "The Continuing Tradition of Reconquest," in *From Reconquest to Empire: The Iberian Background to Latin American History*, ed. H. B. Johnson, Jr. (New York: Alfred A. Knopf, 1970), p. 46.

Another historian, John Ramsey, while not denying the stimulating nature of Castro's ideas, questions Castro's theories, saying their proof "seems to lie more in the realm of the subjective." See John Ramsey, *Spain: The Rise of the First World Power* (Birmingham: The University of Alabama Press, 1973), p. 50.

In Castro's defense is the late Professor Jaime Vicens Vives, the leader of sociological history in Spain, who after twenty years of study eventually endorsed Castro's method of interpreting Spanish history. See Castro, *The Spaniards*, p. 4.

67. As Benardete interprets, "Islam became Spanish"; only the creed remained ("Spiritual Spain," p. 7).

68. Ibid., p. 14.

69. Walsh, review of *Virgin Spain*, p. 134.

70. Carter, *Waldo Frank*, p. 70. Frank's interpretation of the nature of Islam is also a prominent part of this chapter, but it has already been designated as a

part of Frank's teleology. Thus it must be viewed primarily in that light rather than as something separate and original. For even if Frank's interpretation is original, his motivation is clear.

71. Lee, "Speaking of Spain," p. 7.

72. Sitwell, "Virgin Spain," p. 64.

73. It is in this section that Frank describes the racial makeup of the Spaniard, and the effect of Spain on Islam, both subjects that have already been discussed.

74. Frank, *Virgin Spain*, p. 57.

75. Laura Benét, "Spain through Magic Casements," *Literary Digest International Book Review* 4 (May 1926): 395.

76. Baker, *Hemingway*, p. 150.

77. Benardete, "Spiritual Spain," p. 7.

78. Frank, *Virgin Spain*, pp. 67–68.

79. Ibid., p. 77.

80. Dos Passos, "Spain on a Monument," p. 27.

81. Walsh, review of *Virgin Spain*, p. 135.

82. Kloucek, "Waldo Frank," p. 357. Frank's Don Juan, like Barrès's, is the legendary figure first presented by Tirso de Molina. Walsh believes Frank's interpretation of Don Juan is such because this Don Juan "presents the highly cultivated sex appeal so fetching to adolescent readers and book-buyers" (review of *Virgin Spain*, p. 135).

83. Kloucek points out the strong resemblance between Barrès and Frank: they both relate their adventures in the various locales they have visited, chronicling their feelings and explaining the significance of their adventures in terms of their personal interpretations of the native cultures; they both are concerned with the minds and hearts as well as the customs and traditions of the people they encounter so that they might better understand the minds of others ("Waldo Frank," p. 358). Kloucek admits that Frank might have modeled his own work after that of Barrès, but suggests that the parallels between the two are so obvious that Frank's debt to Barrès can be blown out of proportion. After all, Frank was familiar with the work of other French writers who had also found appeal in Barrès's approach and had tried to achieve the same goals ("Waldo Frank," p. 359).

84. Frank, *Virgin Spain*, p. 84.

85. Carter, *Waldo Frank*, p. 72; Baker, *Hemingway*, p. 150; Dos Passos, "Spain on a Monument," p. 27.

86. Benardete, "Spiritual Spain," p. 8.

87. Frank, *Virgin Spain*, p. 86.

88. Ibid., p. 97.

89. Ibid., p. 109.

90. Walsh, review of *Virgin Spain*, p. 135.

91. He states, "the Body of Catholic Europe was bone of Greek logic, flesh of Jewish faith and eye of Arab science" (Frank, *Virgin Spain*, p. 114). Castro, however, shows Spain to have been outside of that Catholic Europe (*The Spaniards*, pp. 517–33).

92. Frank, *Virgin Spain*, p. 119.

93. Ibid., p. 126.

94. Walsh, review of *Virgin Spain*, p. 135.

95. Castro, *The Spaniards*, pp. 9, 23, 52, 57–58, 73–74, 91, 165, 175, 203–4, 206, 213, 513, 518, 538–39, 545–46, 558, 565.

96. Kloucek, "Waldo Frank," p. 357.

97. Frank, *Virgin Spain*, p. 131.

98. Ibid., pp. 132, 134.

99. Benét, "Spain through Magic Casements," p. 395.

100. Benardete, "Spiritual Spain," p. 9.

101. Lee, "Speaking of Spain," p. 7.

102. Dos Passos, "Spain on a Monument," p. 27.

103. Frank, *Virgin Spain*, pp. 157–58.

104. Dos Passos, "Spain on a Monument," p. 27.

105. Ibid.; Sitwell, "Virgin Spain," p. 64; Benardete, "Spiritual Spain," p. 13.

106. Frank, *Memoirs*, p. 146.

107. Dos Passos, "Spain on a Monument," p. 27.

108. Benét, "Spain through Magic Casements," p. 395.

109. Benardete, "Spiritual Spain," p. 13.

110. Ernesto Montenegro, "Waldo Frank before the Riddle of Spain," *Literary Review of the New York Evening Post* (20 March 1926): 2.

111. Lee, "Speaking of Spain," p. 7.

112. Ibid.

113. Benét, "Spain through Magic Casements," p. 395.

114. Plato explained the whole sex drive in terms of an original hermaphrodite being that, because it was too powerful, too complete, had then been split in two by the Creator. Ever since then, there has operated the desire to reaccomplish wholeness—to become, as it were, the hermaphrodite.

115. Dos Passos, "Spain on a Monument," p. 27.

116. Baker, *Hemingway*, pp. 151–52. This Freudian symbolism is really very pre-Freudian. Freud himself picked up on Plato's idea of the hermaphrodite, and he used it to explain the sex drive.

117. Bittner, *Novels of Waldo Frank*, pp. 119–20.

118. Benardete, "Spiritual Spain," p. 15.

119. Dos Passos, "Spain on a Monument," p. 27.

120. Sitwell, "Virgin Spain," pp. 63–64.

121. Chapman, "Waldo Frank in Spanish America," p. 519.

122. Lee, "Speaking of Spain," p. 7.

123. Walsh, review of *Virgin Spain*, p. 135.

124. Bittner, *Novels of Waldo Frank*, p. 120. Bittner misses the real point.

125. For a good description of the situation in Catalonia during the period of Frank's visits to Spain, see Gerald Meaker, *The Revolutionary Left in Spain, 1914–1923* (Stanford: Stanford University Press, 1974). For a good survey of Basque pretensions, see Stanley G. Payne, *Basque Nationalism* (Reno: University of Nevada Press, 1975).

126. Benardete, "Spiritual Spain," p. 17.

127. Ibid.

128. Ibid.

129. Frank, *Virgin Spain*, p. 292.

130. Lee, "Speaking of Spain," p. 7.

131. Chapman, "Waldo Frank in Spanish America," p. 518.

132. Frank, *Virgin Spain*, pp. 1, 282. For a concise account of the moralism of Unamuno that Frank refers to, see John A. Mackay, *The Other Spanish Christ: A Study in the Spiritual History of Spain and South America* (New York: The Macmillan Company, 1932), pp. 146–56.

133. Also, in view of the rapport Frank had established with many leading literary figures, it is scarcely surprising that the book elicited a favorable response in Spain and Spanish America, in contrast with its reception in the United States.

Part of the credit must go to Léon-Felipe, a Spanish poet and admirer of Walt Whitman, who undertook the translation and provided Frank's Hispanic readers with "an unusually readable book." As Arnold Chapman points out, Léon-Felipe toned down many of Frank's emotional expressions about Spain, particularly those that might stir differences of opinion. The circle of readers for Frank and his skillful, diplomatic translator grew considerably when Ortega y Gasset's *Revista de Occidente* reprinted selections from the Spanish version. See Chapman, "Waldo Frank in Spanish America," pp. 516–18.

134. Consider the reaction of the Colombian Baldamiro Sanín Cano. While "lukewarm" to the book "because he is disappointed in Frank's pat explanations," he concedes its readability. Moreover, he credits Frank for desiring a rapprochement between the United States and Spanish America. See Chapman, "Waldo Frank in Spanish America," pp. 516–18.

135. For a concise discussion of this phenomenon, see Mackay, *The Other Spanish Christ*, pp. 177–88.

136. Waldo Frank, *The Death and Birth of David Markand: An American Story* (New York: Charles Scribner's Sons, 1934), pp. 324–25.

137. Bittner, *Novels of Waldo Frank*, p. 150.

138. Madariaga, *Spain*, p. 481.

139. Waldo Frank, "Viva España Libre!" *New Masses* 20 (18 August 1936): 12–13.

140. Bittner, *Novels of Waldo Frank*, p. 150.

141. Waldo Frank, *In the American Jungle*, pp. 265–69.

142. Waldo Frank, "The Artist: Minister of Freedom," *Radical Religion* 2 (Autumn 1937): 9–15.

143. Bittner, *Novels of Waldo Frank*, pp. 151–52.

144. Richard Pells, *Radical Visions and American Dreams*, p. 305; Bittner, *Novels of Waldo Frank*, p. 153.

145. Waldo Frank, "Spain in War: The People," *The New Republic* 95 (13 July 1938): 269–72.

146. Waldo Frank, "Spain in War: Parties and Leaders," *The New Republic* 95 (20 July 1938): 298–301. That Frank's appraisal of the Soviet Union's desires for Spain was at least wrong has been shown in Burnett Bolloten, *The Spanish Revolution: The Left and the Struggle for Power during the Civil War* (Chapel Hill: The University of North Carolina Press, 1979). He presents evidence that "men and methods used to convert . . . countries into Kremlin satellites were tested in Spain" (p. 295).

147. Waldo Frank, "Spain in War: The Meaning of Spain," *The New Republic* 95 (27 July 1938): 325–27.

148. Bittner, *Novels of Waldo Frank*, p. 120. According to Kloucek, Aguilar of Madrid published an edition of *Virgin Spain* in 1950; while it included Alfonso Reyes's introduction to the revised edition, its text was that of the first edition. Thus, the chapter on the Spanish Civil War was omitted from this book ("Waldo Frank," p. 511).

149. Alfonso Reyes, introduction to *Virgin Spain: The Drama of a Great People*, by Waldo Frank (New York: Duell, Sloan and Pearce, 1942), pp. ix–xxiv.

150. Frank, *Virgin Spain*, rev. ed., pp. xxv–xxvi.

151. Ibid., pp. 301–5.

152. Ibid., pp. 306–7.

153. Ibid., pp. 308–10.

154. Ibid., pp. 311–14.

155. M. J. Benardete, "The Genius of Spain," *Nation* 154 (16 May 1942): 577–78.

156. Selden Rose, "The Personality of Spain," *Yale Review* (Autumn 1942): 195–97. The review in the *New York Times* merely describes the book's content, rendering no judgment. See E. L. Tinker, "New Editions, Fine and Otherwise," *New York Times*, 13 September 1942.

Chapter 3. From Courtship to Marriage: Waldo Frank and Latin America, 1919–1931

1. Arnold Chapman, "Waldo Frank in the Hispanic World," p. 626.
2. Van Wyck Brooks, *Days of the Phoenix*, pp. 27–28.
3. Robert Spiller et al., *Literary History of the United States*, vol. 2 (New York: Macmillan Company, 1948), p. 1387.
4. Chapman, "Waldo Frank in the Hispanic World," p. 626.
5. Chapman, "Waldo Frank in Spanish America," pp. 512–13. Chapman also points out the familiarity that Frank's attitude, as well as the title of his book, held for Latin Americans. He develops a comparison that Tablada makes between *Our America* and *Nuestra America* (1903), by the Argentinian Carlos Octavio Bunge. Besides both books having identical titles, and, in Tablada's judgment, being similar in approach, Chapman finds their moods "lyrical, and not impassive; impressionistic and not erudite." Furthermore, he traces the phrase "Our America" back to 1883 and José Martí, who used it then to express the hope that North American journalists were "showing new respect" for Latin America. Martí would later use it in other frames of reference. Chapman concludes that the words were "proud ones" even before Frank used them to acknowledge "that there is another real America."
6. Chapman, "Waldo Frank in Spanish America," p. 513. Undoubtedly, it was as a kindred spirit that Frank was welcomed by Palacios to Argentina when the American arrived in Buenos Aires in 1929.
7. Ibid., p. 514.
8. M. J. Benardete, ed., *Waldo Frank in America Hispana* (New York: Instituto de las Españas, 1930), p. 66.
9. Chapman, "Waldo Frank in Spanish America," p. 514. Chapman also points out the "family resemblance" of Mariátegui's most important work, *Siete ensayos de interpretación de la realidad peruana* (1928), to *Our America*. Of Mariátegui and his book, Jorge Basadre writes: "He linked history to the drama of the present and the imponderables of the future. He pointed out problems that, unsolved in the past, still weigh on present generations, along with other problems that have appeared in the latter's time. He drew attention to lacerating and pathetic realities that many did not or would not see." See Jorge Basadre, introduction to *Seven Interpretive Essays on Peruvian Reality*, by José Carlos Mariátegui, trans. Marjory Urquidi (Austin: University of Texas Press, 1971), p. xxxii. Indeed, what Basadre writes about Mariátegui might well be applied to Waldo Frank and *Our America*.

For more information concerning the life and times of Mariátegui, see Jesús Chavarría, *José Carlos Mariátegui and the Rise of Modern Peru, 1890–1930* (Albuquerque: University of New Mexico Press, 1979).

10. Frank, *Memoirs*, pp. 122–23.

11. Ibid.

12. Chapman, "Waldo Frank in Spanish America," p. 514.

13. Chapman, "Waldo Frank in the Hispanic World," p. 632.

14. Alfonso Reyes, introduction to *Virgin Spain*, rev. ed., by Waldo Frank, pp. x–xii.

15. Chapman, "Waldo Frank in Spanish America," pp. 514–15.

16. Waldo Frank, "Mensaje de Waldo Frank a los escritores mexicanos," *Repertorio Americano* 8 (4 agosto 1924): 305–6.

17. Chapman, "Waldo Frank in Spanish America," p. 514.

18. Chapman, "Waldo Frank in the Hispanic World," p. 632.

19. Chapman, "Waldo Frank in Spanish America," pp. 515–16. Araquistaín called the book a work of art, a historic-dramatic poem. Even though objecting to some of Frank's ideas, he turned his essay into a favorable appraisal of Frank the artist. Sanín Cano's review was dealt with in chapter 2.

20. Chapman, "Waldo Frank in Spanish America," pp. 516–18. Torre's particular emphasis is on Frank's "newness" and avant-gardism.

21. Ibid., p. 518. Frank's comprehension is attributed to his "being a Jew returning as it were to the old home."

One review—that of Xavier Villarrutia, writing for *Contemporáneos* of Mexico—is wholly negative in its appraisal of Frank's work. But Chapman contends that the *Contemporáneos* group suspected "anything resembling nineteenth-century rococo or bourgeois pretentiousness"; therefore, such comment could have been anticipated (p. 519).

22. John Unterecker, *Voyager, a Life of Hart Crane* (New York: Farrar, Straus, and Giroux, 1969), pp. 437–38.

23. Waldo Frank, "Habana of the Cubans," *New Republic* 47 (23 June 1926): 140–41.

24. Chapman, "Waldo Frank in Spanish America," pp. 519–20.

25. Frank, *Memoirs*, p. 134.

26. Waldo Frank, *The Re-discovery of America: An Introduction to a Philosophy of American Life* (New York and London: Charles Scribner's Sons, 1929), pp. 268–70.

Chapman also suggests that the appeal of this book to Latin Americans could be credited to Frank's speaking "much the same accents" as José Enrique Rodó, who preached the doctrine of *arielismo* (from Rodó's 1900 essay *Ariel*, "considered the Magna Charta [*sic*] of South American idealism"; see John A. Mackay, *The Other Spanish Christ*, p. 171). Both men "lamented the specialization which breaks man into jarring splinters" and concerned themselves with "spiritual elevation." Chapman, "Waldo Frank in the Hispanic World," p. 633.

27. William Bittner, *The Novels of Waldo Frank*, p. 124.

28. Chapman, "Waldo Frank in Spanish America," pp. 520–21. The interchange between Frank and Espinoza began in 1924 when the Argentine writer mailed Frank a volume of his own short stories, *La levita gris*. Frank responded by requesting permission to translate one of the stories. Espinoza, of course, consented; and then embarked on a campaign to spread Frank's work throughout Spanish America, and to get Frank to visit the continent.

29. Ibid.

30. Benardete, *Waldo Frank in America Hispana*, p. 3.

31. Spiller et al., *Literary History of the United States*, vol. 2, p. 1387.

32. Reyes, introduction to *Virgin Spain*, rev. ed., by Waldo Frank, pp. x, xiv.

33. Frank, *Memoirs*, p. 157.

34. Ibid., pp. 157–61.

35. Ibid., pp. 63–64.

36. Doris Meyer, *Victoria Ocampo: Against the Wind and the Tide* (New York: George Braziller, 1979), pp. 105–7.

37. Frank, *Memoirs*, pp. 170–71.

38. Meyer, *Victoria Ocampo*, p. 105.

39. Benardete, *Waldo Frank in America Hispana*, pp. 30–31.

40. Frank, *Memoirs*, pp. 168–70. Frank recalls that as the plane increased its altitude he forgot to attach his oxygen tube, and the thin air gave him a feeling of euphoria. Rising to the height of Mount Aconcagua, he spied a condor in the distance and remembered having read about one of those birds getting caught in a plane's propeller, causing the craft to crash. And yet, although he knew that even a safe landing in those mountains would mean death, he was unafraid. His consciousness had become as elevated as he and the plane. He felt his oneness with all things. To him, this was a mystical revelation, the kind that he knew must be revealed in the way man lives (p. 170).

41. Ibid., pp. 171–72.

42. Ibid., p. 171.

43. Chavarría, *Mariátegui*, pp. 165, 177.

44. Frank, *Memoirs*, p. 172.

45. Ibid., p. 167.

46. Meyer, *Victoria Ocampo*, p. 105.

47. Benardete, *Waldo Frank in America Hispana*, pp. 41, 53, 141. The reaction of the public of Buenos Aires was noticed as far away as Spain. In *A.B.C* of Madrid, José Maria Salverría writes that "the applause for Waldo Frank has gone the limit." See Frank, *Memoirs*, p. 166.

48. Benardete, *Waldo Frank in America Hispana*, p. 71.

49. Ibid., p. 48.

50. Francisco Dura, "Waldo Frank, restaurador y profeta," *Criterio* 6 (21 noviembre 1929): 371–73.

51. Kloucek, "Waldo Frank," p. 506.

52. Chapman, "Waldo Frank in the Hispanic World," p. 626.

53. Kloucek, "Waldo Frank," p. 506.

54. Chapman, "Waldo Frank in the Hispanic World," p. 626.

55. Kloucek, "Waldo Frank," p. 506.

56. Benardete, *Waldo Frank in America Hispana*, p. 1.

57. Van Wyck Brooks, *Autobiography* (New York: E. P. Dutton & Company, Inc., 1965), p. 565.

58. Chapman, "Waldo Frank in Spanish America," p. 514.

59. Chapman, "Waldo Frank in the Hispanic World," p. 632.

60. Benardete, *Waldo Frank in America Hispana*, p. 111.

61. Ibid., pp. 7–8, 11.

62. Kloucek, "Waldo Frank," p. 506.

63. Benardete, *Waldo Frank in America Hispana*, p. 16.

64. Mackay, *The Other Spanish Christ*, p. 188.

65. Frank, *Memoirs*, p. 168.

66. Fredrick B. Pike, "Visions of Rebirth: The Spiritualist Facet of Peru's Haya de la Torre," paper presented at the Louisville meeting of the Southern Historical Association, Louisville, Ky., 12 November 1981.

67. Chapman, "Waldo Frank in Spanish America," pp. 514, 521.

68. Mackay, *The Other Spanish Christ*, p. 190.

69. Frank, *In the American Jungle*, pp. 256–60.

70. Waldo Frank, foreword to *Tales from the Argentine*, ed. Waldo Frank, trans. Anita Brenner (New York: Farrar & Rinehart, 1930), p. xi.

71. Chapman, "Waldo Frank in Spanish America," p. 520.

72. Surprisingly, the book did not contain one of Espinoza's stories.

73. Frank, *Memoirs*, p. 167.

74. Chapman, "Waldo Frank in Spanish America," p. 520.

75. Frank, foreword to *Tales from the Argentine*, p. 179.

76. Waldo Frank, "What is Hispano-America to Us?" *Scribner's* 87 (June 1930): 579–86.

77. Waldo Frank, "Contemporary Spanish American Literature," *Publisher's Weekly* 118 (18 October 1930): 1841–43.

78. Meyer, *Victoria Ocampo*, pp. 112–14.

79. Basadre, introduction to *Seven Essays*, p. ix.

80. Bittner, *Novels of Waldo Frank*, p. 125.

81. See the analysis of *Virgin Spain* in chapter 2.

82. Waldo Frank, *America Hispana*, p. ix.

83. Ibid., pp. ix–xi. Frank also lists his most important sources. The books are the following: the correspondence of Simón Bolívar, edited by Rufino Blanco-Fombona, the Venezuelan novelist; the life of José San Martín by Bartolomé Mitre; the works on the Panama Canal by the Colombians Nieto Caballero and A. Rebollado, Howard C. Hill's *Roosevelt and the Caribbean*, Norman Thomson's *Colombia and the United States*, and Leander T. Chamberlain's *A Chapter of National Dishonor*; and the works of leading French, American, and British archaeologists on the Indian cultures. Of periodicals, there are: *El Repertorio Americano* (Costa Rica), *Nosotros*, *La Vida Literaria*, *Criterio*, and *Síntesis* (Buenos Aires), *Indice* (Santiago, Chile), *Indice* (Puerto Rico), *Contemporáneos* (Mexico), *Amauta*, *El Mercurio del Peru*, and *La Nueva Revista Peruana* (Lima), and *La Revista de Avance* (Havana). The books conveyed information, while the periodicals helped Frank maintain contact with the spirituality of the Hispanic world. Characteristically, though, Frank claims he has been helped more by his friendships and journeys. Nonetheless, he includes a pretentious bibliography at the end of the book that contains mention of 179 Latin American authors whose work or works he read (*America Hispana*, pp. xi–xii; 373–80).

84. Frank, *America Hispana*, pp. xiii–xiv.

85. Waldo Frank, "Rediscovering a Nation That Once Was Great," *Travel* 46 (January 1926): 24–25.

86. Jaime Cortesão, "The Portuguese Imprint Upon Brazil," in *From Reconquest to Empire*, p. 212. Frank and Cortesão are also in agreement on the premise that Portugal's "will to separateness" was geographically determined. They part company, however, over the birth of the Portuguese nation. Frank finds Portugal's nationhood a tragedy. As he sees it, though the Spanish element "ruled in Portugal more deeply than an alliance of kings," . . . "it must be denied—though it lived in her own heart." Thus, "in denying her true spirit, Portugal indeed stifled it, so that it festers there" (Frank, "Rediscovering a Nation That Once Was Great," pp. 25–26).

Cortesão sees it differently. Believing that "the living lineage of a people sinks its roots into the soil from which they are born," he concludes that "it was from the close interpenetration of the sea and the land that the Portuguese came to be born with their characteristic way of life, their national character, their language, their religious sensibility, and—as the supreme product of their native spirit— their artistic expression" (p. 263).

Cortesão's attitude might be attributed to nationalism. But what about Frank's? To the American's Hispanophilia can be added the fact that Frank sees Portugal's "partnering" with England against Spain, and her adapting and practicing "what England stood for, the culture of Western Europe and the culture of France" as causing her to lose a profound part of the Hispanic character. See Frank, "Rediscovering a Nation That Once Was Great," p. 26; Frank, *Memoirs*, p. 110.

87. Frank, *America Hispana*, pp. 3–22.

88. Ferner Nuhn, review of *America Hispana*, by Waldo Frank, *Nation*, 30 September 1931, p. 337.

89. One of those "connoisseurs of the Southwest" who has contended for a long time that the Indian and mestizo cultures have not been duly appreciated. See ibid., p. 337.

90. Mary Austin, review of *America Hispana*, by Waldo Frank, *Books* (*New York Herald Tribune*), 20 September 1931, p. 1.

91. Frank, *America Hispana*, p. 20.

92. Austin, review of *America Hispana*, p. 1.

93. Gardner Harding, review of *America Hispana*, by Waldo Frank, *New York Times Book Review*, 18 October 1931, p. 1.

94. Frank, *America Hispana*, pp. 27–33.

95. Austin, review of *America Hispana*, p. 1. In his acknowledgments Frank credits the top American, French, and British archaeologists as his main sources on the Indian cultures, but his conclusions are based on what he has intuited from his firsthand experience. In seeming answer to this, Austin points out that Frank's analysis of the Indians' mind and political organization is "much too sound and authentic to have leaped out of the earth at him, as his writing of it seems to indicate."

96. Frank, *America Hispana*, pp. 34–47.

97. Harding, review of *America Hispana*, p. 1. William Hickling Prescott, author of *The Conquest of Peru*, also wrote *The Conquest of Mexico*. Frank calls Prescott his "great predecessor" to whom he gives "homage" in the acknowledgments.

98. Frank, *America Hispana*, pp. 48–57.

99. Ibid., pp. 58–61.

100. Ibid., pp. 62–69.

101. Harding, review of *America Hispana*, p. 1.

102. Ernest Gruening, review of *America Hispana*, by Waldo Frank, *Saturday Review of Literature*, 3 October 1931, p. 165.

103. Austin, review of *America Hispana*, p. 2.

104. Frank, *America Hispana*, pp. 70–78.

105. Ibid., pp. 79–83.

106. Ibid., pp. 87–88.

107. Ibid., pp. 88–89.

108. Ibid., pp. 90–95.

109. Ibid., pp. 96–101.

110. Ibid., pp. 102–8.

111. Review of *America Hispana*, by Waldo Frank, *Review of Reviews*, November 1931, p. 8.

112. Frank, *America Hispana*, pp. 109–18.

113. Ibid., pp. 119–21.

114. Ibid., pp. 122–25.
115. Ibid., pp. 125–28.
116. Ibid., pp. 131–35.
117. Harding, review of *America Hispana*, p. 17.
118. *Review of Reviews*, p. 8.
119. Carter, *Waldo Frank*, p. 95.
120. Frank, *America Hispana*, pp. 136–40.
121. Carter, *Waldo Frank*, p. 95.
122. Frank, *America Hispana*, pp. 141–54.
123. Ibid., pp. 154–58.
124. Ibid., pp. 159–65.
125. Ibid., pp. 166–71. Frank even tells of an interview Leguía had with Mariátegui; then he adds a footnote to the effect that intimates of Mariátegui deny any such interview ever took place. Frank reveals that he left it in anyway because it "is truth, *virtually*."
126. Ibid.
127. Ibid., pp. 172–77.
128. See Frank, *In the American Jungle*, pp. 248–52.
129. Cf. Basadre, introduction to *Seven Essays*, p. xxix. He writes: "Mariátegui was not basically in disagreement with the leaders of the Communist International; the nature of his objections was tactical, immediate, and incidental."

Mackay perhaps more rightly interprets Mariátegui's communism in terms of the Peruvian's belief "that the true present-day equivalent of the dynamic religions of humanity, which in their time exercised a great influence upon mankind, is revolutionary socialism" (p. 192). Thus Mackay closely follows Frank.

130. Frank, *America Hispana*, pp. 181–82.
131. Gruening, review of *America Hispana*, p. 165.
132. Frank, *America Hispana*, pp. 181–82.
133. Ibid., pp. 183–93.
134. Gruening, review of *America Hispana*, p. 165.
135. Kloucek, "Waldo Frank," p. 522.
136. *Review of Reviews*, p. 8.
137. Frank, *America Hispana*, p. 193.
138. Ibid., pp. 194–97.
139. Ibid., pp. 198–200.
140. Harding, review of *America Hispana*, p. 17.
141. Frank, *America Hispana*, p. xiv.
142. Ibid., pp. 203–10.
143. Ibid., pp. 210–17.
144. Ibid., pp. 217–26.
145. Nuhn, review of *America Hispana*, p. 337.
146. Frederick Bliss Luquiens, review of *America Hispana*, by Waldo Frank, *Yale Review*, Winter 1932, p. 408.
147. Frank, *America Hispana*, p. 227.
148. Ibid., p. 228.
149. Ibid., p. 230.
150. Gruening, review of *America Hispana*, p. 165.
151. Frank, *America Hispana*, pp. 233–55.
152. Ibid., pp. 255–58.
153. Ibid., pp. 258–59.
154. Ibid., pp. 260–70.

155. Ibid., pp. 272–78.
156. Ibid., pp. 279–82.
157. Amy Blanche Greene, review of *America Hispana*, by Waldo Frank, *World Tomorrow*, November 1931, p. 371.
158. Harding, review of *America Hispana*, p. 17.
159. Frank, *America Hispana*, pp. 185–94.
160. Kloucek, "Waldo Frank," p. 524.
161. Gruening, review of *America Hispana*, p. 165.
162. Frank, *America Hispana*, pp. 309–12.
163. Ibid., pp. 312–16.
164. Ibid., p. 317.
165. Ibid., pp. 318–26.
166. Ibid., pp. 326–31.
167. Ibid., pp. 333–36.
168. Ibid., pp. 336–41.
169. Ibid., pp. 342–48.
170. Ibid., p. 360.
171. Nuhn, review of *America Hispana*, pp. 337.
172. Frank, *America Hispana*, pp. 358–60.
173. Nuhn, review of *America Hispana*, p. 337.
174. Frank, *America Hispana*, pp. 361–67.
175. Ibid., pp. 368–71.
176. Harding, review of *America Hispana*, p. 17.
177. Nuhn, review of *America Hispana*, p. 337.
178. Carter, *Waldo Frank*, p. 97.

Chapter 4. Keeping the Faith: Waldo Frank and Latin America, 1932–1943

1. Paul Carter, *Waldo Frank*, p. 102.
2. Waldo Frank, introduction to *Don Segundo Sombra: Shadows on the Pampas*, by Ricardo Güiraldes, trans. Harriet de Onís (New York: Farrar & Rinehart, 1935), pp. x–xiii.
3. Carter, *Waldo Frank*, pp. 102–3.
4. Waldo Frank, *South American Journey* (New York: Duell, Sloan and Pearce, 1943), p. 110.
5. Carter, *Waldo Frank*, p. 103.
6. Ibid., p. 109.
7. Ibid., p. 114.
8. Frank, *South American Journey*, p. 102.
9. Daniel Aaron, *Writers on the Left*, p. 193.
10. Frank, *Memoirs*, p. 192.
11. Ibid., p. 193.
12. Frank, "The Artist: Minister of Freedom," p. 12.
13. Aaron, *Writers on the Left*, p. 305.
14. Frank, *Memoirs*, p. 194.
15. Ibid., p. 190.
16. Waldo Frank, "El proceso de Trotsky," *Repertorio Americano* (4 mayo 1937): 365–66.

17. Waldo Frank, "Waldo Frank rectifica," *Repertorio Americano* (16 julio 1937): 52–53.

18. Carter, *Waldo Frank*, pp. 115–16.

19. Waldo Frank, "Prólogo a la nueva edición de *América Hispana*," in *America Hispana: Un retrato y una perspectiva*, trad. León Felipe (Santiago de Chile: Ediciónes Ercilla, 1937), pp. ix–xvi.

20. Frank, *Memoirs*, p. 195.

21. Carter, *Waldo Frank*, p. 125.

22. Frank, *Memoirs*, p. 194.

23. Waldo Frank, "Mexico Today: The Heart of the Revolution," *Nation* 149 (5 August 1939): 140–41.

24. Ibid., pp. 141–42.

25. Ibid., pp. 142–44.

26. Waldo Frank, "Mexico Today: President Cárdenas and His People," *Nation* 149 (12 August 1939): 171–73.

27. Waldo Frank, "Mexico Today: Danger on the Right," *Nation* 149 (9 September 1939): 265–69.

28. Waldo Frank, "Mexico Today: The Deepest Danger," *Nation* 149 (16 September 1939): 288–90.

29. Waldo Frank, "Cárdenas of Mexico," *Foreign Affairs* 18 (October 1939): 91–101.

30. Quoted from a typescript carbon copy (in Frank's private papers) of the original English version of "Prólogo," *Los perros de abajo (Bottom Dogs)*, por Edward Dahlberg, trad. de E. Elizalde M. C. (Santiago de Chile: Ediciónes Ercilla, 1940), pp. [9]–12. Cited by Jerome Kloucek, "Waldo Frank," p. 389.

31. Carter, *Waldo Frank*, p. 125.

32. Waldo Frank, "Saludo a *Sur* en su cumpleaños," *Sur* 10 (diciembre 1940): 7.

33. Carter, *Waldo Frank*, p. 126.

34. Frank, "Saludo a *Sur*," pp. 7–10.

35. Waldo Frank, "La pintura contemporánea norteamericano," *Nación (Buenos Aires)* (13 julio 1941): 1, 4.

36. Waldo Frank, "The Hispano-American's World," *Nation* 152 (24 May 1941): 615–18.

37. Carter, *Waldo Frank*, p. 132.

38. William Bittner, *Novels of Waldo Frank*, pp. 176–77.

39. Waldo Frank, "La guerra simple y la guerra profunda: Prefacio a la edición castellana," in *Rumbos para América (Nuestra misión en nuevo mundo)*, trad. de María Zambrano, Luis Orsetti y José Basiglio Agosti (Buenos Aires: Editorial Americalee, 1942), pp. 15–21.

40. Ibid., pp. 22–25.

41. Waldo Frank, "The Two American Half-Worlds," *Common Ground* 2 (Spring 1942): 63–70.

42. M. J. Benardete, review of *Virgin Spain: The Drama of a Great People*, by Waldo Frank, *Nation*, 16 May 1942, p. 577.

43. Carter, *Waldo Frank*, p. 132.

44. Waldo Frank, *Ustedes y nosotros*, pp. 19–43.

45. Richard Pells, *Radical Visions and American Dreams*, pp. 210–13.

46. Waldo Frank, *Ustedes y nosotros*, pp. 47–72.

47. Ibid., pp. 75–104.

48. Ibid., pp. 107–35.

49. Ibid., pp. 139–67.

50. Ibid., pp. 171–97.

51. Ibid., pp. 201–13.

52. Ibid., p. 214.

53. Doris Meyer, *Victoria Ocampo*, p. 141.

54. Carter, *Waldo Frank*, p. 132.

55. Bittner, *Novels of Waldo Frank*, p. 177.

56. Ibid.

57. Waldo Frank, "Argentina—Unwilling Enemy," *Collier's* 110 (26 September 1942): 67–68.

58. Bittner, *Novels of Waldo Frank*, p. 177.

59. Characteristically, Frank promoted his newly published work with an article, "Why Good Neighbors?" Appearing in the 28 May issue of New York's *PM* magazine, the piece warns of the danger present in the Good Neighbor policy: it doesn't "go deep enough." Characterizing the Yankee attitude toward Latin America with words like "condescension" and "ignorance," Frank sees the day when the United States will be fighting those very "anti-democratic forces" that it has blindly supported; and he calls for a deepening of our knowledge of our southern neighbors. Furthermore, he suggests implementing goodwill with fundamental economic assistance. Then, characterizing Latin Americans as having a passionate belief in democracy, he claims that they are our allies in "the Deep War for democracy" that will continue beyond Hitler's defeat. Our duty, he says, is to learn from them "those basic personal values without which democracy goes hideously astray," for then, they will truly be "good neighbors." He warns that in the future we will "need them." Meantime the editors of the magazine helped promote *South American Journey* by citing it in a short preface to the article. Significantly, the preface even mentions the attack, thus keeping the incident alive ten months after the fact. See Waldo Frank, "Why Good Neighbors?" *PM (New York)* (28 May 1943): 2.

60. Carter, *Waldo Frank*, p. 133.

61. Bittner, *Novels of Waldo Frank*, p. 178.

62. The list also lends itself to a criticism that extends to the entire book. With incorrect spellings like "Bello Horizonte," "Tucamán," and "Comodore Rivadavia," Frank opens himself to charges of carelessness. See Lincoln Kirstein, review of *South American Journey*, by Waldo Frank, *New Republic*, 28 June 1943, p. 866.

63. Frank, *South American Journey*, p. v. Compare this to Frank's earlier depiction of "democratism" in *America Hispana*, pp. 318–19, 323–26, 331–33.

64. Kirstein, review of *South American Journey*, p. 866.

65. John T. Frederick, review of *South American Journey*, by Waldo Frank, *Chicago Sun Book Week*, 8 August 1943.

66. Frank, *South American Journey*, pp. 3–6.

67. Ralph Bates, review of *South American Journey*, by Waldo Frank, *Nation*, 19 June 1943, p. 870.

68. Frank, *South American Journey*, pp. 7–16.

69. Ibid., pp. 20–22.

70. Kirstein, review of *South American Journey*, p. 866.

71. Frank, *South American Journey*, pp. 23–42.

72. Ibid., pp. 42–44.

73. Ibid., pp. 45–46.

74. Kirstein, review of *South American Journey*, p. 866.

75. Frank, *South American Journey*, pp. 47–57.

76. Bates, review of *South American Journey*, p. 870.

77. It seems that Ifigenia was not the only woman with whom Waldo Frank sought a symbolic union. He confesses in his *Memoirs* that his second marriage was to him an allegory, with his wife Alma Magoon representing Anglo-America's acceptance of the Jew (Frank, *Memoirs*, p. 206). This marriage was over long before August of 1943 (some three months after the publication of *South American Journey*), when Frank and Alma Magoon were divorced in Reno; that same month he married his third wife, Jean Klempner, who had been his secretary throughout the book's composition (Carter, *Waldo Frank*, p. 135).

78. Richard Slotkin, *Regeneration Through Violence: The Mythology of the American Frontier, 1600–1860* (Middletown, Conn.: Wesleyan University Press, 1973), p. 343.

79. Frank, *South American Journey*, pp. 58–60.

80. See Jacques Lafaye, *Quetzlcoatl et Guadalupe: La formation de la conscience nationale au mexique (1531–1813)*, Pref. d'Octavio Paz (Paris: Gallimard, 1974).

81. Julia Sabine, review of *South American Journey*, by Waldo Frank, *Library Journal*, 15 May 1943, p. 428.

82. Frank, *South American Journey*, pp. 63–73.

83. Ibid., p. 80.

84. Lewis Gannett, review of *South American Journey*, by Waldo Frank, *New York Herald Tribune "Books and Things,"* 20 May 1943.

85. Hubert Herring, review of *South American Journey*, by Waldo Frank, *Yale Review*, Autumn 1943, p. 151.

86. Frank, *South American Journey*, pp. 100–110.

87. Lewis Mumford, review of *South American Journey*, by Waldo Frank, *New York Times*, 23 May 1943.

88. Frank, *South American Journey*, p. 103.

89. Ibid., pp. 111–29.

90. Kirstein, review of *South American Journey*, p. 866.

91. Frank, *South American Journey*, pp. 130–41.

92. Ibid., pp. 145–50.

93. Ibid., pp. 150–61.

94. Mumford, review of *South American Journey*, p. 5.

95. Frank, *South American Journey*, p. 168.

96. Ibid., pp. 172–74.

97. Ibid., pp. 175–82.

98. Ibid., pp. 183–90.

99. Ibid., pp. 191–98.

100. Ibid., pp. 198–203.

101. Mumford, review of *South American Journey*, p. 5.

102. Bittner, *Novels of Waldo Frank*, p. 178.

103. Gannett, review of *South American Journey*, n.p.

104. Frank, *South American Journey*, pp. 204–19.

105. Meyer, *Victoria Ocampo*, p. 141.

106. Frank, *South American Journey*, pp. 223–30.

107. Bates, review of *South American Journey*, p. 869.

108. Frank, *South American Journey*, pp. 231–34.

109. Ibid., pp. 235–38.

110. Ibid., p. 239.

111. Ibid., pp. 241–44.
112. Ibid., pp. 244–45.
113. Ibid., pp. 246–55.
114. Ibid., pp. 259–61.
115. Bates, review of *South American Journey*, p. 869.
116. Fredrick Pike, *The Politics of the Miraculous in Peru*, p. 50.
117. Frank, *South American Journey*, pp. 263–68.
118. See Pike, *The Politics of the Miraculous in Peru*.
119. Frank, *South American Journey*, pp. 271–79.
120. Kirstein, review of *South American Journey*, p. 866.
121. Frank, *South American Journey*, p. 279.
122. Hubert Herring, review of *South American Journey*, by Waldo Frank, *Saturday Review of Literature*, 19 June 1943, p. 15.
123. Frank, *South American Journey*, pp. 283–98.
124. Ibid., pp. 299–310.
125. Bates, review of *South American Journey*, p. 870.
126. Frank, *South American Journey*, pp. 311–20.
127. Ibid., pp. 321–40.
128. Ibid., pp. 341–50.
129. Ibid., pp. 353–59.
130. Kirstein, review of *South American Journey*, p. 866.
131. Frank, *South American Journey*, pp. 355–59.
132. Ibid., pp. 359–63.
133. Ibid., pp. 364–74.
134. J. McS., review of *South American Journey*, by Waldo Frank, *Catholic World*, August 1943, p. 557.

Chapter 5. A Dream Deferred: Waldo Frank and Latin America, 1943–1967

1. Waldo Frank, "Rubén Darío and the Jews," *Contemporary Jewish Record* 6 (August 1943): 348–49.
2. Frank's interpretation of Latin America is, of course, consistent with his earlier writings. He finds Ibero-America, its strength derived from the medieval church and the Renaissance, weak in technical development and strong in the humanistic disciplines. Moreover, that world has the "organic sense of wholeness." See Waldo Frank, *The Jew in Our Day* (New York: Duell, Sloan and Pearce, 1944), pp. 115–21.
3. Ibid., pp. 122–27.
4. Ibid., pp. 126–27.
5. Frank has added several new elements to his program. The Estrada Doctrine (conceived by Genaro Estrada, Mexico's "genial" foreign minister) seeks the routine recognition of de facto American governments. The U.S. has departed from the doctrine with regard to Argentina's "nationalist" government ruled by the generals, thus helping those we should be opposing. Frank suggests we adhere strictly to the doctrine until we begin to move toward economic and racial democracy at home (this is an about-face from his earlier call for nonrecognition of obvious dictatorships). He wants to broaden the Estrada Doctrine to the economic field by placing economic help on a "strict quota basis" and by having economic

sanctions voted on by a congress of American foreign ministers. He wants a college for the consular and diplomatic services in Latin America; its training would emphasize "ethnography and Latin American cultures." Finally, he wants an ambassador to Buenos Aires who would be "a liberal of the highest record and a profound student of Latin America, a man who can communicate with the Argentines in inter-American terms." See Waldo Frank, "Policy for Argentina," *Nation* 159 (21 October 1944): 471–73.

6. William Bittner, *Novels of Waldo Frank*, p. 202.

7. Waldo Frank, *Memoirs*, p. 214.

8. Bittner, *Novels of Waldo Frank*, p. 203.

9. Ibid.

10. Paul Carter, *Waldo Frank*, p. 148.

11. Bittner, *Novels of Waldo Frank*, p. 203.

12. The program included: socialization of the national wealth; universalization of health and educational services; building communications between towns and countryside, between the productive classes, between Latin American nations; and, the abolition of the army. See Waldo Frank, "To the Youth of Latin America," *Nation* (19 March 1949): 343–45.

The year 1949 also saw Frank being named honorary professor by the Central University of Ecuador, as well as the publication in the *Saturday Review* of "Latin America: A Cultural Inventory." The article is merely a reiteration of the message contained in the Prospect section of *America Hispana*. Again, he characterizes Latin America as weak in means, the United States in ends; and he calls for a better understanding of and more cooperation with Latin America as Latin Americans are "potentially" North America's "big brothers." See Waldo Frank, "Latin America: A Cultural Inventory," *Saturday Review of Literature* 32 (9 April 1949): 7–9, 29–31.

13. Waldo Frank, "Necesitamos crear un mundo nuevo," *Cuadernos Americanos* 9 (julio/agosto 1950): 40–44.

14. Waldo Frank, *Birth of a World: Bolívar in Terms of His Peoples* (Boston: Houghton Mifflin Company, 1951), pp. v–viii.

15. Ibid., pp. ix–x.

16. Edmund Wilson, *Letters on Literature and Politics* (New York: Farrar, Straus and Giroux, 1977), pp. 500–501.

17. Review of *Birth of a World*, by Waldo Frank, *Kirkus Reviews*, 15 July 1951, p. 372.

18. Milton Byam, review of *Birth of a World*, by Waldo Frank, *Library Journal*, 1 September 1951, p. 1328.

19. Claude G. Bowers, review of *Birth of a World*, by Waldo Frank, *New York Times Book Review*, 16 September 1951.

20. Hubert Herring, review of *Birth of a World*, by Waldo Frank, *New York Herald Tribune Book Review*, 16 September 1951.

21. J. Fred Rippy, review of *Birth of a World*, by Waldo Frank, *Chicago Sunday Tribune "Books"*, 23 September 1951.

22. Richard H. Dillon, review of *Birth of a World*, by Waldo Frank, *San Francisco Chronicle*, 25 November 1951.

23. Arturo Uslar Pietri, review of *Birth of a World*, by Waldo Frank, *Americas*, January 1952, p. 38.

24. Erna Fergusson, review of *Birth of a World*, by Waldo Frank, *Saturday Review of Literature*, 22 September 1951, p. 18.

25. Frank, *Birth of a World*, p. 3.

26. Ibid., pp. 13–15.
27. Ibid., p. 19.
28. Ibid., p. 31.
29. Ibid., pp. 37–47.
30. Ibid., pp. 66–67.
31. Ibid., pp. 67–68.
32. Ibid., pp. 114–18.
33. Ibid., pp. 143–45.
34. Ibid., pp. 147–48.
35. Ibid., pp. 242–45.
36. Ibid., pp. 246–48.
37. Ibid., p. 249.
38. Ibid., pp. 253–55.
39. Ibid., pp. 370–78.
40. Ibid., pp. 378–86.
41. Ibid., pp. 387–90.
42. Ibid., pp. 410–12.
43. Ibid., pp. 412–13.
44. Ibid., p. 414.
45. Waldo Frank, introduction to *Dom Casmurro*, by Joaquím Machado de Assís, trans. Helen Caldwell (New York: Noonday Press, 1953), pp. 6–12. That same year, on 14 June, Frank, as a member of the Committee for the Liberation of Argentine Intellectuals, had published in the *New York Times* a long letter on behalf of those arrested in Juan Perón's attempt to stem the tide of revolution. The victims, according to Frank, had "all expressed their love of liberty and their hate of totalitarian regimes." See Doris Meyer, *Victoria Ocampo*, pp. 159–60.

Then, on 15 August, Frank's article entitled "Latin America: Shall We Lose It?" appeared in the *Nation*. Here he contends that we in the United States subjectively view the Latin American situation; thus, we arm Latin America for defense of the hemisphere, and the weapons get "turned by the despisers of democracy against their people, teaching them to hate us." He concludes that while Latin America needs a "new radicalism, both practical and creative," to survive, *our* need is to let Latin America solve her own problems. Because our interference has its basis in an ignorance that stems from deep "spiritual and intellectual shortcomings in our culture," the only cure for our ignorance is "self-knowledge." Otherwise, "American ignorance means isolation." See Waldo Frank, "Latin America: Shall We Lose It?" *Nation* 177 (15 August 1953): 125–28.

46. Waldo Frank, "Puerto Rico and Psychosis," *Nation* 178 (13 March 1954): 210–11.
47. Carter, *Waldo Frank*, p. 157. Frank must have relished this assignment, for it meant that at least he had some semblance of an audience somewhere. In the United States the market for his articles was shriveling as were the invitations to lecture. He blamed this situation on the twin realities of the day: the cold war and McCarthyism. See Frank, *Memoirs*, p. 234.
48. Waldo Frank, *Bridgehead: The Drama of Israel* (New York: George Braziller, 1957), p. 92.
49. Waldo Frank, "Gabriela Mistral (Lucila Godoy y Alcayaga: 7 April 1889–10 January 1957)," *Nation* 184 (26 January 1957): 84. For the remainder of 1957, Frank kept in touch with Latin America both in body and in spirit. In addition to lecturing in Guatemala (Carter, *Waldo Frank*, p. 159), he wrote a long essay on Mexico (no more than a reiteration of everything he had ever written about that

country) for a book entitled *The Romance of North America*. See Waldo Frank, "Mexico," in *The Romance of North America*, ed. Hardwick Moseley (Boston: Houghton Mifflin Company, 1958), pp. 107–54.

The following year, Frank's article, "Venezuela: Hour of Promise," appeared in the *Nation*. Prompted by the overthrow of the Pérez-Jiménez dictatorship by the people of Venezuela, the article is a survey of the South American political situation. In citing the various problems that the continent faces in building a "workable democratic system," Frank focuses on the army, and he offers the same solution he did in his 1949 article, "To the Youth of Latin America": as the producing classes become conscious, they can frontally attack the army and win. Then, he urges the republics to move toward economic union and political federation, concluding with an ominous note: "There must be no delay. In every organic being, there is a time for growth. Neglected, it vanishes forever." See Waldo Frank, "Venezuela: Hour of Promise," *Nation* 186 (8 February 1958): 115–16.

50. Carter, *Weldo Frank*, p. 164.

51. Ibid., p. 165.

52. Ibid., pp. 165–66. Losada of Buenos Aires enthusiastically published a Spanish edition in advance of the United States edition. When Frank finished the rough draft at the end of October 1961, he found the Beacon Press willing to consider publishing the book. Beacon was the only American publisher he could find, possibly because of the general hostility toward Castro by that time. Frank neglected to tell Beacon that he had been compensated by the Cuban government for authoring the book. The General Council of the Unitarian church (which owned the press), upon discovering this information, declared the contract void, maintaining "that Frank had in effect invalidated it by his silence" (pp. 165–66).

53. Waldo Frank, *Cuba: Prophetic Island* (New York: Marzani and Munsell, 1961), p. 11.

54. Ibid., pp. 11–14.

55. Ibid., p. 60.

56. Ibid., pp. 67–69, 74.

57. Ibid., pp. 24–25.

58. Ibid., pp. 26–29.

59. Ibid., pp. 30–33.

60. Ibid., p. 33.

61. Ibid., pp. 36–37.

62. Ibid., pp. 45–47.

63. Ibid., p. 52.

64. Ibid., pp. 14, 18, 21.

65. Ibid., pp. 77–79.

66. Ibid., p. 31.

67. Ibid., pp. 76, 140–41.

68. Ibid., pp. 142–43.

69. Ibid., p. 116.

70. Ibid., p. 164.

71. Ibid., p. 81.

72. Ibid., pp. 124–26.

73. Ibid., p. 132.

74. Ibid., p. 135.

75. Ibid., pp. 136–37.

76. Ibid., p. 140.

77. Ibid., p. 144.

78. Ibid., pp. 149–53.

79. Ibid., pp. 153–56.

80. Ibid., pp. 157–58.

81. Ibid., p. 159.

82. Ibid., p. 166.

83. Ibid., p. 167.

84. Joseph Newman, review of *Cuba: Prophetic Island*, by Waldo Frank, *New York Herald Tribune Books*, 11 March 1962.

85. Daniel James, review of *Cuba: Prophetic Island*, by Waldo Frank, *Saturday Review*, 24 February 1962, p. 26.

86. Carter, *Waldo Frank*, p. 166.

87. Frank, *Memoirs*, pp. 233–34.

88. Bittner, *Novels of Waldo Frank*, p. 18.

89. Kloucek, "Waldo Frank," pp. 1, 508.

90. Carter, preface to *Waldo Frank*.

91. Lewis Mumford, introduction to *Memoirs of Waldo Frank*, p. xvi.

92. Kloucek, "Waldo Frank," p. 505; Bittner, *Novels of Waldo Frank*, p. 125.

93. Carter, *Waldo Frank*, p. 178.

94. M. J. Benardete, *Waldo Frank in America Hispana*, p. 241.

95. Kloucek, "Waldo Frank," p. 509.

96. Fredrick Pike, *The Politics of the Miraculous in Peru*, p. 192.

97. Thomas E. Skidmore and Peter H. Smith, eds., *Modern Latin America*, 2d ed. (New York and Oxford: Oxford University Press, 1989), p. 266.

98. Benardete, *Waldo Frank in America Hispana*, pp. ix, 223–24.

99. Quoted in Américo Castro, *The Spaniards*, p. 302.

100. Alexander DeConde, *A History of American Foreign Policy*, 2d ed. (New York: Charles Scribner's Sons, 1971), p. 538.

101. Benardete, *Waldo Frank in America Hispana*, pp. 111, 127.

102. See chapter 2.

103. DeConde, *A History*, p. 540.

104. Waldo Frank, *The Rediscovery of Man*, p. 202.

105. Benardete, *Waldo Frank in America Hispana*, p. 111.

106. Ibid., p. 123.

WORKS CITED

Writings by Waldo Frank

Frank, Waldo. *America Hispana: A Portrait and Prospect*. New York and London: Charles Scribner's Sons, 1931; reissued with the title *America Hispana: South of Us; The Characters of the Countries and the People of Central and South America*. Garden City, N.Y.: Charles Scribner's Sons, 1940.

————. "Argentina—Unwilling Enemy." *Colliers* 110 (26 September 1942): 17, 67–68.

————. "The Artist: Minister of Freedom." *Radical Religion* 2 (Autumn 1937): 9–15.

————. *Birth of a World: Bolívar in Terms of His Peoples*. Boston: Houghton Mifflin Company, 1951.

————. *Bridgehead: The Drama of Israel*. New York: George Braziller, 1957.

————. "Cárdenas of Mexico." *Foreign Affairs* 18 (October 1939): 91–101.

————. *Chart for Rough Water: Our Role in a New World*. New York: Doubleday, Doran and Company, 1940.

————. "Contemporary Spanish American Literature." *Publisher's Weekly* 118 (18 October 1930): 1841–43.

————. *Cuba: Prophetic Island*. New York: Marzani and Munsell, 1961.

————. *The Death and Birth of David Markand: An American Story*. New York: Charles Scribner's Sons, 1934.

————. Foreword to *Tales from the Argentine*. Edited by Waldo Frank. Translated by Anita Brenner. New York: Farrar & Rinehart, 1930.

————. "Gabriela Mistral (Lucila Godoy y Alcayaga: 7 April 1889–10 January 1957)." *Nation* 184 (26 January 1957): 84.

————. "La guerra simple y la guerra profunda: Prefacio a la edición castellana." In *Rumbos para América: Nuestra misión en un nuevo mundo*. Segunda edición. Traducción de María Zambrano, Luis Orsetti y José Basiglio Agosti. Buenos Aires: Editorial Americalee, 1942.

————. "Habana of the Cubans." *New Republic* 47 (23 June 1926): 140–41.

————. "The Hispano-American's World." *Nation* 152 (24 May 1941): 615–18.

————. *Holiday*. New York: Boni & Liveright, 1923.

————. *In the American Jungle (1925–1936)*. New York: Farrar & Rinehart, 1937.

————. Introduction to *Dom Casmurro*, by Joaquím Machado de Assís. Translated by Helen Caldwell. New York: Noonday Press, 1953.

————. Introduction to *Don Segundo Sombra: Shadows on the Pampas*, by Ricardo Güiraldes. Translated by Harriet de Onís. New York: Farrar & Rinehart, 1935.

———. *The Jew in Our Day*. New York: Duell, Sloan and Pearce, 1944.

———. "Latin America: A Cultural Inventory." *Saturday Review of Literature* 32 (9 April 1949): 7–9, 29–31.

———. "Latin America: Shall We Lose It?" *Nation* 177 (15 August 1953): 125–28.

———. "Letter to J. García Monge." *Repertorio Americano* 33 (19 junio 1937): 365.

———. *Memoirs of Waldo Frank*. Edited by Alan Trachtenberg. Introduction by Lewis Mumford. Amherst: University of Massachusetts Press, 1973.

———. "Mensaje de Waldo Frank a los escritores mexicanos." *Repertorio Americano* 8 (4 agosto 1924): 305–6.

———. "Mexico." In *The Romance of North America*, edited by Hardwick Moseley, 107–54. Boston: Houghton Mifflin Company, 1958.

———. "Mexico Today." *Nation* 149 (1939), 4 installments as follows: "The Heart of the Revolution" (5 August): 140–44; "President Cárdenas and His People" (12 August): 171–73; "Danger on the Right" (9 September): 265–69; "The Deepest Danger" (16 September): 288–90.

———. "Necesitamos crear un mundo nuevo." *Cuadernos Americanos* 9 (julio/agosto 1950): 40–44.

———. *Not Heaven: A Novel in the Form of Prelude, Variations, and Theme*. New York: Hermitage House, 1953.

———. *Our America*. New York: Boni & Liveright, 1919.

———. "La pintura contemporánea norteamericano." *Nación* (Buenos Aires) (13 julio 1941): 1, 4.

———. "Policy for Argentina." *Nation* 159 (21 October 1944): 471–73.

———. *Primer mensaje a la América Hispana*. Madrid: Revista de Occidente, 1930.

———. "El proceso de Trotsky." *Repertorio Americano* (4 mayo 1937): 365–66.

———. "Prólogo a la nueva edición de *América Hispana*." In *América Hispana: Un retrato y una perspectiva*. Traducido por León Felipe. Santiago de Chile: Ediciónes Ercilla, 1937.

———. "Puerto Rico and Psychosis." *Nation* 177 (13 March 1954): 210–11.

———. "Rediscovering a Nation That Once Was Great." *Travel* 46 (January 1926): 21–24, 42.

———. *The Re-discovery of America: An Introduction to a Philosophy of American Life*. New York and London: Charles Scribner's Sons, 1929.

———. *The Rediscovery of Man: A Memoir and a Methodology of Modern Life*. New York: George Braziller, 1958.

———. "Rubén Darío and the Jews." *Contemporary Jewish Record* 6 (August 1943): 348–49.

———. "Saludo a *Sur* en su cumpleaños." *Sur* 10 (diciembre 1940): 7–10.

———. "Sobre *Chart for Rough Water*." *Sur* 11 (febrero 1941): 69–72.

———. *South American Journey*. New York: Duell, Sloan and Pearce, 1943.

———. "Spain in War." *New Republic* 95 (1938), 3 installments as follows: "The

People" (13 July): 269–72; "Parties and Leaders" (20 July): 298–301; "The Meaning of Spain" (27 July): 325–27.

———. "To the Youth of Latin America." *Nation* (19 March 1949): 343–45.

———. "The Two American Half-Worlds." *Common Ground* 2 (Spring 1942): 63–70.

———. *Ustedes y nosotros: Nuevo mensaje a Ibero-America.* Buenos Aires: Editorial Losada, 1942.

———. "Venezuela: Hour of Promise." *Nation* 186 (8 February 1958): 115–16.

———. *Virgin Spain: Scenes from the Spiritual Drama of a Great People.* New York: Boni & Liveright, 1926.

———. *Virgin Spain: The Drama of a Great People.* Rev. ed. Introduction by Alfonso Reyes. New York: Duell, Sloan and Pearce, 1942.

———. "Viva España Libre!" *New Masses* 20 (18 August 1936): 12–13.

———. "Waldo Frank rectifica." *Repertorio Americano* 34 (31 julio 1937): 52–53.

———. "What is Hispano-America to Us?" *Scribner's* 87 (June 1930): 579–86.

———. "Why Good Neighbors?" *PM* (New York) (28 May 1943): 2.

Writings Concerning Waldo Frank

Austin, Mary. Review of *America Hispana*, by Waldo Frank. *New York Herald Tribune Books*, 20 September 1931.

Bates, Ralph. Review of *South American Journey*, by Waldo Frank. *Nation*, 19 June 1943, pp. 869–70.

Benardete, M. J. Review of *Virgin Spain*, rev. ed., by Waldo Frank. *Nation*, 16 May 1942, pp. 577–78.

———. "Spirltual Spain—A Synthesis." *Hispania* 10 (February 1927): 1–21.

———, ed. *Waldo Frank in America Hispana.* New York: Instituto de las Españas, 1930.

Benét, Laura. "Spain through Magic Casements." *Literary Digest International Book Review* 4 (May 1926): 395.

Bittner, William. *The Novels of Waldo Frank.* Philadelphia: University of Pennsylvania Press, 1958.

Blake, Casey Nelson. *Beloved Community: The Cultural Criticism of Randolph Bourne, Van Wyck Brooks, Waldo Frank, & Lewis Mumford.* Chapel Hill and London: The University of North Carolina Press, 1990.

Bowers, Claude G. Review of *Birth of a World*, by Waldo Frank. *New York Times Book Review*, 16 September 1951.

Byam, Milton. Review of *Birth of a World*, by Waldo Frank. *Library Journal*, 1 September 1951, p. 1328.

Carter, Paul J. *Waldo Frank.* Twayne's United States Authors Series. New Haven, Conn.: Twayne Publishers, Inc., 1967.

Chapman, Arnold. "Waldo Frank in the Hispanic World: The First Phase." *Hispania* 44 (December 1961): 626–34.

———. "Waldo Frank in Spanish America: Between Journeys, 1924–1929." *Hispania* 47 (September 1964): 510–21.

Dillon, Richard H. Review of *Birth of a World*, by Waldo Frank. *San Francisco Chronicle*, 25 November 1951.

Dos Passos, John. "Spain on a Monument." *New Masses* 1 (July 1926): 27.

Dura, Francisco. "Waldo Frank, restaurador y profeta." *Criterio* 6 (21 noviembre 1929): 371–73.

Fergusson, Erna. Review of *Birth of a World*, by Waldo Frank. *Saturday Review of Literature*, 22 September 1951, p. 18.

Frederick, John T. Review of *South American Journey*, by Waldo Frank. *Chicago Sun Book Week*, 8 August 1943.

Gannett, Lewis. Review of *South American Journey*, by Waldo Frank. *New York Herald Tribune "Books and Things,"* 20 May 1943.

Greene, Amy Blanche. Review of *America Hispana*, by Waldo Frank. *World Tomorrow*, November 1931, p. 371.

Gruening, Ernest. Review of *America Hispana*, by Waldo Frank. *Saturday Review of Literature*, 3 October 1931.

Harding, Gardner. Review of *America Hispana*, by Waldo Frank. *New York Times Book Review*, 18 October 1931, p. 165.

Herring, Hubert. Review of *Birth of a World*, by Waldo Frank. *New York Herald Tribune Book Review*, 16 September 1951.

———. Review of *South American Journey*, by Waldo Frank. *Yale Review*, Autumn 1943, pp. 150–51.

———. Review of *South American Journey*, by Waldo Frank. *Saturday Review of Literature*, 19 June 1943, p. 15.

James, Daniel. Review of *Cuba: Prophetic Island*, by Waldo Frank. *Saturday Review*, 24 February 1962, pp. 26–27.

Kirstein, Lincoln. Review of *South American Journey*, by Waldo Frank. *New Republic*, 28 June 1943, pp. 866–67.

Kloucek, Jerome W. "Waldo Frank: The Ground of His Mind and Art." Ph.D. diss., Northwestern University, 1958; Ann Arbor, Michigan: University Microfilms, Inc., 1981.

Lee, Muna. "Speaking of Spain, Here Is Waldo Frank." *New York Times Book Review*, 18 April 1926.

Luquiens, Frederick Bliss. Review of *America Hispana*, by Waldo Frank. *Yale Review*, Winter 1932, pp. 407–8.

McS., J. Review of *South American Journey*, by Waldo Frank. *Catholic World*, August 1943, p. 557.

Montenegro, Ernesto. "Waldo Frank before the Riddle of Spain." *Literary Review of the New York Evening Post*, 20 March 1926.

Mumford, Lewis. Review of *South American Journey*, by Waldo Frank. *New York Times*, 23 May 1943.

Newman, Joseph. Review of *Cuba: Prophetic Island*, by Waldo Frank. *New York Herald Tribune Books*, 11 March 1962.

Nuhn, Ferner. Review of *America Hispana*, by Waldo Frank. *Nation*, 30 September 1931, p. 337.

Peixotto, Ernest. "The Soul of Spain." *Saturday Review of Literature* 2 (17 April 1926): 719–20.

Review of *America Hispana*, by Waldo Frank. *Review of Reviews*, November 1931, p. 8.

Review of *Birth of a World*, by Waldo Frank. *Kirkus Reviews*, 15 July 1951, p. 372.

Rippy, J. Fred. Review of *Birth of a World*, by Waldo Frank. *Chicago Sunday Tribune "Books,"* 23 September 1951.

Rose, Selden. "The Personality of Spain." *Yale Review* (Autumn 1942): 195–97.

Sabine, Julia. Review of *South American Journey*, by Waldo Frank. *Library Journal*, 15 May 1943, p. 428.

Sitwell, Sacheverell. "Virgin Spain." *Dial* 82 (January 1927): 63–65.

Tinker, E. L. "New Editions, Fine and Otherwise." *New York Times*, 13 September 1942.

Uslar Pietri, Arturo. Review of *Birth of a World*, by Waldo Frank. *Américas*, January 1952, pp. 36–38.

Walsh, Thomas. Review of *Virgin Spain*, by Waldo Frank. *Commonweal*, 9 June 1926, pp. 134–35.

Willingham, John R. "The Achievement of Waldo Frank." *Literary Review* 1 (Summer 1958): 465–77.

Other Works Cited

Aaron, Daniel. *Writers on the Left: Episodes in American Literary Communism*. New York: Harcourt, Brace and World, 1961.

Baker, Carlos. *Hemingway: The Writer as Artist*. Princeton: Princeton University Press, 1952.

Baudet, Henri. *Paradise on Earth: Some Thoughts on European Images of Non-European Man*. Translated by Elizabeth Wentholt. New Haven: Yale University Press, 1965.

Berkhofer, Robert F., Jr. *The White Man's Indian: Images of the American Indian from Columbus to the Present*. New York: Alfred A. Knopf, 1978.

Billington, James H. *Fire in the Minds of Men: Origins of the Revolutionary Faith*. New York: Basic Books, Inc., 1980.

Bolloten, Burnett. *The Spanish Revolution: The Left and the Struggle for Power during the Civil War*. Chapel Hill: The University of North Carolina Press, 1979.

Braunthal, Alfred. *Salvation and the Perfect Society: The Eternal Quest*. Amherst: University of Massachusetts Press, 1979.

Brenan, Gerald. *The Literature of the Spanish People*. Cambridge: Cambridge University Press, 1951.

———. *The Spanish Labyrinth: An Account of the Social and Political Background of the Spanish Civil War*. Cambridge: Cambridge University Press, 1943; reprint ed., New York: The Syndics of the Cambridge University Press, 1976.

Brooks, Van Wyck. *Autobiography*. New York: E. P. Dutton & Company, Inc., 1965.

————. *Days of the Phoenix*. New York: E. P. Dutton & Company, Inc., 1957.

————. *Scenes and Portraits: Memories of Childhood and Youth*. New York: E. P. Dutton & Company, Inc., 1954.

Campbell, Bruce F. *Ancient Wisdom Revived: A History of the Theosophical Movement*. Berkeley and Los Angeles: University of California Press, 1980.

Carr, Raymond. *Spain: 1808–1939*. Oxford: Oxford University Press, 1966.

Castro, Américo. *The Spaniards: An Introduction to their History*. Translated by Willard F. King and Selma Margaretten. Berkeley: University of California Press, 1971.

Chavarría, Jesús. *José Carlos Mariátegui and the Rise of Modern Peru, 1890–1930*. Albuquerque: University of New Mexico Press, 1979.

DeConde, Alexander. *A History of American Foreign Policy*. 2d ed. New York: Charles Scribner's Sons, 1971.

Doctorow, E. L. *Ragtime*. New York: Random House, 1975; Bantam edition, 1976.

Dudley, Edward, and Maximilian E. Novak, eds. *The Wild Man Within: An Image in Western Thought from the Renaissance to Romanticism*. Pittsburgh: University of Pittsburgh Press, 1972.

Gornick, Vivian. *The Romance of American Communism*. New York: Basic Books, 1978.

Green, Martin. *Children of the Sun: A Narrative of "Decadence" in England After 1918*. New York: Basic Books, 1976.

Hemingway, Ernest. *Death in the Afternoon*. New York and London: Charles Scribner's Sons, 1932.

————. *Ernest Hemingway, Selected Letters 1917–1961*. Edited by Carlos Baker. New York: Charles Scribner's Sons, 1981.

Hoffman, Frederick J. *Freudianism and the Literary Mind*. Baton Rouge: Louisiana State University Press, 1945.

Hoffman, Frederick J., Charles Allen, and Caroline F. Ulrich, *The Little Magazine*. Princeton: Princeton University Press, 1946.

Johnson, H. B., Jr., ed. *From Reconquest to Empire: The Iberian Background to Latin American History*. New York: Alfred A. Knopf, 1970.

Jones, Howard Mumford. *Guide to American Literature and Its Backgrounds Since 1890*. Cambridge: Harvard University Press, 1953.

Kazin, Alfred. *On Native Grounds: An Interpretation of Modern American Prose Literature*. New York: Reynal & Hitchcock, 1942.

Lafaye, Jacques. *Quetzalcoatl et Guadelupe: La formation de la conscience rationale au mexique (1531–1813)*. Preface by Octavio Paz. Paris: Gallimard, 1974.

Lasch, Christopher. *The New Radicalism in America, 1889–1963: The Intellectual as a Social Type*. New York: Alfred A. Knopf, 1965.

Lasky, Melvin J. *Utopia and Revolution: On the Origins of a Metaphor, or Some Illustrations of the Problem of Political Temperament and Intellectual Climate and How Ideas, Ideals, and Ideologies Have Been Historically Related*. Chicago and London: The University of Chicago Press, 1976.

Lawrence, D. H. *The Plumed Serpent*. Introduction by Richard Aldington. London: William Heinemann Ltd., 1955.

Mackay, John A. *The Other Spanish Christ: A Study in the Spiritual History of Spain and South America*. New York: The Macmillan Company, 1932.

Madariaga, Salvador de. *Spain: A Modern History*. New York: Frederick A. Praeger, 1958; second printing, 1960.

Mariátegui, J. C. *Seven Interpretive Essays on Peruvian Reality*. Introduction by Jorge Basadre. Translated by Marjory Urquidi. Austin: University of Texas Press, 1971.

May, Henry F. *The End of American Innocence: A Study of the First Years of Our Time, 1912–1917*. New York: Alfred A. Knopf, 1959.

Meaker, Gerald. *The Revolutionary Left in Spain, 1914–1923*. Stanford: Stanford University Press, 1974.

Meyer, Doris. *Victoria Ocampo: Against the Wind and the Tide*. New York: George Braziller, 1979.

Moses, Wilson J. *The Golden Age of Black Nationalism, 1850–1925*. Hamden, Conn.: The Shoe String Press, Inc., 1978.

Munson, Gorham. "The Fledgling Years, 1916–1924." *Sewanee Review* 40 (1932): 24–54.

Oppenheim, James. "The Story of the *Seven Arts*." *American Mercury* 20 (1930): 156–64.

Payne, Stanley G. *Basque Nationalism*. Reno: University of Nevada Press, 1975.

————. *Spain & Portugal*. Vol. 1. Madison: University of Wisconsin Press, 1973.

Pells, Richard H. *Radical Visions and American Dreams: Culture and Social Thought in the Depression Years*. New York: Harper & Row, 1973.

Pike, Fredrick B. "Dabbling in Psychohistory: A Look at United States-Spanish Mutual Images from the 1920s to the 1970s." *Red River Valley Historical Journal* 4 (Summer 1980): 372–98.

————. *The Politics of the Miraculous in Peru: Haya de la Torre and the Spiritualist Tradition*. Lincoln and London: University of Nebraska Press, 1986.

————. "Visions of Rebirth: The Spiritualist Facet of Peru's Haya de la Torre." Paper presented at the Louisville meeting of the Southern Historical Association, Louisville, Ky., 12 November 1981.

Ramsey, John. *Spain: The Rise of the First World Power*. Birmingham: The University of Alabama Press, 1973.

Rosenfeld, Paul. *Men Seen: Twenty-Four Modern Authors*. New York: The Dial Press, 1925.

————. *Port of New York: Essays on Fourteen American Moderns*. New York: Harcourt, Brace and Company, 1924.

Santayana, George. *The Genteel Tradition: Nine Essays*. Introduction by Douglas L. Wilson. Cambridge: Harvard University Press, 1967.

Skidmore, Thomas, and Peter Smith. *Modern Latin America*. 2d ed. New York and Oxford: Oxford University Press, 1989.

Slotkin, Richard. *Regeneration Through Violence: The Mythology of the American Frontier, 1600–1860*. Middletown, Conn.: Wesleyan University Press, 1973.

Spiller, Robert, et al. *Literary History of the United States*. Vol. 2. New York: Macmillan and Company, 1948.

Unterecker, John. *Voyager, a Life of Hart Crane*. New York: Farrar, Straus, & Giroux, 1969.

Webb, James. *The Harmonious Circle: The Lives and Work of G. I. Gurdjieff, P. D. Ouspensky, and Their Followers*. New York: G. P. Putnam's Sons, 1980.

Williams, Stanley T. *The Spanish Background of American Literature*. 2 vols. New Haven: Yale University Press; London: Oxford University Press, 1955.

Wilson, Edmund. *Letters on Literature and Politics*. New York: Farrar, Straus & Giroux, 1977.

Index

DATE DUE

DEMCO 38-297